Many Parts, One Body

MANY PARTS, ONE BODY

How the Episcopal Church Works

JAMES DATOR
WITH JAN NUNLEY

© 2010 by James Dator and Jan Nunley
All rights reserved.

No part of this book may be reproduced, stored in a retrieval system, or transmitted in any form or by any means, electronic or mechanical, including photocopying, recording, or otherwise, without the written permission of the publisher.

Library of Congress Cataloging-in-Publication Data
Dator, James Allen.
Many parts, one body: how the Episcopal Church works / James Dator; with Jan Nunley.
   p.   cm.
Includes bibliographical references.
ISBN 978-0-89869-640-0 (pbk.)
1. Episcopal Church—Government. I. Nunley, Jan. II. Title.
BX5950.D38 2010
262'.0373—dc22
                            2009044110

Cover design by Jennifer Glosser
Interior design and typesetting by Vicki K. Black

Printed in the United States of America

Church Publishing, Incorporated
445 Fifth Avenue
New York, New York 10016
www.churchpublishing.org

5 4 3 2 1

CONTENTS

Preface: The Future Has a Long Fuse. ix

Preface to the Original Work. xiii

1. What Difference Does It Make?. 1
    The Controversy / 1
    Unitary, Federal, and Confederal Government Defined / 6
    Resolving the Controversy / 11

2. The Constitution and Canons 13
    The Church in America in 1776 / 13
    Plans for Reconstituting the Church / 16
    Conventions to Reconstitute the Church / 23
    The Constitution of 1789 / 26
    The Canons of 1789 / 29
    How the Constitution Was Enacted / 31
    How the Constitution May Be Amended / 46
    Conclusions / 50
    Separation of Powers? / 52

3. The Structure of General Convention 54
    Overview / 54
    Who Are the Members? / 59
    Whom Do They Represent? / 63
    How Do They Vote? / 69
    Is General Convention Bicameral? / 72
    Conclusions / 73

4. Executive, Administrative, and Judicial Powers............75
   What Are Bishops? / 75
   Bishops' Jurisdiction, Mission, Selection, and the General Church / 79
   The Presiding Bishop / 89
   The Executive Council / 93
   Finances / 96
   The Judicial System / 99

5. Provinces, Dioceses, and the General Church...............109
   Provinces / 109
   Dioceses / 114
   May Dioceses Nullify or Secede? / 117
   The Church in the Confederate States / 118
   Admitting New Dioceses / 125
   Who Is a Member of the Church? / 129

6. Summary and Conclusions............................133
   The Written Constitution / 133
   General Convention / 136
   Executive and Judiciary / 139
   Membership / 141
   Locus of Sovereignty / 142
   Final Conclusion / 144

Bibliography...146

Appendix..165
   I. Controversy Concerning the Source of Canon Law 166
      The Ancient Canons Do Apply to the Episcopal Church
         Hoffman's View
         "The Ancient Canons"
         Analogy to Common Law
         Summary of Hoffman's Position
      The Ancient Canons Do Not Apply to the Episcopal Church
         Andrews's View
         Opinion of Kevin and Brydon
      The Importance of This Controversy

   II. The Constitution of the Confederate Episcopal Church ...174
      The Official Draft of October 1861
      The Accepted Constitution

   III. The Reformed Episcopal Church 178
      The Constitution of the Reformed Episcopal Church

IV. Notes and Comments on the Church's Government 180
   On the Name of the Church
   On Church Parties
   On Parish Government
   On "Divided Votes" in the House of Deputies
   On the Use of the Word "Mission"
   Quotations Showing Conflicting Opinions Regarding the Meaning
      of the Constitution Enacted in 1789
   Quotations Showing Conflicting Opinions Regarding the Extent
      of General Convention's Power
   Official Church Acts Showing the Relationship of the Episcopal
      Church to the Church of England
   Civil Court Cases Involving the Episcopal Church
   On "Sovereignty"

PREFACE

THE FUTURE HAS A LONG FUSE

The story of how this book came to be is a case study in the law of unintended consequences. Let author James Dator and editor Jan Nunley tell the story together.

JD: When I completed and defended my doctoral dissertation in political science at The American University in 1959, no one was interested in publishing it. Even though it dealt with a topic that had long been discussed within the church, not even the church presses of the time were interested. It simply did not deal with an issue of interest. Eventually I dropped the topic and went on to other things.

JN: I met Jim Dator by mistake.

In my former position as the Episcopal Church's Deputy for Communication, part of my job was to monitor for accuracy the stories being written and posted on websites by reporters about the Episcopal Church.

After the 2003 General Convention consented to the election of Gene Robinson as bishop of New Hampshire, I was submerged under a flood of stories of people, parishes, and institutions supporting and opposing the Episcopal Church's action—not to mention the newest element, bloggers. Every day was taken up with the twists and turns of the story, and the reactions, threats, proposals, manifestos, position papers, and the like that were churned out daily.

Dator's name was a footnote in an opinion by Robert G. Devlin, then Chancellor of the Episcopal Diocese of Pittsburgh, circulated throughout that diocese and on their website in support of a resolution to revise the diocese's accession clause to the Constitution and Canons of the Episcopal Church.[1] Devlin maintained that "there is no authority that expressly forbids a diocese from nullifying an act of General Convention," and cited Dator's 1959 doctoral dissertation, "The Government of the Protestant Episcopal Church in the United States of America: Confederal, Federal or Unitary?" for support.

Out of curiosity, I ran Dator's name through a search engine. It turned out he was now professor and director of the Hawaii Research Center for Futures Studies at the Department of Political Science of the University of Hawaii at Manoa.

And he had an email address.

JD: On September 29, 2004, I received an email from one Jan Nunley wanting to know if I was the James Allen Dator who had written a doctoral dissertation on the government of the Protestant Episcopal Church in the United States of America, and if so, did I had a copy of it that she could review?

I replied: "I am thunderstruck! After all these years, someone wants to look at my dissertation? What's this all about?"

She wrote back: "You're cited in a footnote to a discussion of a proposed constitutional amendment to the constitution of the Diocese of Pittsburgh, effectively authorizing them to nullify any action of General Convention."

I replied back that I wasn't even sure where my copy of the dissertation was, much less what I had concluded. It was so long ago, and my scholarship had moved into completely different directions. However, I said, "I am interested in reading what I wrote lo these many years ago, and so will keep digging. The more I think about it, the more I may have come down on the side of a 'confederal' structure."

JN: My heart sank. But then....

JD: After several failed searches for the manuscript, my wife finally remembered where the copy was. After we retrieved it, I looked for the passage in question. On October 2, I wrote to the Reverend Nunley: "I am

---

1. "Discussion of Proposed Constitutional Amendment, Article I, Section 1," September 4, 2004: http://parishtoolbox.org/media/chancellorconstitutionalamendment.pdf.

holding in my hand a copy of my dissertation. Thanks to my wife, Rosemary McShane, for digging through many boxes to find it. I am now looking at page 200, and in fact I am relieved to discover that I do NOT state what the authors of the document you quote in your email below have me saying. Indeed, I state the opposite!"

JN: When the original dissertation arrived in New York, it dawned on me how far we've come from the cutting-edge technology of 1959. In my lap were pages of scholarly prose, typewritten in a tiny font on onion-skin typing paper. A member of my staff volunteered for the monotony of placing each delicate page on the glass of a copying machine, then running the copy through a scanner to create an electronic file. When it was done, I returned the original to Hawaii and sat down to read the photocopied file.

Almost fifty years ago, as a young graduate student—long before the culture-war controversies over the ordination of women, lesbians, and gay men in the Episcopal Church—James Dator laid out a carefully reasoned argument that what the Episcopal Church had was really a unitary government, with all its temporal authority resting in the triennial General Convention. Like a restorationist gently brushing away the dust and grime from a hidden masterpiece, Dator carefully discarded the assumptions and accretions of the years until the real structure of the Episcopal Church emerged.

JD: Frankly speaking, I was astonished at what the evidence led me to conclude—and impressed with my long-ago research! At the outset, I had more or less assumed, as so many have, that the church had a structure similar to that of the U.S. government, since they were both created at the same time, with the same ideas of governance in the air, and with some people active in the creation of both polities.

But the facts were beyond dispute, it seemed to me, and so I presented them and successfully defended my dissertation before a committee composed of Dr. Edgar Robinson, the chair of my committee, Dean Richard van Wagenen, Dean Ralph John, and Dr. Chester Earle, all of The American University, and Canon Theodore Wedel, of the Washington Cathedral, College of Preachers, and President of the House of Deputies of the General Convention of the PECUSA.

And there the matter stood, silent and still, buried away in my dissertation until people who chose to misquote it resurrected it in 2004, and it became a subject of discussion and controversy beyond my wildest dreams.

JN: For several years, a PDF of those original pages was downloaded, passed around, studied, and discussed while the controversy over governance moved from the blogs to the courts. I was convinced it needed a wider audience, and Dr. Dator generously offered to have the dissertation retyped into more readable computer files. My task was to streamline and update the information for a new and more extended readership.

My thanks go to Dr. James Dator, who continued to encourage me on this project; to Robert Devlin, without whose mistake I might never have met Dr. Dator; to Daphne Mack, whose tirelessness in copying and scanning the original made it possible to bring it to the attention of many; to James Naughton, who hosted the dissertation PDF files on the website of the Diocese of Washington; to the staff at Church Publishing Incorporated, who saw the wisdom of offering it to the church; and to my life partner and most rigorous editor, Susan Erdey, who has seen me through it all, and more. May it bring the light of clarity to the church in times to come.

JD: I offer my thanks to Elizabeth Allen, Leroy Lawson, Albert Mollegen, Cliff Stanley, Charlie Price, Edgar Robinson, and Tish Yancey for provoking the doctoral dissertation upon which this book is based, and to Bob Devlin, Jan Nunley, Joan Gundersen, Susan Erdey, Rosemary McShane, and Ginny Arnold for provoking and enabling the publication of the book itself.

The future has a long fuse.

Or, as Leo Tolstoy reminded us: "God sees the truth, but waits."

James Allen Dator
Hawaii Research Center for Futures Studies
Department of Political Science
University of Hawaii at Manoa
Honolulu, Hawaii

The Reverend Jan Nunley
Peekskill, New York

July 2009

PREFACE *to the* ORIGINAL WORK

Research into the constitutional structure of the government of the Episcopal Church was first suggested to me while I was studying the history of American Christianity as a special student at the Protestant Episcopal Theological Seminary in Virginia. One of the texts of the course, Dr. Addison's *The Episcopal Church in the United States,* suggested a close theoretical and structural analogy between the Constitution of the United States and the Constitution of the church, both having been written during the same period of American history:

> In making these courageous innovations the leaders of the church were certainly aided by the previous labors of their political contemporaries. None can fail to remark the analogies between the ecclesiastical and federal constitutions—Diocesan conventions corresponding to state legislatures, the House of Deputies answering to the House of Representatives, the House of Bishops to the Senate, and the like. But only to statesmen would such statesmanlike models appeal.[1]

This is an intriguing coincidence. Is there really a structural identity between the two constitutions? The Reverend Allen J. Green, instructor of the course, and the Reverend Henry Rightor, who for some time had been interested in both the theoretical and practical aspects of the problem, submitted there was not. Indeed, they suggested that the church's constitu-

---

1. James Thayer Addison, *The Episcopal Church in the United States, 1789–1931* (New York: Charles Scribner's Sons, 1951), 73.

tional structure is more nearly confederal than federal: the National Church has no central executive, no national system of courts, and little control over the dioceses. Yet, on the very page where Dr. Addison cites apparent similarities between the Episcopal Church and the United States government was a quote by Francis Wharton: "It is difficult to see any limit, on the page of the Constitution, to the powers of the General Convention."

What kind of a federation—or confederation—is it that places no constitutional limits whatsoever upon the power of the central government? The problem of the nature of the church's government became more interesting. Subsequent research showed that the controversy over the nature of the church's constitutional structure was not new; that, indeed, it was as old as the oldest commentaries on the American Episcopal Church. Almost always, moreover, the dispute centered on the politically important questions of whether General Convention did or did not have the constitutional power to enact a given canon, and whether that was a power belonging to the "sovereign dioceses."

It soon became evident that a decision could not be reached as to whether the church's government was federal, confederal, or unitary until these terms had been rather precisely defined and distinguished. After this was done, the church's constitutional structure could be compared with the definitions and a more specific appraisal of the church's Constitution could be reached. The following pages are the result of this method of analysis.

Several persons deserve an expression of special recognition for their parts in this study. Primary thanks belong to Dr. Edgar S. Robinson of the School of Government of The American University, chairman of the committee for this thesis, who gave more than ordinary assistance in his careful guidance in all phases of this project. Appreciation is also given to Canon Theodore O. Wedel of the College of Preachers and President of the House of Deputies of the General Convention, for his kindness in allotting time from his usual duties to serve on the thesis committee and read and comment upon several drafts of this study.

To Dean Richard W. van Wagenen, Dean Ralph C. John, and Dr. Chester B. Earle, all of The American University, gratitude is also expressed for their several contributions of criticism and encouragement, particularly in the development of the criteria. Final thanks are given to Mr. Jack H. Goodwin, Librarian of the Virginia Theological Seminary, for unlocking to the writer many periodical and documentary sources that were not otherwise accessible.

It is hoped that this study will be helpful to persons concerned with both the government of the Episcopal Church and ecclesiastical polity as a whole, as well as to those students of government who are interested in comparing and contrasting public and private governance.

James Allen Dator
1959

CHAPTER ONE

WHAT DIFFERENCE DOES IT MAKE?

Why does it matter whether the structure of the Episcopal Church is federal, confederal, or unitary? In order to answer this question, it is necessary to show the conflicting nature of the evidence concerning the structure of the church and the significance of the resulting controversy regarding the church's polity. Contradictory statements about the church's government abound.

The Controversy

It is possible to extract a considerable number of statements from the literature about the Episcopal Church to support a federal hypothesis. These quotations fall into three categories. There are statements that simply call the polity of the church "federal" without further justification. For example:

> Actually, the Episcopal Church was a federal union of independent diocesan units and each diocese a federation of independent parishes, rather than a single, closely-knit ecclesiastical institution.[1]

---

1. Powel Mills Dawley, *Chapters in Church History* (New York: The National Council, 1950), 222. See also William S. Perry, *History of the Constitution of the American Church* (New York: T. Whittaker, 1891), 99, 118; Samuel D. McConnell, *History of the American Episcopal Church*, tenth edition (Milwaukee: Young Churchman, 1916), 264; and William W. Manross, *A History of the American Episcopal Church*, second edition (New York: Morehouse-Gorham, 1950), 190.

Others cite certain selected constitutional features of the church's polity that they present as exhibiting the federal nature of the church's government:

> Because the government of the Episcopal Church is that of a federated union of dioceses, the analogy of the federal government of the United States in this respect is very striking.[2]

> The American Church adapted herself entirely to the body politic of the United States. Certain features in her construction are in exact parallel with the structure of the federation. The parallelism between General Convention and Congress, Diocesan Convention, and State Legislature, is so evident as to need no discussion.[3]

> The Episcopal Church is organized in a similar way to the United States Federal Government. Both received their Constitutions in the same year and place, and many of the same people participated in both transactions.[4]

Quotations also exist, however, which deny that there is any significant similarity between the government of the United States and that of the church, as far as their constitutional structure is concerned:

> The true analogy therefore, is not to be found between the Church and the Federal Government, but between the Church and its dioceses on the other hand, and any one State and its several counties on the other hand.[5]

> It is nonsense to say that [the Church's] governing power is patterned after that of the Republic.[6]

---

2. G. MacLaren Brydon, *Shall We Accept the Ancient Canons as Canon Law?* (Richmond, Va.: Virginia Diocesan Library, 1955), 36.
3. Richard G. Salomon, "Mother Church—Daughter Church—Sister Church," *Historical Magazine of the Protestant Episcopal Church* 21 (1952): 420.
4. *Ibid.*, 131. For other examples, see also Perry, *History of the Constitution,* 108; John W. Andrews, *Church Law* (New York: T. Whittaker, 1883), 50–62; McConnell, *History,* 242; Francis L. Hawks, *The Constitution and Canons of the Protestant Episcopal Church in the United States, Annotated* (New York: Stanford and Swords, 1841), 5–6, 51–58; Leighton Coleman, *The Church in America* (New York: James Pott, 1895), 134; William S. Perry, *The History of the American Episcopal Church,* vol. 2 (Boston: J. R. Osgood, 1885), 90; William H. Wilmer, *The Episcopal Manual* (Philadelphia: R. S. H. George, 1841), 37–38; Calvin Colton, *The Genius and Mission the Protestant Episcopal Church in the United States* (New York: Stanford and Swords, 1853), 8–9; George Hodges, *Three Hundred Years of the Episcopal Church in America* (Philadelphia: G. W. Jacobs, 1906), 95–96; James Thayer Addison, *The Episcopal Church in the United States, 1789–1931* (New York: Charles Scribner's Sons, 1951), 73; and Percy V. Norwood, "Constitutional Developments Since 1789," *Historical Magazine of the Protestant Episcopal Church* 8 (1939): 282–84.
5. Christopher Stuart Patterson, "The Sources and Scope of the Law of the Church," *Church Review* 43 (1884): 124.
6. John H. Stotsenburg, "The Governing Power of the Church," *Virginia Seminary Magazine* 4 (1891): 322.

The few resemblances between the Church and the nation sink into insignificance, however, when we compare the differences between them.[7]

Sources can also be found to support the contention that the government of the Episcopal Church is confederal:

> In the days of White and Seabury it was the prevailing opinion that the Church was a confederation of independent dioceses, just as the nation was a confederation of the independent states, and no national executive was provided for in the Church's Constitution.[8]

> The Church of the States collectively—that is, of the nation—has no head, no governing power, no administration, no guide, no leader; but it is merely a collection of confederated dioceses.[9]

Moreover, there are those sources that state that the General Convention is supreme, and thus tacitly show that the church is unitary:

> The history of the legislation of General Convention since its formation shows that the Convention has again and again taken to itself powers which once belonged to the diocese, and in some cases to the individual parish. This fact demonstrates the correctness of the theory, as we have before stated, upon which the General Convention has ever acted from the beginning of its history: that it has the power to legislate on any subject unless expressly forbidden to do so by the Constitution. The General Convention not only makes the Constitution and amends it, but it interprets the Constitution. The General Convention limits its own power, and it can remove that limitation. It assumes that all power is in the General Convention which the Constitution itself does not limit. The one conclusion that follows from these facts is, that the General Convention is the ultimate seat of authority in American Church government.[10]

---

7. Edwin A. White and Jackson A. Dykman, *Annotated Constitution and Canons for the Government of the Protestant Episcopal Church*, vol. 1 (Greenwich, Conn.: Seabury, 1954), 140. This two-volume work, with triennial pocket parts, is an indispensable source for the student of the church's government. It is a revision by Dykman of the 1924 annotation by White. White and Dykman, as it shall be referred to hereinafter, was further updated in 1981, and a supplement was last issued in 1991. See also Murray Hoffman, *A Treatise on the Law of the Protestant Episcopal Church in the United States* (New York: Stanford and Swords, 1850), 115; and Francis Vinton, *A Manual Commentary on the General Canon Law and the Constitution of the Protestant Episcopal Church in the United States* (New York: E. P. Dutton, 1870), 48, 75.
8. James A. Muller, *The Government of the Episcopal Church* (Cambridge, Mass.: Episcopal Theological School, 1929), 19.
9. Stotsenburg, "Governing Power," 322.
10. White and Dykman (1954), 1:142. See also 1:33, 92–94, 100, 139–42; 2:55–56.

> The General Convention *possesses the acknowledged power of supreme legislation, as a corollary of the supreme and sole authority to make, and to alter the Constitution of the Protestant Episcopal Church in the United States.*[11]

> I must say that after a careful and anxious scrutiny of the Constitution and Canons of our General Church, the power of the General Convention seems to be unlimited, while that of the Diocesan Convention is only that which the General Convention is pleased to concede.... That the sovereignty of the Church is in the General Convention is shown by an almost unbroken current of legislation. It is difficult to see any limit, on the face of the Constitution, to the powers of the General Convention.[12]

How is it possible to reach such contradictory opinions regarding the structure of the church's government? There seem to be three main reasons. First, there have been few systematic and comprehensive analyses of the governmental structure of the church. Equally important, no writer in his description of the Episcopal Church's government has stated what he meant by "federal," "confederal," or "unitary." Thus the structure of the church has been described in these terms without their definition. Finally, some of the crucial points concerning the church's constitutional structure are genuinely open to varying interpretations because the facts about them are inconclusive. Whether the persons who wrote the church's Constitution between 1784 and 1789 were delegates of diocesan governments or merely representatives of the church in the several states has been frequently disputed. In part, this is because the definition of a "diocese" is controvertible. Whether all the framers of the Constitution were delegates of diocesan governments or not depends upon the observer's analysis of the completeness of diocesan organization at the time, the "spirit of the time," the framers' intention, and the dependence of the church upon bishops.

Indeed, whether or not bishops are essential to the church—whether or not there can be a true church without bishops, and whether or not governing power flows from the bishops downward to the clergy and laity, or upward from the individual churchmen through the various conventions—has affected judgments on the question of the church's constitutional structure.

Likewise, the almost irresistible temptation to analogize from the American State to the American Episcopal Church, and to transfer feelings about

---

11. Vinton, *A Manual Commentary,* 124. Italics in source.
12. Francis Wharton, "How Far Are We Bound by English Canons?" in Perry, *History of the American Episcopal Church,* 2:398, 400, 401–2.

"states' rights" and related questions to the polity of the church, may have influenced some analyses of the church.

The question of the church's structure has generally been connected with the problem of whether the General Convention or the dioceses are supreme. The confederal, federal, or unitary nature of the government has been denied or affirmed in the interest of showing that either the General Convention or the dioceses, constitutionally and/or inherently, possess political powers upon which the other cannot impinge.

The controversy of General Convention versus diocesan convention supremacy has not been merely an academic question among church historians. Persons protesting an act proposed or done by General Convention often insisted that the act was unconstitutional because the constitutional structure of the church is federal or confederal, and the power exercised was one belonging by constitutional right to the dioceses. For example, when the Constitution was amended in 1943 to require all bishops to resign upon reaching age seventy-two, Bishop William Manning of New York protested heatedly:

> The rights of a diocese are analogous to those of a sovereign state under our American Constitution, and by this legislation, for the first time in any branch of the Catholic Church, the rights of the diocese are encroached upon by the General Church.[13]

One of the most strongly political statements cited above was that made by a committee on "Diocesan Autonomy and Federal Relations" of the 1877 Council (Convention) of the Protestant Episcopal Church in the Diocese of Virginia. This report strongly insisted that the Diocese of Virginia had the legal right to secede from the American Episcopal Church for theological reasons, if necessary, although it did not recommend secession itself. Hill Burgwin illustrated the seriousness of the controversy in this statement:

> I have seen very strong and ultra claims asserted by most respectable writers, in behalf of diocesan rights; and have never attended a General Convention where objections have not been made to this or that proposed legislation, for the reason that it would be an invasion of the rights of the Dioceses, or, if not, that it was beyond the scope of the National Church's legislative powers, and on the other hand I observe, in looking over the legislative acts of this National Church, that there is scarcely found a sin-

---

13. Excerpt from an editorial, "Episcopal Retirement," in *Chronicle* 44 (1944): 183. See also White and Dykman (1954), 1:46–47.

gle subject naturally to be regarded as belonging exclusively to diocesan control, which has not been assumed to be within that of the National Church, and acted on accordingly.[14]

Research for this book was not begun in order to prove that the government of the Episcopal Church is either federal, confedal, or unitary in structure. No attempt was made to find justifications for predispositions of this nature. Instead, the conflict over the nature of the church's Constitution was so intense that the wish to attempt to solve the controversy was sufficient of itself to provoke serious study into the problem.

It should be emphasized that this study is focused upon the formal structure and not upon the behavior within that structure. There often is considerable behavioral divergence from the formal norm in governments. No attempt has been made in this book to determine the extent to which this is the case in the government of the American Episcopal Church.

Unitary, Federal, and Confederal Government Defined

Internally speaking only, and in relation to the concentration versus the geographic dispersion of political power, governments may only be classified as unitary, federal, or confederal.[15] There are many forms and types of each, and the dividing line between them is by no means perfectly clear in real governments. The difference between a highly decentralized unitary government and a closely knit federal or confederal government, for example, may be difficult to determine without careful analysis.

But what do these terms mean? What is a unitary government, a federation, a confederacy? To define or explain any one of these three types is impossible without reference to the other two.

However, it would seem that the normal type of governmental organization is the unitary form. Kenneth Wheare, one of the great students of modern federalism, says:

> It is commonly assumed that federal government is called upon to justify its existence. The unitary form of government is regarded as normal and self-explanatory and self-justifying; if there is to be government at all for an area, it is assumed that, unless strong reasons to the contrary can be shown, that government will and should be unitary.[16]

---

14. Hill Burgwin, "The National Church and the Diocese," *Church Review* 45 (1885): 423.
15. William Anderson, *Federalism and Intergovernmental Relations* (Chicago: Public Administration Service, 1946), 6.
16. Kenneth C. Wheare, in Geoffrey Sawer, ed., *Federalism: An Australian Study* (Melbourne: F. W. Cheshire, 1952), 110.

What, then, is a unitary government? Sidgwick defines it as one

> in which the ordinary exercise of the highest powers of government belongs to a central organ or organs, exercising control over all the members of the state; while only matters of secondary importance are handed over to the independent management of local governing bodies.[17]

It must be emphasized that these "matters of secondary importance are handed over" by the central government. They are not inherently possessed by the local governments. Thus, all political decisions are ultimately referable to a single, territorially inclusive, all-powerful, and, if explicitly limited at all, self-limited central government.

The principle of unitary government is that of the legal supremacy of a central government over all other exercisers of government in a given geographic area. Unitary governments, however, may be considered in terms of the amount of power actually exercised by the central governments and that exercised by the local governmental units.

Because of political, economic, or simply philosophical reasons, a unitary government actually may exhibit the possession of considerable political powers by the local governments. That is, political power may be *centralized,* in which case considerable power is held and exercised by the central government, or *decentralized,* so that the local governments possess a great deal of power. The distinguishing feature of a unitary government, again, is the legal supremacy of the central government. The mere distribution of powers within a state where the central government is legally supreme over all other exercisers of political power only indicates the degree of centralization or decentralization.[18]

What is a confederate government? A confederacy is an association of governments that have agreed to delegate to a common governmental authority the exercise of certain of their governmental powers. The association, though intended to be permanent, is characterized by the retention in the associated governments of the right to nullify acts of the common government agency, and to secede from the association at will. Supreme power thus lies in the member governments severally. The powers of the common government are usually partial, and are related to those problems that are the overarching concern of the confederacy as a whole. To some extent, a confederacy is a "state" itself; to some extent it is nothing more than

---

17. Henry Sidgwick, *The Elements of Politics,* second edition (London: Macmillan, 1897), 331–32. See also Herman Finer, *Theory and Practice of Modern Government,* revised edition (New York: Henry Holt, 1949), 166; and Albert V. Dicey, *Introduction to the Study of the Law of the Constitution,* eighth edition (London: Macmillan, 1924), 153.
18. Sidgwick, *Elements of Politics,* 333–34.

a rather rigid alliance of states that have set up a common governmental system over some mutual area.[19]

Federal government lies between a closely knit confederacy and a decentralized unitary government and must be defined in reference to the two preceding systems.[20] Federalism is a principle of governmental organization, designed to be permanent,[21] which manifests a constitutional division of governmental powers between a central (common, national, or general) government and two or more regional (constituted or associated) governments in the following manner.

The general and associated governments are coordinate and, regarding the powers assigned to them, independent in their own governmental jurisdiction.

> That the real key to the nature of a federation is in the distribution of powers seems to be agreed upon by nearly every writer who addresses himself to the question. Federalism implies the existence of two coordinate sets of government operating at two different levels in two different spheres.[22]

The constitution that defines the distribution of governmental powers between the general and regional governments has a supremacy and rigidity over all other acts and bodies. Thus the constitutional distributions of powers between and among the several governments cannot be modified by the central government or by a state government alone, but only by each operating independently and coordinately. This amending process not only must be substantially more difficult than ordinary legislative processes, but also must involve the concurrent consent of both the central and associated governments.[23]

---

19. Westel W. Willoughby, *The Fundamental Concepts of Public Law* (New York: Macmillan, 1924), 189–96.
20. Edward A. Freeman, *A History of Federal Government in Greece and Italy*, second edition (New York: Macmillan, 1893), 1: "Federal government . . . is, in its essence, a compromise between two opposite political systems. Its different forms occupy the whole middle space between two widely distant extremes. It is therefore only natural that some of these intermediate forms should shade off imperceptibly into the extremes of either side. Controversies may thus easily be raised both as to the correct definition of a federal government, and also whether this or that particular government comes within the definition." See also Carl J. Friedrich, *Constitutional Government and Democracy*, revised edition (New York: Ginn, 1950), 190.
21. Albert B. Hart, *Introduction to the Study of Federal Government* (Boston: Ginn, 1891), 17.
22. William S. Livingston, *Federalism and Constitutional Change* (Oxford: Clarendon, 1956), 10.
23. *Ibid.*, 11–15. See also George B. Adams, *Federal Government: Its Function and Method* (New York: Knickerbocker Press, 1919), 59, 83–101; Arthur B. Keith, *Federation: Its Nature and Conditions* (London: Historical Association, 1942), 536; Friedrich, *Constitutional Government*, 6; Kenneth C. Wheare, *Federal Government* (London: Oxford, 1947), 10–11, 96; Sidgwick, *Elements of Politics*, 220; and Dicey, *Introduction to the Study of the Law*, 140–53.

Disputes between the regional and the general government or among the regional governments as to the meaning of the division and distribution of powers (that is, problems of constitutional interpretation) are settled by an authority independent of both state and central governments. However, if no authority is provided in the written constitution, the function belongs to the courts.[24]

Thus, there can be no "nullification" by a component part of the acts of the central government, or the government is confederate. On the other hand, if the central government unilaterally can eradicate or modify the structure or powers of the associated governments, the government is unitary.[25]

Sovereignty, or ultimate legal supremacy, lies in the federation as a whole rather than in either the regional or the central governments alone, with the main expression of this sovereignty being found in the constitution of the federation. If the central government were wholly sovereign, the government would be unitary. If the regional governments were wholly sovereign, the government would be confederate.

The exercise of sovereign power must be divided between central and regional governments so that each is supreme, independent, and coordinate in its own sphere; but there is no necessary formula of how the division is to be made, what powers each shall have, or whether the regional governments or the central have residual or enumerated powers. However, the powers of both central and regional governments should be substantial and not merely trivial.[26]

Since sovereignty lies in the federation as a whole, secession of the member governments from the union is impossible.

On the basis of coordinate independence, the central government and the several governments each should possess constitutionally sufficient manpower and resources to carry out the constitutional powers and duties allotted to each governmental jurisdiction. Thus, neither a constituent government nor the central government should be forced by the constitution to be dependent financially upon the other federal components for the exercise of its constitutional authorities and requirements.

---

24. John A. R. Marriott, *Federalism and the Problem of the Small State* (London: George Allen and Unwin, 1943), 90. See also Adams, *Federal Government,* 84, 97–100; Wheare, *Federal Government,* 64–88; Dicey, *Introduction to the Study of the Law,* 153–61; Livingston, *Federalism and Constitutional Change,* 14–15, 295–318; and Arthur W. Macmahon, "Federation," in *Encyclopedia of the Social Sciences,* vol. 6, ed. Edwin R. A. Seligman (New York: Macmillan, 1931), 175.
25. Robert M. MacIver, *The Modern State* (London: Oxford, 1926), 379–81; Willoughby, *Fundamental Concepts,* 210–18, 195–203; and Wheare, *Federal Government,* 91–92.
26. Arthur W. Macmahon, *Federalism: Mature and Emergent* (Garden City, N.Y.: Doubleday, 1955), 4; Wheare, *Federal Government,* 3.

The governmental powers of the central government must be able to extend directly to the persons in the member governments rather than indirectly to them through the component governments.[27] There should be a dual citizenship or membership, moreover. A person should be a citizen, or member, of both the federation and of the member governments, rather than of one or the other only.[28]

The separateness and independent political power of the associated governments as such should find substantial expression in the central government, especially by representation of the governments-as-such in part or all of the central legislature. There should also be a genuine legal equality among the constituent governments themselves.[29] The participation of the associated governments should be had also in the election of the central executive.[30]

A bicameral legislature and the separation of the powers of the central government into executive, legislative, and judicial branches are taken as marks of federalism by some writers.[31] The general government and the member governments, moreover, should each possess a complete complement of governmental institutions. Thus, if a separation of powers is assumed, each government should possess for itself an independent executive, legislature, and judiciary.[32]

Finally, there should be a provision to allow new members to enter the federation on an equal basis with the old. However, there may also be a provision made for "colonies," "protectorates," "dependent governments," or other part-members to the federation, probably under the control of the central government until they become equal members.[33]

---

27. Freeman, *A History of Federal Government*, 9; Sidgwick, *Elements of Politics*, 538; Macmahon, *Federalism*, 5; Wheare, *Federal Government*, 2. But see, to the contrary, Willoughby, *Fundamental Concepts*, 198–200.
28. Robert M. MacIver, *The Web of Government* (New York: Macmillan, 1947), 160–61; J. Rivero, "Introduction to a Study of the Development of Federal Societies," *International Social Science Bulletin* 4 (1952): 42; Marriott, *Federalism and the Problem of the Small State*, 100; Willoughby, *Fundamental Concepts*, 205, 273.
29. Marriott, *Federalism and the Problem of the Small State*, 96; Macmahon, *Federalism*, 5.
30. Livingston, *Federalism and Constitutional Change*, 11.
31. John A. R. Marriott, *Second Chambers* (Oxford: Clarendon, 1910), 241–53; Dorothy Schaffter, *The Bicameral System in Practice* (Iowa City: State Historical Society of Iowa, 1929), 18–19; Franz L. Neumann, "Federalism and Freedom: A Critique," in Macmahon, *Federalism*, 44; Frank J. Goodnow, *Principles of Constitutional Government* (New York: Harper, 1916), 152–66; Macmahon, "Federation," 176; Wheare, *Federal Government*, 85, 92–96; Friedrich, *Constitutional Government*, 19; Keith, *Federation*, 9–13.
32. Willoughby, *Fundamental Concepts*, 276.
33. Keith, *Federation*, 8.

Resolving the Controversy

After describing the government of the church and comparing its structure with these criteria, it should be possible to conclude whether or not the Episcopal Church is confederal, federal, or unitary. Having made this determination, the problem of the supremacy of the general church, in General Convention, over the dioceses, or of the diocesan churches over General Convention can be affirmed or denied.[34]

Four of the remaining chapters of this book examine specific parts of the governmental structure of the Episcopal Church with reference to the constitutional question. Chapter 2 comprises an introduction of the Constitution and Canons. After an historical introduction, this chapter undertakes an investigation of the source, scope, and purpose of the Constitution and Canons of the Episcopal Church from 1782 until the time of the original writing of this work (1959), with canonical updates indicated where necessary to bring the information to the current day. The scope and purpose of the Constitution and Canons are analyzed, including the important problems concerning how and by whom the Constitution and Canons are enacted, how and by whom they may be amended or repealed, and whether or not there is a constitutional separation of powers.

Chapter 3 examines the history, development, and present status of the structure and powers of General Convention. The constitutional and canonical provisions concerning General Convention from 1782 to the present are analyzed. Implications of the system of representation and the method of legislative apportionment are evaluated. Finally, the problem of the extent of the General Convention's powers is studied.

The fourth chapter analyzes the status and exercise of the executive powers in the church as they relate to the question of the structure of the Constitution and the distribution of governmental powers in the church.

---

34. Historically, the use of the words "federal" and "confederal" has not always been precise. Especially in the early part of the United States' history—at least before the Civil War period—the terms were used interchangeably, and did not convey the distinction that has been stated in the definition. For a good example, see Alexander Hamilton, *et al.*, *The Federalist Papers*, Modern Library edition (New York: Random House, [n.d.]), especially Number 9 and Number 39, as well as *passim*. The interchangeable use of the two words is most striking in this volume, which is now taken as the most powerful early statement of federal, as opposed to unitary, government, as defined above. Thus, it may be possible to find instances when the church is called "federal" or "confederal" even in the Journals of the General Convention. But simply calling the church a confederation does not mean that it actually exhibits the governmental structure that confederal governments, by definition, must have. It is primarily to the structural realities of the church, rather than to opinions about the church's structure, that this book is directed.

The development of the governing role of bishops, in both their diocesan and national duties and powers, is examined. Special consideration is given to the governing role of the Presiding Bishop and the Executive Council (and its predecessor, the National Council) in the past and at present.

Also, the constitutional and canonical requirements for the judicial system of the church, in development to the present, are examined in this chapter. The implications of the absence of a Supreme Court either as a final court of appeal or as the source of authoritative constitutional and canonical interpretation is discussed, and the relation of the civil courts in the United States to the church's courts is described.

The governing role of diocesan and provincial governments in relation to the wider church is examined in chapter 5. The scope and nature of constitutional and canonical requirements affecting dioceses and provinces are analyzed. Consideration is also given in this chapter to the question of nullification and secession, with the example being the Episcopal Church in the Confederate States of America; the governmental role of foreign and domestic missionary districts [now called missionary dioceses], with special attention to the locus of their responsibility; the method of admitting new dioceses into the association; and the problem of the definition of membership, considering especially the question of whether or not there is dual membership.

The last chapter, in connection with a brief summary of the major findings of this thesis, compares the criteria developed in the first chapter with the data summarized in order to determine whether the government of the Episcopal Church is federal, confederal, or unitary in structure.

CHAPTER TWO

THE CONSTITUTION *and* CANONS

THE CHURCH IN AMERICA IN 1776

The American Revolution and the Declaration of Independence of 1776 severed the flimsy ties of ecclesiastical government that bound the Anglican churches in the American colonies to the Church of England.[1] Prior to the Revolution, no bishop was resident in the churches in the colonies. The Bishop of London had been assigned jurisdiction over the colonial churches and had administered supervision in varying degrees.[2] Episcopal oversight, however, had been always exercised *in absentia*.

Several factors contributed to the crisis of 1776. Included among them were the lack of resident episcopal authority, the localism of each of the American colonies themselves, the varying ecclesiastical and social arrangements of the church in the several colonies—especially differences between colonies where the church was established and where it was not—the shortage of ordained and adequately trained clergy and the considerable influence of the laity in ecclesiastical government, the differences in churchmanship that mirrored and fluctuated in proportion to the varieties and successes of church parties in England, and the general ineffectualness

---
1. See Clara O. Loveland, *The Critical Years: The Reconstitution of the Anglican Church in the United States of America: 1780–1789* (Greenwich, Conn.: Seabury, 1956). This is an indispensable source for this period of the church's history.
2. See any history of the Episcopal Church listed in the Bibliography regarding the use of "commissaries" (clerical representatives of the Bishop of London in the colonies).

and unpopularity of the church in the colonies before the Revolution. All contributed to creating a crisis in the church's government when the American colonies broke away from England.[3]

The crisis was made more acute because of the uncertainty concerning an aspect of one theory of the relationship between church and state extant in the Church of England at the time. This theory, based essentially upon Richard Hooker's *Ecclesiastical Polity* and Article Thirty-Four of the *Thirty-Nine Articles*,[4] assumed that while the Holy Catholic Church was indeed one in faith and doctrine, variations in government and discipline might be permitted from place to place. In fact, church and nation being one in substance, differences in ecclesiastical government could be allowed within churches in different countries as local circumstances required. Thus, governmentally, each church was organized on a country-to-country basis. The church, while universal in faith, was national in government.

While England retained political control over the colonies, the church in England and the church in the colonies were under the same ecclesiastical discipline. When the political association was ended, so did the ecclesiastical. This assumption, then, necessitated a "reconstitution" of the government of the church in the states pursuant to the change in civil government.

The characteristics of the church at the Declaration of Independence and the theory of a national church resulted in a governmental arrangement atypical of Anglican polity when these two factors were combined with the confusing complexion of civil governance of the same period. The several states, being, to some extent, sovereign and independent countries and only eventually forming the more inclusive governmental arrangement of the Articles of Confederation, presented the church in the states a model of disintegration and insularity.

It should be borne in mind, then, that the reconstitution of the Anglican church in the United States was contemporaneous with the reconstitution of the English colonies into the United States of America. Some have made claims that the "Founding Fathers" of both the church and the state were the same persons. Thus:

> A comparison is often drawn between the constitution of the church and that of the Republic, with a view of showing the similarity between the

---

3. Besides Loveland, *The Critical Years*, see the church histories also regarding this important period in the church's development.
4. Article Thirty-Four was cited in the 1782 edition of William White's *The Case of the Episcopal Churches in the United States Considered*. See the annotated edition by Richard G. Salomon (Philadelphia: Church Historical Society, 1954), 21.

two instruments—a similarity not to be wondered at, when it is recollected that a number of those who were concerned in framing the one were also concerned in framing the other. But it also must be remembered that the church's constitution was first adopted.[5]

A number of the "fathers" of the civil government were, in fact, nominal Episcopalians,[6] and there perhaps were a few persons active in the constitutional conventions of both church and state, but there appears to have been no close interrelationship between the two conventions.[7]

In any event, the constitutional documents of both church and state were formed during the same period and there may have been at least an indirect cross-fertilization of ideas. Indeed, that both church and state delineated their governments by means of a formal, written constitution is perhaps the most striking coincidence of all. Apparently, no church had ever resorted to a written constitution to define its polity before.[8]

The practical locus of ecclesiastical authority in the church in the colonies was the parish. While legal authority over the church in all the colonies lay in the Bishop of London, there was such a measure of parochial freedom and such an absence of episcopal or even colony-diocesan control that the operation of colonial church government was far more nearly congregational than hierarchical.[9] At the same time, pursuant to the national church theory, after the Revolution, the church within each state, or diocese,[10] severally began to assume the incipient characteristics of a complete and independent ecclesiastical polity.

---

5. Leighton Coleman, *The Church in America* (New York: James Pott, 1895), 134. See also Samuel D. McConnell, *History of the American Episcopal Church*, tenth edition (Milwaukee: Young Churchman, 1916), 242.
6. See Anson Phelps Stokes, *Church and State in the United States*, vol. 1 (New York: Harper, 1950), 292–357.
7. Sydney A. Temple, Jr., *The Common Sense Theology of Bishop White* (Morningside Heights, N.Y.: King's Crown, 1956), 23: "It is not true that the men who made the federal government also formed the Episcopal Church. Some Episcopalians were active in forming the Government, but it is doubtful if any of the men who attended the Constitutional Convention were delegates to the early conventions of the Episcopal Church."
8. Louis C. Sanford, *The Province of the Pacific* (Philadelphia: Church Historical Society, 1949), 1.
9. Loveland, *The Critical Years*, 6.
10. The words "state" or "diocese" were used interchangeably during the early history of the American Episcopal Church. Indeed, the Constitution of 1789 used "state" almost exclusively. It was not until 1835–1838, with the division of the State of New York into two dioceses, that the Constitution and Canons were amended to read at every point "diocese." Before this time, each diocese's boundaries had been coterminous with the state in which it was located. Indeed, even today the boundaries of the states of the United States, with some exceptions, are also the boundaries of the dioceses. Where a single state embraces two or more dioceses, the state and county lines generally define the dioceses' limits as well.

Thus, there was contemporaneously a situation of parochial centeredness within a theoretical structure of diocesan supremacy and independence, all without benefit of episcopal guidance or control. As there had been little intercourse of ideas or persons between the churches in the colonies before the Revolution, there was difficulty in determining the bases and conditions of communication afterward. Although nominally all under the discipline of the See of London, and thus in theory part of a governmental unity, the churches in the colonies had, in fact, been separated on a parochial or at best colony-diocesan base. The parochial-and-diocesan-centeredness continued and expanded after 1776.[11]

Plans for Reconstituting the Church

There were, however, several programs eventually presented by various persons and groups for the purpose of reconstituting the Church of England in the American States. Three major approaches to reorganization are exhibited in the plans, begun and continued after 1780, of the church in Maryland, Pennsylvania, and Connecticut.[12]

The original attitude of the church in Maryland is illustrative of churches chiefly concerned with establishing their identity as successors to the Church of England so that they might retain legal control over property that had been held by the church before the Revolution as a first step toward perfecting their government. At the same time, they also wished to demonstrate that they were independent of any foreign ecclesiastical control. The church in Maryland also was careful to see that its actions toward these ends were either expressly sanctioned by the government of the State of Maryland or at least not requiring or able to have state approval or disapproval. This cautiousness was found, not unreasonably, among Episcopalians in most of the states, because of fears that actions by American churchmen might be interpreted in America or in England as such departures from Anglican faith or practice as to sever the bonds of continuity between the church in America and the Church of England.

In short, the church in Maryland was first concerned with developing its government within the state, not with establishing a nationwide Episcopal Church. Toward this end, Dr. William Smith, leader of the church's

---

11. The few clergy conventions that were held were almost all intra-colony. See Edgar L. Pennington, "Colonial Clergy Conventions," *Historical Magazine of the Protestant Episcopal Church* 8 (1939): 178–218. "The Conventions were more or less informal. This was to be expected since the conventions lacked authority and remained voluntary to the end. No one was empowered to enforce their decisions" (p. 217).
12. Loveland, *The Critical Years*, 21–22.

movement for reorganization in Maryland, was, in 1773, elected "*to go to Europe to be ordained an antistes,* President of the Clergy, or Bishop (if that name does not hurt your feelings)."[13] Because of a number of reasons, Dr. Smith was never consecrated, and Maryland did not have a bishop until after the organization of the Protestant Episcopal Church in 1789.

Though having several points of similarity with the Maryland approach, the church in Connecticut (and New England generally) manifested an essentially different conception of the role of the Episcopal Church. Theologically "High Church,"[14] politically Tory, dependent upon the aid of the Society for the Propagation of the Gospel in Foreign Parts (SPG),[15] the church in Connecticut was predisposed to react differently to the situation brought on by the defeat of England. Unlike Maryland, and the church in the South, and, as shall be seen, unlike the Pennsylvania Plan, the church in Connecticut felt that no departure in ecclesiastical faith or discipline could legitimately be made until a valid episcopate had been secured. The "government" of the church *was* the bishop, it was believed. Authority to govern the church flowed from Christ through the apostles to the bishops. To have ecclesiastical government without bishops was impossible.

Hence, Connecticut's energies were consumed, at least after March 1783, in obtaining the consecration of Samuel Seabury, at first unsuccessfully at Canterbury, and then successfully in November 1784 by nonjuring but valid bishops in Scotland.[16] Until Bishop Seabury arrived back in Connecticut in August 1785, the church in Connecticut rejected overtures from the church in the other states to join in an ecclesiastical union for the revision of faith and discipline as the times required. "Really, Sir," the New England clergy wrote William White in reference to his plan, "we think an Episcopal Church without Episcopacy, if it be not a contradiction in terms, would, however, be a new thing under the sun."[17]

---

13. Letter from the Rev. Thomas John Claggett to William Duke of September 20, 1783, in William Stevens Perry, ed., *Journals of General Conventions of the Protestant Episcopal Church in the United States, 1785–1835,* vol. 3 (Claremont, N.H.: Claremont Manufacturing Company, 1874), 34. Italics in source. This work will hereinafter be cited as Perry, *Journals,* plus the volume number and page.
14. For a note about the church's "parties," see the Appendix.
15. The Society for the Propagation of the Gospel in Foreign Parts (SPG) was a private English missionary society of considerable importance to the history of the Church of England in America.
16. See Walter H. Stowe, "The Scottish Episcopal Succession and the Validity of Bishop Seabury's Orders," *Historical Magazine of the Protestant Episcopal Church* 9 (1940): 322–48. See also Arthur Lyon Cross, *The Anglican Episcopate and the American Colonies* (New York: Longmans, Green, 1902).
17. William White, *Memoirs of the Protestant Episcopal Church in the United States of America,* DeCosta edition (New York: E. P. Dutton, 1880), 337.

Moreover, the New England clergy were horrified at suggestions of clerical consecration of bishops. Only valid, episcopal consecration of bishops would do: "We think that the uniform practice of the whole American Church, for a near a century, sending their candidates three thousand miles for Holy Orders, is more than presumptive proof that the Church here are, and ever have been" of the opinion that validly consecrated bishops are essential to a valid church.[18]

The Pennsylvania Plan was the only major scheme that sought first to reorganize the church in all the states into a single ecclesiastical entity. This plan, developed by William White, who is generally considered to be the "founding father" of the American Episcopal Church,[19] has been called the "Federal Plan."[20]

The theoretical basis of White's plan, according to Loveland, was that "the authority to govern the Episcopal Church in America had to be derived from elected representatives from all the churches throughout the United States, united by the voluntary acceptance of a federal constitution."[21] White's program was first outlined in *The Case of the Episcopal Churches in the United States Considered.*[22] This document generally is considered to be the initial precursor to the Constitution of 1789 and hence must be examined in close detail in order to see whether Loveland's verdict is correct or not.

Written during the summer of 1782 at a time when White, along with many others, thought England might not recognize the independence of the American States, the *Case* was primarily concerned with outlining a scheme of union for the church in the United States. White assumed that it would be completely impossible to secure consecration of an American bishop from the English line. Thus, although he lamented the necessity of so acting, he felt that the need of a continuing witness to the Christian

---

18. *Ibid.,* 338.
19. E. Clowes Chorley, "The General Conventions of 1785, 1786, 1789," *Historical Magazine of the Protestant Episcopal Church* 4 (1935): 265: "In a very real sense his memory should be venerated at the Father of the American Church." See also Richard G. Salomon, "Mother Church—Daughter Church—Sister Church," *Historical Magazine of the Protestant Episcopal Church* 21 (1952): 418; William J. Seabury, *An Introduction to the Study of Ecclesiastical Polity* (New York: Crothers and Korth, 1894), 193–94; James A. Muller, *The Government of the Episcopal Church* (Cambridge, Mass.: Episcopal Theological School, 1929), 1. Similar statements are made in most of the church histories listed in the Appendix.
20. Chapter 3 of Loveland, *The Critical Years,* is entitled, "The Federal Plan for Reorganization," and is an analysis of White's position in the *Case*. Dr. Loveland acknowledges that she took the term "federal" from Samuel D. McConnell, *History of the American Episcopal Church,* 1904 edition.
21. Loveland, *The Critical Years,* 62.
22. The edition of White's *Case* used in this book is that by edited and introduced by Richard G. Salomon, cited in note 4 above.

faith dictated that the reorganization of the former Church of England in America be conducted in the absence of a bishop.[23]

Events contemporary with the publication of the *Case* in fact negated the basic assumption. In early August 1782 it became apparent that England was willing to recognize American independence.[24] If this were so, then it was more likely that the Church of England could be persuaded to consecrate an American candidate to the episcopacy. Nonetheless, the *Case* was printed and widely distributed among the exiguous American Church, and had considerable influence on subsequent constitutions.

Chapter 3 of White's *Case* contains the "sketch of a frame of government" as follows:

> As the churches in question extend over an immense space of country, it can never be expected, that representatives from each church should assemble in one place; it will be more convenient for them to associate in small districts, from which representatives may be sent to three different bodies, the continent being supposed divided into that number of larger districts. From these may be elected a body representing the whole.
>
> In each smaller district, there should be elected a general vestry or convention, consisting of a convenient number (the minister to be one) from the vestry or congregation of each church, or of every two or more churches, according to their respective ability of supporting a minister. They should elect a clergyman their permanent president; who, in conjunction with other clergymen to be also appointed by the body, may exercise such powers as are purely spiritual, particularly that of admitting to the ministry; the presiding clergyman and others to be liable to be deprived for just causes, by a fair process, and under reasonable laws; meetings to be held as often as occasion may require.
>
> The assemblies in the three larger districts may consist of a convenient number of members, sent from each of the smaller districts severally within their bounds, equally composed of clergy and laity, and voted for by those orders promiscuously; the presiding clergyman to be always one, and these bodies to meet once in every year.
>
> The continental representative body may consist of a convenient number from each of the larger districts, formed equally of clergy and laity, and among the clergy, formed equally of presiding ministers and others to meet statedly once in three years. The use of this and preceding representative bodies is to make such regulations, and receive appeals in such mat-

---

23. White, *Case*, 29–30.
24. *Ibid.*, 9; annotation by Salomon.

ters only, as shall be judged necessary for their continuing one religious communion."[25]

White's plan is cited in all major sources as being substantially identical with the final form of the church's polity, "The Constitution of the American Episcopal Church to this day bears the imprint of his hand, more than that of any one man."[26] If so, the question is crucial: what was White's purpose in recommending the three-tiered governmental framework?

The answer seems to be provided in the first paragraph of his third chapter: because the parish churches extend over such a great expanse of territory, it is difficult to secure a single convention with representatives from each parish, so there must be instead a series of ascending conventions. Nowhere does White declare, in the *Case*, his intention of establishing a federal government; of securing a distribution of governing power between a central and member governments. Rather, he is concerned with how to achieve a satisfactory system of representation within what is a unitary government. Since the territorial extent of the church is considerable, and transportation and communication difficult, he concludes that a system of interrelated, multiple, representative conventions rising from the local congregation to the "continental representative body" is the best solution. He does not attempt to protect the sovereign powers of the church in the states by limiting the power of the continental convention in favor of diocesan power. Rather, he would limit governing powers of all the bodies: "The use of this and preceding representative bodies is to make such regulations, and receive appeals in such matters only, as shall be judged necessary for their continuing one religious communion."[27]

If White favored the possession of residual powers by any single unit, it could be argued that he favored congregational or parochial supremacy. He felt it was good "to retain in each church every power that need not be delegated for the good of the whole."[28]

---

25. *Ibid.*, 25.
26. Walter H. Stowe, "William White: Ecclesiastical Statesman," *Historical Magazine of the Protestant Episcopal Church* 22 (1953): 374. Consult also Muller, *The Government of the Episcopal Church*, 7–8. Muller states, in reference to the "Fundamental Principles of 1784": "This is essentially the plan which had been proposed in White's pamphlet." Salomon, in White's *Case*, says, "It contains the first draft of the organization of the Church as it is today" (p. 1).
27. White, *Case*, 26.
28. Salomon here, in annotating White's *Case*, footnotes Article II of the Articles of Confederation: "Each state *retains* its sovereignty, freedom and independence, and *every power*, jurisdiction and right which is not by this confederation expressly *delegated* to the United States, in Congress assembled" (p. 25, footnote 43; italics in source). To quote a contemporary source that was designed to guarantee the sovereignty of the states in the Confederation for an inferential interpretation of White's statement is very misleading. There is no objective reason to believe that White was stressing either parochial or diocesan supremacy in the *Case*. If he

At another place in the *Case,* he says that "there is great truth and beauty in the following observation of the present Bishop of St. Asaph, 'the great art of governing consist in not governing too much.'"[29] Consequently, White was interested in protecting the individual churchman from "too much" ecclesiastical legislation by setting up an elaborate system of representation; building from the individual parish member, through a series of more-inclusive representative bodies, to a final group continental in its composition and scope.

In White's *Memoirs of the Protestant Episcopal Church,* last revised by him in 1836, shortly before his death, the then long-time Bishop of Pennsylvania, Presiding Bishop of the church, and widely respected "father" of the American Episcopal Church contradicted those who believed that it was impossible to depart from the practice of having the boundaries of dioceses coextensive with the boundaries of the several states and to divide populous dioceses into several dioceses within one state—something which, indeed, was not achieved until the 1835–1836 General Conventions. He rejected the notion that the boundaries of the dioceses had to be identical with the boundaries of the several states, or that the dioceses were essential bodies of residual powers. He wrote:

> When the constitution was framed, the public mind had not yet raised itself above that excessive attachment to the peculiarities of the different states, which is in the way of consistent adherence in practice, to the principle contended for in theory, the founding of law on public will.[30]

The principle for which he contended was unitary government by representative majority rule, although constitutional and limited, based upon John Locke's governmental theories.[31] White foresaw the time when the principle of equal voting by dioceses in General Convention would mean that "measures may be adopted by a majority, according to the constitution, but dissented from by an acknowledged majority of our Episcopal population. It can hardly be supposed, and is contrary to our observation

---

were interested in protecting sovereignty, it is highly significant that he did *not* follow the obvious model of the Articles of Confederation that Salomon cites, and include this protection specifically in his "sketch of a frame of government."
29. *Ibid.,* 27.
30. White, *Memoirs,* 465.
31. See Temple, *Common Sense Theology of Bishop White,* 10, 12, 24, 27, and "the American Episcopal Church took its form from an outline laid down in White's *Case,* which likewise found its basis in Locke's theory of government" (p. 23). Also, Loveland, *The Critical Years*: "William White was a Lockian. . . . His firm support of a contract theory of government was derived from his belief in the importance of natural as well as revealed religion" (p. 9). Salomon says that the *Case* was "conceived under the influence of Locke's political theories" (White, *Case,* 1).

of human nature, that the measure would be submitted to."[32] Thus, by dividing the dioceses so that they were roughly equal in population, or by apportioning the representation of the House of Deputies according to population, the "founding of law on public will" would be more nearly assured.[33]

In any event, the contemporary controversy concerning White's *Case* was not over the distribution of political power, but over its quasi-Presbyterian plan of government and the introduction of the laity on an equal footing with the clergy to ecclesiastical councils.[34] The possibility of clerical, even if conditioned, consecration of a person who was to exercise episcopal duties was rejected by the New England clergy and other persons. This group was also hesitant to accept the idea of lay representation as well. However, the main disagreement arose over the question of the episcopacy.

Essentially, then, there were two main views toward the reconstitution of the church after the Revolution, inasmuch as Maryland was willing to participate in the Pennsylvania Plan. Connecticut and New England, on the one hand, felt that no discussion for organization among the churches could be had until there was a bishop in the Episcopal Church. White and the churches of the East and South felt that the congregations should organize, make whatever minor revisions were essential in Anglican discipline and liturgy to continue the church, and secure a bishop as soon as it was possible to do so.[35]

---

32. White, *Memoirs*, 466.
33. *Ibid.*
34. The laity have always played a prominent and official role in the American Episcopal Church, and the propriety and catholicity of this has often been both challenged and defended. While the implications of lay participation are manifold, they will not be developed systematically in this thesis, though occasional reference will be made to lay governmental responsibilities and duties at various points. For varied discussions, see G. MacLaren Brydon, "The Origin of the Rights of the Laity in the American Episcopal Church," *Historical Magazine of the Protestant Episcopal Church* 12 (1943): 313–38; C. C. Edmunds, Jr., "The Revival of Minor Orders—The True Method of Enlisting Lay Help," *Church Eclectic* 17 (1889): 219–29; Investigator, "Permanent Deacons as Assistants in Large Parishes," *Protestant Episcopalian* 7 (1836): 383–86; "The Laity in the Church: Has the Experiment of the American Church Succeeded?" *Church Eclectic* 7 (1879): 374–80; R. W. Norman, "Women's Work in the Church," *Church Review* 36 (1881): 213–40; Albion K. Parris, "The Place of the Laity in the Church," *Protestant Episcopal Review* 13 (1900): 301–11; "Report of a Meeting of the Standing Committee of the Diocese of M———," *Church Eclectic* 9 (1881): 842–45; Walter H. Stowe, *More Lay Readers than Clergy: A Study of the Office of Lay Reader in the History of the Church* (Philadelphia: Church Historical Society, 1956).
35. See Loveland, *The Critical Years*, 166–67, for the best discussion of the progress of these two schemes. She feels that the union was very nearly impossible, and only precariously achieved by the compromise of both groups and the alteration in the plans of each, in part due to changes in the environmental situation. Structurally and essentially, nonetheless, it was White's plan that prevailed.

Conventions to Reconstitute the Church

The first meeting of members of the Episcopal Church from various states that included a consideration of ways of reorganizing the church was held in New Brunswick, New Jersey, in May 1784. In New York in October 1784 a larger group met, called by the New Brunswick Assembly. Present were clergy and/or lay men from Massachusetts, Rhode Island, Connecticut, New York, New Jersey, Pennsylvania, Delaware, Maryland, and Virginia. This convention of only twenty-seven members presented the following "Fundamental Principles":

I. That there shall be a General Convention of the Episcopal Church in the United States of America.

II. That the Episcopal Church in each State send Deputies to the Convention, consisting of Clergy and Laity.

III. That associated congregations in two or more States may send Deputies jointly.

IV. That the said Church shall maintain the doctrines of the Gospel as now held by the Church of England; and shall adhere to the Liturgy of the said Church, as far as shall be consistent with the American Revolution and the Constitution of the respective States.

V. That in every State where there shall be a Bishop duly consecrated and settled, he shall be considered as a member of the Convention ex officio.

VI. That the Clergy and Laity, assembled in Convention, shall deliberate in one body, but shall vote separately. And the concurrence of both shall be necessary to give validity to every measure.

VII. That the first meeting of the Convention shall be at Philadelphia, the Tuesday before the Feast of St. Michael next; to which it is hoped and earnestly desired that the Episcopal churches in the respective States, will send their clerical and lay deputies, duly instructed and authorized to proceed on the necessary business herein proposed for their deliberation.[36]

As in White's *Case*, the question of federalism does not appear to have been the concern of the persons who wrote these "principles of ecclesiastical union." There is no division of power. However, a case can be made for the position that the union proposal does have several federal or confederal characteristics, with the church in the several states being the basis of the federation, because the voting procedure in the Sixth Principle was

---

36. Perry, *Journals*, 1:12–13.

held, in the Convention of 1785, to mean that voting was counted by states and not by individuals.[37]

In the church in several of the states there were drawn up during this period various proposed articles of union for Episcopal parishes within the state. It is informative to examine these proposals to see whether they evidence a concern for protection of diocesan political powers.

The recounts of various state conventions of the time lead again, as in the instance of White's *Case,* to the conclusion that if the government of the national church were to be one of restricted powers, the residue of the governing power should rest in the parish churches and not in the dioceses.[38] Thus, the proposed principles each of Massachusetts, Virginia, Pennsylvania, South Carolina, and Maryland contain the hope that "no powers be delegated to a general ecclesiastical government, except such as cannot conveniently be exercised by the clergy and laity in their respective congregations."[39]

The same wording was used in one of the six "Articles of Convention" of the church in Pennsylvania in May 25, 1784, and was cited by the convention of the church in Maryland in June 1784 as being the basis of Maryland's "Declaration of Religious Rights" of June 23, 1784.[40] It also appears in Article VI of the articles of the Massachusetts convention of September 8, 1784,[41] and of the South Carolina convention of May 1786.[42]

On May 23, 1785, a convention "consisting of thirty-six clergy and upward of seventy laymen" in Virginia[43] approved the "Fundamental Principles" of October 1784 after modifying the Fourth and Sixth Articles. The convention added "that this convention will however accede to the mode of voting recommended in the Sixth Article, with respect to the convention to be holden in Philadelphia, reserving the right to approve or disapprove their proceedings."[44] Virginia thereby attempted specifically to reserve for herself the right to "nullify" any decisions of the Philadelphia Convention of 1785, which were contrary to her wishes.

---

37. *Ibid.,* 1:18.
38. Perry, *Journals,* vol. 3, and White's *Memoirs,* as well as Walter H. Stowe, "State or Diocesan Conventions of the War and Post War Period," *Historical Magazine of the Protestant Episcopal Church* 8 (1939): 220–50 and the major sources used here.
39. White, *Memoirs,* 93.
40. Perry, *Journals,* 3:14–15, especially 29–30.
41. *Ibid.,* 3:64.
42. Frederick Dalcho, *An Historical Account of the Protestant Episcopal Church in South Carolina* (Charleston: E. Thayer, 1820), 474.
43. Perry, *Journals,* 3:47.
44. *Ibid.,* 3:48.

The New Jersey convention of July 6, 1785, also accepted the "Fundamental Principles" and elected deputies to the Philadelphia Convention, "with power to accede, on the part of this convention, to the fundamental principles...and to adopt such measures, as said general convention may deem necessary for the utility of the said church, not repugnant to the aforesaid fundamental principles."[45]

A convention of the church in Maryland on June 22, 1784, added a statement of what it considered to be the necessary scope of the powers of the governing bodies of the church.[46] But significantly, the Maryland convention did not attempt to divide the powers between the Convention of the national church and the diocesan conventions. There was no attempt to protect the diocesan powers from exercise by the national church.

On September 27–28, 1785, the convention called for by Article VII of the "Fundamental Principles" was held in Philadelphia. One solution toward the problems of securing an American bishop had been met in the consecration of Connecticut's Samuel Seabury on November 14, 1784, but, as Connecticut had not participated officially in the previous national conventions,[47] no Connecticut deputy was at the Philadelphia meeting in 1785.

The Philadelphia Convention drafted "A General Ecclesiastical Constitution of the Protestant Episcopal Church in the United States of America."[48] This Constitution, consisting of a preamble and eleven articles, had substantial identity with the "Fundamental Principles" of the year before. No mention was made concerning a distribution of governing powers among the state conventions and the General Convention, and neither the First Article, which declared simply "that there shall be a General Convention of the Protestant Episcopal Church in the United States of America" nor any other article defined the scope or nature of General Convention's powers.

However, several important functions were assigned to the church in the states as such. Article II said that each state should send from one to four deputies to a unicameral convention, and that voting there would be by states, and not by individuals. Bishops were to be chosen agreeable to state rules, and no bishop would exercise his office outside his own jurisdiction (here, his own state) except by invitation (Article VI). Thus, while

---

45. *Ibid.*, 3:56.
46. *Ibid.*, 3:30–31.
47. Those persons from Connecticut and New England who had attended previous conventions had not been taken to be representatives of the church in these areas, but simply observers.
48. Perry, *Journals*, 1:21–23.

silent on the question of a division of powers, considerable essential governing duties were specifically delegated to the church in the states.

On June 20, 1786, according to agreement at the 1785 meeting, another convention was held, in Philadelphia, once again without the New England churches sending deputies. The question of the possibility of a basis of agreement between the two major plans of organization was still in doubt. Especially was there considerable reluctance on the part of some to recognize Bishop Seabury's consecration by Scottish, nonjuring bishops as being valid. However, the Convention as a whole was primarily concerned with adopting a set of principles of constitution agreeable to all the churches in all the states, and toward this end, still another constitutional document was drawn up. Again, while there were important changes in the governing power granted to bishops and in the process of amendment, both of which will be discussed later in this book, and in the role of the laity in church government, no attempt was made to define either a distribution of power or the governing power of General Convention.[49]

The adjourned Convention of 1786, meeting at Wilmington, Delaware, October 10–11, as a continuation of the June meeting, was essentially concerned only with concluding a series of letters between the American Church and the English archbishops for the purpose of securing an episcopate through Anglican consecration.[50] When the English bishops were finally convinced by the correspondence that the American Church did not intend to depart in any essential way from the doctrine, discipline, or worship of the Church of England, Samuel Provoost of New York and William White of Pennsylvania were ordered bishop by the Archbishops of Canterbury and York with the participation of the Bishops of Bath and Wells and of Peterborough, in the Chapel of the Archepiscopal Palace of Lambeth on February 4, 1787.[51]

The Constitution of 1789

It was during the two sessions in July and September of 1789 that the reorganization of the Episcopal Church was finally settled. Previous constitutional documents had been but proposals for union. On August 8, 1789, a constitution was adopted of which later revisions were only in the way of amendment. White says that there was a "conviction generally prevailing in the convention, that the formerly proposed constitution was inadequate to the situation of this Church"[52] because of the possibility of the

---

49. *Ibid.*, 1:38–42.
50. *Ibid.*, 1:47–62.
51. White, *Memoirs*, 27.
52. *Ibid.*, 166.

two English-consecrated bishops and the single Scottish-consecrated one now joining into a single ecclesiastical organization.

Indeed, the proceedings of this session were largely conditioned by that possibility. After drawing up preliminary canons and a constitution, and preparing a report of their actions for the English archbishops,[53] the Convention adjourned until September 29, a month and a half later, sending an especial request to Bishop Seabury and the New England clergy for their presence at the coming convention. The hope was that the time was propitious for the formation of a lasting union of all the Episcopal churches in the several states.

The expectation of the summer Convention was not proven false. On September 20, 1789, when the adjourned Convention met once again in Philadelphia, Samuel Seabury, Bishop of Connecticut, and three other New England clergymen[54] were in attendance. On October 2, after securing the modification of Article III,[55] the New England clergy accepted the Constitution as drawn up by the summer Convention. Thus, October 2, 1789, may be considered to be the date when the former Church of England in America reconstituted itself into the Protestant Episcopal Church in the United States of America. The Constitution was somewhat revised from earlier constitutional proposals, especially, as shall be seen, in regard to the governing role of bishops, the composition of General Convention, and to some extent, in the amending process.

But still there was no statement as to a division of powers between the General and diocesan conventions or as to the limits of the governing power of General Convention itself. It is true that the Constitution rested upon and operated primarily through the actions of the church in the states. This is a significant change from the scheme outlined in White's *Case,* which was based essentially upon parochial action. But, as was the situation in the proposals since 1784, on the face of the 1789 Constitution, no article or section was included for the purpose of defining a constitutional division of powers between the church's central government and the governments of the dioceses.

Therefore, in contradiction to those who believe the government of the church to be either confederal or federal on the basis of an alleged analogy between the Articles of Confederation or the United States Constitution's division of power, it can be said that there is not explicit in the church's

---

53. Perry, *Journals,* 1:63–90.
54. "The Rev. Dr. Samuel Parker, Deputy from the churches in Massachusetts and New Hampshire, and the Rev. Mr. Bela Hubbard and the Rev. Mr. Abraham Jarvis, Deputies from the church in Connecticut" (*ibid.,* 1:93).
55. The article referred to bishops' powers.

Constitution of 1789 any definition of a division of powers, even though the framers of the Constitution had the models of both the Articles and the United States Constitution before them. This is not to say that the essence of such a section meant the Convention of 1789 specifically rejected the intention of a division of powers. It is not within the scope of the book to determine what the framers' intentions might or might not have been, if it is not written into the formal law of the church. All that can be determined here is whether the formal Constitution of the church is federal, confederal, or unitary.

In summary, neither Bishop White's *Case,* nor the "Fundamental Principles" of 1785, nor the "General Constitution of 1786," nor the Constitution of 1789 provided explicitly for a constitutional division of powers. Such a division of powers is an essential manifestation of both federal and confederal government. Neither is there any other evidence to indicate that the Constitution is one of a confederation. Indeed, as far as the written Constitution is explicitly concerned, the church's government is unitary.

If there was no explicit division of powers provided for at the inception of the Episcopal Church, has such a provision been added to the Constitution subsequently? If not, can a division of powers be reasonably inferred from the totality of the Constitution of 1789 and as amended?

An examination of the constitutional amendments accepted by General Convention shows that no section has been added to the Constitution either for the specific or incidental purpose of affirming or denying the federal or confederal structure of the church or of a division of power between the central and diocesan governments.[56]

The answer to the second question will be found in each of the subsequent chapters of this thesis wherein the particular institutions provided for by the Constitution and Canons are evaluated. The Constitution has undergone considerable revision and reorganization. Aside from changes in substance since 1789, there has been considerable change in form. Whereas the original Constitution was only two or three pages long and consisted of nine brief and single-paragraphed articles, the Constitution after the 1958 Convention was about fourteen pages long and had eleven more

---

56. Article III, Section 4 of the revised Constitution as proposed by the Joint Commission on Revision in March 1895, said in part, "The powers not committed to the General Synod or to the Provincial Synods by this Constitution, nor prohibited by it to the dioceses are reserved to the dioceses respectively, save that no diocese or province shall legislate in regards to doctrine or worship" (*Churchman* 71 [March 16, 1895]: 379). This clause apparently was not the object of public discussion. It was not debated in the 1895 General Convention and was not reported on the floor of either House of the Convention for action. It died, for reasons unascertainable, in the Bishops' Committee on the Constitution.

lengthy and multiparagraphed articles, many of which were themselves divided into subsections.

Until 1901, there had been no reorganization of the order of the 1789 Constitution in spite of many amendments to it. However, in 1892, a joint commission was appointed by the General Convention to revise the Constitution and Canons.[57] The result was the most inclusive revision the Constitution has had until the present day.[58]

The Canons of 1789

The summer session (July 20–August 8) of the 1789 Convention adopted ten canons,[59] prepared largely by a committee appointed to draw up a body of canons.[60] Actually, these canons were passed by the Convention one day *before* the Constitution was finally accepted.[61] This fact has been used by some students of the church's government to show that the canons are not necessarily made pursuant to the Constitution; that there is, indeed, no subject about which General Convention cannot legislate.[62]

The canons were concerned only with establishing the qualifications of candidates to Holy Orders throughout the church. Consequently it was clearly determined that while candidates were required to have the approval of and guarantee of support from the ecclesiastical authorities in their diocese, General Convention was competent to set any qualification supplementing or obliterating those of the dioceses. The canons ensured, for example, the approval or disapproval of a candidate to the episcopacy by representatives of the bishops, clergy, and laity in all dioceses of the church, even though after consecration he would be jurisdictionally restricted to the exercise of his office within his own diocese only, except by invitation.[63]

These first canons also showed that General Convention could significantly control the internal instruments of government of the dioceses even though the Constitution did not give them specific authority so to do. As

---

57. White and Dykman (1954), 1:11.
58. Reference will be made to this revision frequently. For the best single source, see William J. Seabury, *Notes on the Constitution of 1901* (New York: T. Whittaker, 1902).
59. Perry, *Journals*, 1:79–82.
60. *Ibid.*, 1:72.
61. *Ibid.*, compare 1:79 with 83.
62. See Murray Hoffman, *A Treatise on the Law of the Protestant Episcopal Church in the United States* (New York: Stanford and Swords, 1850), 105; Seabury, *Ecclesiastical Polity*, 222; Francis Vinton, *A Manual Commentary on the General Canon Law and the Constitution of the Protestant Episcopal Church in the United States* (New York: E. P. Dutton, 1870), 79–80.
63. More will be said about this and other implications of the governing role of bishops in relation to the question of federalism in chapter 4.

but one example, Canon 7 stated in part, "In every state in which there is no Standing Committee, such Committee shall be appointed at its next ensuing Convention."[64] The very committee that drafted these first canons recognized that they were quite incomplete.

> Mr. Andrews moved the following resolve:
> Whereas it appears that sundry other Canons are necessary for the good government of the Church,
> Resolved that... a Committee [be appointed] to prepare and report to the next meeting of this Convention, such additional Canons as to them shall seem necessary.
> Which was agreed to.[65]

The fall session of this Convention, at which the New England churches were for the first time present, agreed to a list of seventeen canons.[66] The first nine canons were identical to the ten of the previous sessions.[67] Canons 10 through 17 were newly passed, and were concerned with guiding the conduct of the parish clergy in their liturgical and pastoral relations, and in establishing minimal discipline for the laity, or regulating aspects of parish government by clergy and laity.[68]

Thus, the first General Convention not only presumed competence for controlling diocesan governments and the qualifications of ministers, but for the operation of parochial government as well. Such far-reaching authority is more typical of a unitary than of a federal or confederal government, especially inasmuch as the Constitution did not specifically or by reasonable inference give General Convention these powers.

The enactment of canons by General Convention is equivalent to the passing of laws by civil governments. That is, a canon, as far as the American Episcopal Church is concerned, is a law for the church.

After the 1955 Convention there were sixty-two canons in force in the church, arranged under five general topics, which occupied 177 pages of an appendix to the 1955 journal. This is in contrast to the seventeen canons, not arranged in any apparent sequence, of six pages, in 1789. Moreover, all but 142 pages of the 1,065 pages in White and Dykman's two-volume annotation of the Constitution and Canons are devoted to a

---

64. Perry, *Journals*, 1:81.
65. *Ibid.*, 1:82.
66. *Ibid.*, 1:125–30.
67. The only exceptions were that Canon 7 of the first session was joined to Canon 6, and to Canon 8 (now 7), which required that candidates for Holy Orders know Greek and Latin, was appended a clause for exemption under certain circumstances.
68. Canons 10, 11, 12, 14, 15, and 16; Canons 12 and 14; and Canons 19, 17, respectively.

discussion of the canons leading up to and including those in effect as of 1952.

The canons have been codified, revised, and rearranged many times in the church's history. But at no time, either by canonical legislation or constitutional amendment, have there been enacted provisions designed fundamentally to limit the power of the General Convention in favor of diocesan power, or establish a division of governing authority between the central and the affiliate governments.

Moreover, the Constitution of the church not only does not specifically restrict the power of General Convention, but also does not specifically empower the Convention to act in many significant areas. This lack of specific constitutional authority itself has only rarely been successfully invoked to attempt to prevent General Convention from passing canonical legislation. Thus, General Convention has enacted canons touching on almost all matters of ecclesiastical governance, and has preempted various fields from diocesan legislation. Consequently, the point has been made that there is little of significance about which the dioceses possess exclusive jurisdiction—and that even this may at any time be removed by General Convention through canonical legislation or constitutional amendments.[69]

How the Constitution Was Enacted

The method of constitutional enactment and amendment is crucial for any federal government.[70] If the process is such that the persons who participate in the enactment are not primarily and specifically representatives of member governments, and not simply representatives of the people in a geographic region, grave doubts are cast upon the validity of the federal assumption. That is, if the original member governments do not themselves participate in the proceedings leading up to the enactment of a constitution through their specific representatives and by themselves formally ratifying the document upon submittal by the deputies, an important prerequisite for a federal, as well as a confederal, government is lacking and the government is probably unitary.

Similarly, if the constitution can be amended by the central government alone without specific approval, or over the specific disapproval, of a constitutionally predetermined number of member governments, the

---

69. Hill Burgwin, "The National Church and the Diocese," *Church Review* 45 (1885): 423–55.
70. William S. Livingston, *Federalism and Constitutional Change* (Oxford: Clarendon, 1956). Livingston considers the very test of a federal government to be the way in which the constitution is amended.

federal or confederal hypothesis is in doubt and the unitary principle emphasized. If the constitution can be amended or altered by the affiliate governments without the approval, or over the disapproval, of the central government, then the government is probably confederal.

The period between 1782 and 1789 saw the development of four major constitutional drafts before the adoption of the 1789 Constitution, which remains, as revised, the church's Constitution today. To whom did the participants in the conventions that drew up these drafts owe accountability? Were they representatives of diocesan governments, or of the church in the dioceses? How and by whom were they chosen? Were they given strict instructions, which they followed closely? If so, from whom did the instructions come?

The first interstate meeting of Episcopalians for the purpose of ecclesiastical union was in 1784 at New Brunswick, New Jersey. This assembly, held at the special insistence of William White and Abraham Beach,[71] was called to coincide with a meeting of the Corporation for the Relief of the Widows and Children of Clergymen in Pennsylvania, New York, and New Jersey, so that the greatest number of clergy and laity from the several states might attend. However, only persons from New York, Pennsylvania, and New Jersey did attend.[72]

Although the church in Pennsylvania (and elsewhere) was in the process of reorganizing itself into a state convention at this time, no such convention had actually been held. A clergy convention in Connecticut had already sent Samuel Seabury to England for consecration, a fact that most Episcopalians in other states had not known until informed of it at the New Brunswick meeting.[73] None of the persons at the New Jersey meeting, then, were "official" deputies, appointed by the dioceses themselves. Rather, they were simply interested Episcopalians who were able to spend two days in New Brunswick.

Indeed, White observes that while most of the persons at the meeting had come in response to his and Beach's previous invitation,[74] "there happened to be in town, on civil business, some lay gentlemen, who, being presented by the clergy from New York and New Jersey as taking an interest in the welfare of the church, were requested to attend."[75] At this meeting, a

---

71. See the correspondence between Beach and White in Perry, *Journals*, 3:8–12, and Loveland, *The Critical Years*, 64–65.
72. White, *Memoirs*, 84.
73. *Ibid.*
74. The announcement had apparently been published in Philadelphia and New York newspapers. See Perry, *Journals*, 3:11.
75. White, *Memoirs*, 84.

committee of correspondence was appointed to write church members "for the purpose of forming a continental Representation of the Episcopal Church, and for the better management of other concerns of the Church."[76]

October 6, 1784, the next meeting of the Corporation for the Relief of Widows and Orphans, in New York, was the time and place suggested for the Convention. In addition to twenty clergy and laity from New York, New Jersey, and Pennsylvania, three were present from Delaware, and one each from Maryland, Massachusetts and Rhode Island, Connecticut, and Virginia.[77]

> The present meeting, like that in May is here spoken of as a voluntary one, and not an authorized convention, because there were no authorities from the churches in the several states, even in the appointments of the members, which were made from the congregations, to which they respectively belonged; except to Mr. Parker from Massachusetts, of Mr. Marshall, from Connecticut, and of those who attended from Pennsylvania: even from these states, there was no further authority, than to deliberate and propose. Accordingly, the acts of the body were in the form of recommendation and proposal.[78]

The proposals were in the form of the "Fundamental Principles of Ecclesiastical Union" which began:

> The Body now assembled, recommend to the clergy and congregations of their Communion in the States represented as above, and propose to those of the other States not represented, that as soon as they shall have organized or associated themselves in the States to which they respectively belong, agreeably to such Rules as they shall think proper, they unite in a general ecclesiastical constitution, on the following Fundamental Principles.[79]

and closed:

> VIII. That the first meeting of the Convention shall be at *Philadelphia*, the Tuesday before the Feast of St. Michael next; to which it is hoped, and earnestly desired, that the Episcopal churches in the respective States, will send their Clerical and Lay Deputies, duly instructed and authorized to proceed on the necessary business herein proposed for their deliberations.[80]

---

76. Perry, *Journals*, 3:8.
77. *Ibid.*, 3:3.
78. White, *Memoirs*, 86.
79. Perry, *Journals*, 3:4.
80. *Ibid.*

Thus, union was made dependent upon the parish churches forming state ecclesiastical organizations. Members of the next convention, a year later, were to be "duly instructed" by the state ecclesiastical governments.

On September 27, 1785, "A Convention of the Protestant Episcopal Church in the States of New York, New Jersey, Pennsylvania, Delaware, Maryland, Virginia, and South Carolina"[81] was held in Philadelphia. On the first day of business, on September 28, it was resolved, that the

> Deputies from the several States produce the testimonials of their appointment; which being done, and the testimonials read,
> *Resolved*,— that the testimonials produced from the Church in the several States ... are satisfactory.[82]

All of the deputies to the 1785 Convention had been appointed by conventions of the church in the states. However, only one or possibly two of the seven conventions specifically instructed their deputies, and four of the conventions did not bother to develop ecclesiastical governments for their states, merely gathering primarily for the purpose of electing the deputies to the Philadelphia Convention.

Virginia was the first state to hold a convention in 1785.[83] This meeting not only chose two laymen and two clergy, but also specifically instructed them. However, the instructions related only to liturgical and theological matters, and did not refer at all to church government or to the locus and distribution of the governing power of the church. Most significantly, however, the convention declared itself to be "at liberty to approve or disapprove the proceedings of General Convention."[84] Also, the Virginia convention proceeded fully to form its diocesan governmental organization.

In Philadelphia the first Pennsylvania state convention, which set up a diocesan government under "an act of association of the Clergy and Congregations of the Protestant Episcopal Church in the state of Pennsylvania," chose five clerical and seventeen lay deputies to the 1785 General Convention, completely uninstructed in any way.[85]

The churches in South Carolina, too weak to establish a diocesan government, did manage to form a convention to choose four lay and one clerical deputies.[86] Though they instructed their deputies to declare that

---

81. *Ibid.*, 1:14–29.
82. *Ibid.*, 1:17.
83. *Ibid.*, 3:44–51.
84. *Ibid.*, 3:47.
85. *Ibid.*, 3:40–43. Held May 24, 1785, in Philadelphia.
86. *Ibid.*, 3:51–53. Held May 12, 1785, in Charleston.

South Carolina wanted no bishop resident in the state, the deputies were otherwise specifically "left to act according to their judgment."[87]

The New York convention of June 22, 1785,[88] appointed three clerical and lay deputies "authorized to proceed on the necessary business of the said convention, so far as they conform to the general principles [of 1784] which are established to regulate their conduct in this matter."[89] Taking no action in the foundation of a diocesan government other than choosing a president for the convention, it was "resolved, that the president be requested to call another convention, at such time and place as he shall deem most conducive to the interest of the church."[90]

A convention in New Brunswick, New Jersey, held July 6, 1785, appointed deputies

> with power to accede, on the part of this convention, to the fundamental principles published by the convention of the Protestant Episcopal Church, held in New-York, the 6th and 7th days of October, 1784; and to adopt such measures, as the said General Convention may deem necessary for the utility of the said Church, not repugnant to the aforesaid fundamental principles.[91]

Scarcely more was done than in the case of New York toward the formation of a diocesan government.

Apparently no records of Delaware's convention exist, but Loveland says "as the delegates from there were officially accepted, it is probable that a preliminary convention had been held."[92] Maryland, however, may not have held a convention in 1785, perhaps considering the 1784 meeting sufficient. At any rate, no records of a 1785 meeting exist.[93] In North Carolina and Georgia, the church was, and remained for some time, too weak to participate in any scheme of union. But the New England churches, supporting Bishop Seabury's opposition to several changes wrought by the middle and southern states in General Convention, refused to attend, though aware of the Convention's existence. For example, a convention of the churches in Massachusetts, Rhode Island, and New Hampshire[94] "voted, that is the

---

87. *Ibid.*, 3:53.
88. *Ibid.*, 3:53–55.
89. *Ibid.*, 3:54–55.
90. *Ibid.*, 3:55.
91. *Ibid.*, 3:56.
92. Loveland, *The Critical Years*, 134.
93. Protestant Episcopal Church in Maryland, *Journal of the 72nd Annual Convention of the Protestant Episcopal Church in Maryland* (Baltimore: Joseph Robinson, 1855). Journals of the 1783 through 1788 Maryland conventions are bound after the index of the 1855 convention (see pp. 168–69).
94. Perry, *Journals*, 3:92–99.

opinion of this Convention, that it is not necessary nor convenient to send a deputy or deputies to the Convention, to be holden at Philadelphia."[95]

Thus it can be doubted that the members of the 1785 General Convention, as a whole, were delegates of the diocesan governments, or that they were under any specific instructions from their diocesan governments concerning the structure or the distribution of power in the proposed union, and particularly that there were no instructions indicating that the deputies were to set up either a federal or confederal union. Indeed, there is strong evidence that many of the deputies to the 1785 Convention in Philadelphia were merely representatives of the church in the states, and not of the ecclesiastical governments of the states.

Among the first business of substance engaged in by the Convention was a review and reaffirmation of the "Fundamental Principles of 1784." These were accepted with but few revisions.[96] It should be noted again, however, that Article VI, concerning voting in General Convention, was interpreted "as meaning that the Deputies are to vote according to the States from which they come, and not individually."[97]

In the "General Ecclesiastical Constitution" adopted by the 1785 Convention, a new Convention was called for June 1786. This convention met, from June 20 to 26, with representatives from the same seven states as in 1785.[98]

Again, the journals of the General Convention indicated that the deputies' credentials were read and approved, though the substance of the credentials is not included in the official record. What does an examination of the diocesan journals show? Were the representatives deputies of the ecclesiastical governments of the states, or simply of governmentally unorganized clergy conventions? Were the delegates instructed by the governments or conventions, or left to act at their own discretion?

According to the journals of the Virginia convention,[99] it was "resolved that the delegates be appointed to the General Convention to be held at Philadelphia in June next, and that their powers be defined by instructions."[100] A committee of ten persons was appointed toward this end. The resulting instructions said, in part:

---

95. *Ibid.*, 3:98.
96. *Ibid.*, 1:18.
97. *Ibid.*
98. *Ibid.*, 1:31–46.
99. Convention reports for Virginia are in Francis L. Hawks, *Contributions to the Ecclesiastical History of the United States*, vol. 1 (New York: Harper & Brothers, 1836), Appendix, 12–18.
100. *Ibid.*, 14.

> We consider the Protestant Episcopal Church in America as an incorporate society, and therefore unity in doctrine and worship its characteristics: Conformably to this, you will not carp at expression, nor carry your objections to unessential points; guarding against schism by all possible means, and giving our church every benefit and strength it can acquire from union.[101]

The other instruction simply asked for the "necessary character" of the "benefit of episcopal superintendence."[102]

In South Carolina on April 26, 1786, four persons were chosen as deputies to the Philadelphia Convention "on behalf of the several churches represented in this Convention."[103] No instructions were explicitly given, although it is implicit that they were to communicate alterations to the Constitution suggested by the South Carolina conventions and to try to get those provisions changed. The most important constitutional change regarding federalism was:

> Rule 6 [*i.e.*, Article VI of the Constitution of 1785] Objected to; so far as relates to the establishment of a Bishop in South-Carolina. But recommend that the word *State* be inserted between the words *respective* and *Conventions*.[104]

The inference here is that South Carolina wanted that it should be left up to each state convention to decide whether or not the state should have a bishop.

A second convention was held in 1786 in South Carolina; this from May 29 to 31. After rather extensive liturgy and Prayer Book alterations, it was resolved that deputies to General Convention "are desired to use their endeavors to get them adopted."[105] Also at this convention a constitution was adopted for the diocese, ending:

> Article 6. That no power be delegated to a General Ecclesiastical Government, except such, as cannot be exercised by the Clergy and Vestries, in the respective Congregations.[106]

Similar provisions were found in the contemporary Maryland and Pennsylvania constitutions.

---

101. *Ibid.*, 15.
102. *Ibid.*
103. Dalcho, *An Historical Account*, 470.
104. *Ibid.*, 469.
105. *Ibid.*, 473.
106. *Ibid.*, 474.

In New York, two conventions were also held in 1786. At the first, four clerical and four lay deputies were elected to the June General Convention. Their only instruction: "*Resolved.* That the persons appointed to represent this Church be instructed not to consent to any act that may imply the validity of Dr. Seabury's ordinations."[107] At the second convention, on September 20 and 21, 1786, four deputies were appointed to the Wilmington Convention, and it was:

> *Resolved.* That the representatives of this Church in the General Convention, be instructed to move, that the name of every person who makes a motion in the said Convention, upon which a question is put, be entered on the minutes of said Convention, and that the ayes and noes be also entered on the determination of the question, in the said minutes, if any member should require it.[108]

More importantly, it was also

> *Resolved.* That the Deputies to the General Convention have discretionary power, with respect to any matters which may come into debate in the said General Convention.[109]

From May 16 to 19, 1786, a convention was held for consideration of the proceedings of the 1785 General Convention, for election of deputies to the June 1786 General Convention, and for the establishment of a more complete diocesan government. Among the first order of business was the consideration of the 1785 Constitution. The New Jersey meeting rejected this Constitution because the members felt that Prayer Book and general ecclesiastical revision and reformation was improper without the presence and support of a bishop.[110] The convention did not show any particular objection to the organization proposed in the 1785 Constitution, but only that it was agreed upon without episcopal supervision. Moreover, while specifically accepting General Convention's work, though also saying it should not have been done, the New Jersey convention also elected eleven deputies to the 1786 General Convention. It thus was willing to continue

---

107. Protestant Episcopal Church in New York, *Journals of the Conventions of the Protestant Episcopal Church in the Diocese of New York, 1785–1819* (New York: Henry M. Onderdonk, 1844), 9.
108. *Ibid.*, 11.
109. *Ibid.*
110. Protestant Episcopal Church in New Jersey, *Journals of the Conventions of the Protestant Episcopal Church in the State of New Jersey, 1785–1816* (New York: John Polhemus, 1890), 7–9 and 13–15.

participation in this plan of ecclesiastical reorganization. At the same convention, the constitution of the diocese was presented and accepted.[111]

No record of the April 1786 meeting in Maryland exists, according to the Maryland journals of 1855, where the early diocesan records are collected.[112] The journal of the 1789 Maryland convention shows that a convention was held in April 1786 and that two deputies were chosen by Maryland to the June 1786 General Convention, but no other information is given.[113]

In 1786, the evidence indicates a slightly different situation than in 1785. Mainly, the dioceses had moved farther along toward the establishment of their own ecclesiastical governments. Thus, the deputies to the two 1786 Conventions were more nearly representatives of the diocesan governments and not simply of diocesan clergy meetings.

However, again, not all of the diocesan conventions instructed their deputies in any positive way. Some deputies were left completely uninstructed; others were expressly given discretionary powers. In some instances the instructions seemed to mean that the deputies were representatives of the churches in the dioceses and not of the diocesan conventions. Virginia's statement concerning the "incorporate" nature of the church in the United States implies that Virginia viewed the church as logically and organically one throughout the nation and its present condition as unnatural and lacking its normal character as a unified body. Moreover, of those who were instructed, the orders were usually pertaining only to one or two issues, and, again, none referred to the distribution of governing powers between the General and diocesan conventions.

While the first General Convention is generally considered to have been that of 1785, it seems that even the Convention of 1786 did not feel itself fully qualified and empowered to handle authoritatively many governing problems. This Convention was still concerned with constructing a prayer book and a form of government that would satisfy all Episcopal churchmen in the United States. On June 23,

> A Memorial from the Convention of the Church in the State of New Jersey was presented, and sundry communications from the Conventions in the other States were made, relative to the business of this Convention. Whereupon,
> *Resolved.*—That the said Memorial and communications be referred to the first General Convention which shall assemble with sufficient powers to de-

---

111. *Ibid.*, 9–12.
112. Protestant Episcopal Church in Maryland, *Journal*, 17.
113. *Ibid.*, 18.

termine on the same; and that, in the meantime, they be lodged with the Secretary.[114]

The Constitution of the 1786 Convention was read twice and fully discussed, only a few amendments being made.[115] One of the most significant resolutions of the 1786 Convention was made on June 24:

> *Resolved.*—That it be recommended to the Conventions of this Church, in the several States represented in this Convention, that they authorize and empower their Deputies to the next General Convention, after we shall have obtained a Bishop or Bishops in our Church, to confirm and ratify a general constitution, respecting both doctrine and discipline of the Protestant Episcopal Church in the United States of America.[116]

This resolution was introduced to implement the newly written Article XI of the Constitution of 1786.[117] As shall be seen, this resolution has considerable ramifications for the question of federalism.

The 1786 adjourned Convention met at Wilmington, Delaware. As this was an adjourned and not a new convention,[118] no credentials of the deputies were sought, though there were some changes in personnel. The primary business of this meeting was to receive and evaluate letters from the Archbishops of England regarding the American Episcopal Church. However, at one point,

> A question was then proposed and seconded, viz., whether this convention hath authority to admit as members persons deriving their appointment, not from a State Convention, but from one particular parish or parishes only.
>
> On the question being put, it was determined in the negative.
>
> Another question was then proposed and seconded, viz., whether this Convention can, consistently with its fundamental articles, admit a State to be represented by a Clerical or Lay deputy only. Which was also determined in the negative.[119]

This ruling immediately affected the Reverend William Smith, who alone represented Maryland. Virginia had no deputies at all.[120] The church in

---

114. Perry, *Journals*, 1:38.
115. *Ibid.*, 1:38–40.
116. *Ibid.*, 1:42.
117. The full quotation is given later.
118. Perry, *Journals*, 1:51.
119. *Ibid.*, 1:57.
120. *Ibid.*, 1:49.

these states had sent deputies to previous Conventions. Since they were absent, it was

> *Resolved.*—That the Secretary be desired to transmit a copy of the proceedings of this Convention to the Standing Committees of the Protestant Episcopal Church in the States of Maryland and Virginia, with the affectionate hope of this body, that their brethren of the said States after duly considering the principles of which these proceedings have been held, will approve and adopt the same.[121]

On July 28, 1789, another General Convention opened in Philadelphia. Delegates were present from the seven states, though throughout the session, only a single lay deputy represented Virginia.[122] Virginia's clerical deputy, the Reverend David Griffith, died in Philadelphia during the fifth day, without attending any meetings. Thus, the ruling of the previous Convention was not invoked in this instance against Virginia, nor was the question raised, according to the journal record. However, an important piece of business on the first day was taken in pursuance to the resolution made in 1786:

> The deputies from the several States being called upon to declare their powers, relative to the object of the [resolution cited earlier[123]] gave information that they came fully authorized to ratify a Book of Common Prayer, etc., for the use of the Church.[124]

On July 30, late-arriving deputies "were requested to state their powers relative to the ratification of a Book of Common Prayer, etc., which were deemed sufficient."[125]

Thus the Constitution of 1789, adopted after considerable study, was enacted by deputies authorized and empowered, as far as the state conventions were concerned, to act fully on their own discretion in confirming and ratifying that Constitution. At no point does the record indicate that the Constitution of 1789 was necessarily to be submitted to the diocesan governments for their approval or disapproval. It was apparently assumed to be binding on the church in all the states whose deputies signed it.[126] As shall be seen, several of the states did in fact record their approval of the Constitution, but it would seem that this was not necessary.

---

121. *Ibid.*, 1:61.
122. *Ibid.*, 1:66.
123. *Ibid.*, 1:67.
124. *Ibid.*, 1:69.
125. *Ibid.*
126. *Ibid.*, 1:84–85.

While the journal of the 1789 Convention indicated that all the deputies "gave information" that they were fully authorized to accept the Constitution, that "information" is not detailed in the journals. Then, what indication of this authorization can be found in the journals of the diocesan conventions before July 1789?

In Virginia, the Sixth Resolution of May 19, of the 1787 diocesan convention states:

> That the recommendation from the General Convention to the Convention of the United States, to authorize and empower their deputies to the next General Convention, after a bishop or bishops shall be obtained in the Church, to confirm and ratify a General constitution respecting both the doctrine and discipline of the Protestant Episcopal Church of the United States of America, ought to be complied with.[127]

Two deputies were elected under this resolution.[128]

No indication is given in the South Carolina record of any consideration being given to the General Convention resolution.[129] However, the three persons signing the Constitution from South Carolina were three of five persons originally chosen at the South Carolina convention of May 1789.[130]

In the New York convention of November 1788, eight deputies were elected. No action was taken regarding the authorization of the deputies to act in pursuance to the 1786 resolution. However, New York did make this resolution:

> That the union of the Protestant Episcopal Church, in the United States of America, is of great importance, and much to be desired; and that the delegates of this State, in the next General Convention, be instructed to promote that union by every prudent measure, consistent with the constitution of the Church, and the continuance of the Episcopal succession in the English line.[131]

The Convention had previously resolved that it was "highly necessary... to preserve the Episcopal succession in the English line."[132] These resolutions were introduced at the urgent insistence of Bishop Provoost of New York, who was emphatic in his wish that Samuel Seabury's consecration not be accepted by the General Convention. Thus he endeavored to bind very

---

127. Hawks, *Contributions to the Ecclesiastical History*, 20.
128. *Ibid.*
129. Dalcho, *An Historical Account*, 475–77.
130. Compare Perry, *Journals*, 1:85 with Dalcho, *An Historical Account*, 477.
131. Protestant Episcopal Church in New York, *Journals*, 28–29.
132. *Ibid.*, 28–29.

strongly New York's deputies to the 1789 General Convention to the explicit instructions at the New York convention on this matter. However, the New York deputies specifically contradicted their instructions.[133] Provoost protested this action bitterly. "The delegates from New York," he wrote, "have grossly deviated from their instructions, which were worded with their consent, and at my particular request."[134]

In another letter he asserted that the New York convention "had an undoubted right to restrict their delegates from consenting to any alteration" in the Constitution of 1786.[135] The three representatives from New York to the first 1789 Convention were three of eight persons who had originally been chosen in November 1788 by the New York convention.

Three conventions were held in New Jersey between the 1786 Convention and the first Convention of 1789. At each of the three, deputies were chosen to the next General Convention, in the event one should be called before the diocesan convention could meet again. In the June convention of 1787, instructions to four chosen deputies were read, amended, and adopted by the diocesan convention. But the substance of the instructions is not given in the record.[136]

In June 1789, eight deputies were chosen to General Convention, and:

> *Resolved.* That the Convention will give no instructions to their delegates; But leave them to act as they shall think most conducive to the general interests of the Protestant Episcopal Church in America.[137]

In a meeting held only one month before the 1789 General Convention, it was:

> Resolved unanimously, that it is the opinion of this convention, that the union of the Protestant Episcopal Church in the United States of America is necessary for its prosperity, and ought to be promoted by all Episcopalians; and that the delegates to be appointed to represent this convention in the next general convention, be instructed to move for and promote a coalition and union of all Protestant Bishops in the said states, and that the government, rules and orders of the Church throughout the same may be similar and uniform as nearly as may be.... The basis of the instructions

---

133. See Perry, *Journals,* 1:61. Here it was "resolved unanimously—That it is the opinion of this Convention, that the consecration of the Right Rev. Dr. Seabury to the Episcopal office is valid." Similarly see *ibid.,* 1:74–75.
134. Perry, *Journals,* 3:408. This is one of a number of letters Provoost wrote White about Seabury. See *ibid.,* 3:408–12.
135. *Ibid.,* 3:410.
136. Protestant Episcopal Church in New Jersey, *Journals,* 38–41.
137. *Ibid.,* 48.

be the instructions of this convention to our delegates to the General Convention of the 8th of June, 1787—the promoting of the union of the Protestant Episcopal Church in the United States of America, together with uniformity in its doctrine and discipline.[138]

The instructions themselves simply stressed that the identity of the American Church with the Church of England had to be maintained, and that everything necessary to achieve a "union of the Protestant Episcopal Church in the United States of America, and uniformity in its government" ought to be done.[139]

Thus, once again, the record does not indicate federalism or confederalism. From the state journals it appears that the state conventions either acted specifically and positively on the 1786 resolutions of General Convention or did not act on them at all. No state refused to authorize its deputies to ratify the Constitution without referring it to the diocesan convention.

In "instructing" their deputies, no diocesan convention evidenced a concern for protecting any "diocesan sovereignty." Indeed, the statements of the conventions seem to show once again the desire to reunite an abnormally separated body rather than to create a new entity by the uniting of independent organizations. Therefore, once the deputies had signed the Constitution of 1789, it was in effect and binding on all the dioceses whose deputies had participated in the signing. It was unnecessary and, indeed, impossible for the diocesan conventions to have then "ratified" it. Nonetheless, several of the states did formally assert their allegiance to the Constitution, while others, in more indirect ways, manifested their adherence thereunto.[140]

For example, New York and South Carolina both adopted resolutions approving the Constitution of 1789. The journals of the 1790 convention of South Carolina said simply, "The General Constitution and Canons being read, were unanimously agreed to."[141] New York, in November 1789, unanimously affirmed "that this Convention do approve of, and consider

---

138. *Ibid.*, 53–54.
139. *Ibid.*, 57.
140. Hoffman remarks in his tract on schism in the Episcopal Church, "And it is very striking, as an historical fact, that in both Massachusetts and Connecticut, the constitution was submitted to the several parishes for approbation. In Massachusetts the parishes were requested to instruct their deputies to the state convention, on the subject of adopting the Constitution and form of prayer, set forth by General Convention" (Murray Hoffman, *What Is Schism? According to the Law of the Protestant Episcopal Church in the United States of America* [New York: E. Jones, 1863], 16).
141. Dalcho, *An Historical Account*, 478.

the Church in this State as bound by the Constitution lately adopted by the General Convention at Philadelphia."[142]

Virginia, on the other hand, did not act on the Constitution *per se*.[143] However, approval was indirectly granted when it was ordered that "the General Constitution and Canons framed by the late General Convention, be annexed to the Journal" of the state convention along with the diocesan canons, as being "in force" in Virginia.[144]

In New Jersey, during the June 1790 convention, the deputies to the 1789 Convention reported and it was resolved:

> That, agreeably to the powers committed to them, they have, among other matters in said Convention, concurred in forming and establishing a Constitution for the Protestant Episcopal Church in these states.... *Resolved unanimously,* that the Convention and the Church of this State are bound by said proceedings; and further resolved that the thanks of this Convention by given to the deputies for their services in the *General* Convention.[145]

Many of the changes in the Constitution of 1786 incorporated into the Constitution of 1789 were designed to make that document acceptable to Bishop Seabury and the New England clergy. What was the method used to indicate the acceptance of the Constitution of 1789 by these New England churches?

In September 1789, the adjourned session of the 1789 Convention met, representatives of the New England churches being present. "Being an adjourned convention, testimonials were only required from new members" of the Convention.[146] The first and main business of the Convention was an alteration by the Convention of the Constitution passed in the preceding session in order to make it acceptable to the New England deputies. When this was done:

> Ordered, that the General Constitution of this Church, as altered and amended, be laid before the Right Rev. Dr. Seabury, and the deputies from the Churches in the Eastern States, for their approbation and assent. After a short time, they delivered the following testimony of their assent to the same viz.:

---

142. Protestant Episcopal Church in New York, *Journals,* 33.
143. Hawks, *Contributions to the Ecclesiastical History,* 29–36.
144. *Ibid.,* 32.
145. Protestant Episcopal Church in New Jersey, *Journals,* 63–64.
146. Perry, *Journals,* 1:93.

> Oct. 2, 1789
> We do hereby agree to the Constitution of the Church, as modified this day in Convention.[147]

Again, this action on the Constitution was taken by an adjourned session of the same convention, and not by a new convention. Thus the Constitution was not amended in the way prescribed in Article IX. Also, the alterations made in this October session were part of the substance of the Constitution that the dioceses above mentioned were considering in their "ratifications."

How the Constitution May Be Amended

Bishop White's *Case*, being only a sketch of a plan of government and not a constitution itself, did not provide for any method of amendment nor discuss how any future plan might be amended.[148] The "Fundamental Principles of 1784" also did not contain an amending clause, as the Principles were meant to serve only as guides for the deputies to the 1785 Convention.[149]

The General Ecclesiastical Constitution drawn up by the 1785 Convention had, in its Article XI, the first indication of an amending process. However, the entire article simply said: "This General Ecclesiastical Constitution, when ratified by the Church in the different States, shall be considered as fundamental, and shall be unalterable by the Convention of any State."[150] This sentence of course does not say by whom the Constitution may be amended, but by whom it may not. Thus the inference is left that the Convention itself alone was unquestionably able to amend the Constitution. Care only was taken to see that there would not be unilateral amendments by a state convention.

The first 1786 session expanded the sentence of the 1785 Constitution by inserting a provision for ratification of the Constitution thus:

> The Constitution of the Protestant Episcopal Church in the United States of America, when ratified by the Church in a majority of the States assembled in General Convention, with sufficient power for the purpose of such ratification, shall be unalterable by the Convention of any particular State, which hath been represented at the time of such ratification.[151]

---

147. *Ibid.*, 1:96–97.
148. See portion of chapter 3 of White's *Case*.
149. Perry, *Journals*, 1:12–13.
150. *Ibid.*, 1:23.
151. *Ibid.*, 1:42.

However, the article still did not state how the Constitution might be amended but was concerned only with seeing that the dioceses could not themselves amend it. The presumption still remains that the Convention could amend the Constitution on its own action without recourse to the dioceses for approval or ratification.

The Ninth Article of the Constitution of 1789 was the first to state how the Constitution might be amended. The provision, as adopted in the first session, was not changed by the second of 1789:

> This Constitution shall be unalterable, unless in General Convention by the Church in a majority of the States which may have adopted the same; and all alterations shall be first proposed in one General Convention, and made known to the several State Conventions, before they shall be finally agreed to, or ratified, in the ensuing General Convention.[152]

This is the way the article stood until 1838 when, as elsewhere in the Constitution, the words "State" and "States" were changed respectively to the words "Dioceses" and "Diocesan."[153]

In the major constitutional revision of 1901, the article was thoroughly revised. The alteration was needed due to the uncertainties that had arisen in General Convention over the meaning of the original article. There were two main questions asked about Article IX of 1789.

What does the phrase "in General Convention, by the Church, in a majority of the States" mean? White and Dykman, in considering this problem, show that the interpretation by General Convention has been inconsistent. A number of different methods of voting on amendments have been used in General Convention. Sometimes the Convention has voted by dioceses and at other by a simple resolution.[154] Even the reports by the Committee on Amendments to the Constitution of the House of Deputies have given contradictory interpretations.[155] The Committee reported in 1877 that while voting on amendments should be by orders, and that the vote in the affirmative should be equal to a majority of the dioceses, it was not necessary for a majority of both orders in each diocese to concur.[156]

In 1889 the same committee this time held that "on amendments to the Constitution, *the Diocese must act affirmatively as a unity in both orders,* as

---

152. *Ibid.*, 1:84 and 100.
153. The reason for this change was stated earlier, in footnote 115.
154. White and Dykman (1954), 1:134.
155. *Ibid.*, 1:135–36.
156. *Ibid.* This is an ordinary "vote by orders."

in no other way can it be determined that a majority of the Dioceses which have adopted the Constitution consent to the change."[157] In neither 1877 nor 1889 did the House of Deputies act upon these committee reports. Thus they are not an official position of the House, much less of General Convention.

Then, in answer to this first question, it cannot be determined exactly what the phrase in question meant. There has been no authoritative interpretation from General Convention, nor a uniform practice established by that body.

What do the phrases "made known to the several State Conventions" and "agreed to, or ratified, in the ensuing General Convention" mean? The dispute over the meaning of these phrases is one of the oldest disputes among church canonists in the United States.

Francis L. Hawks, the first person to do a commentary on the Constitution and Canons of the Episcopal Church, devoted more space to a consideration of Article IX than any other constitutional article.[158] Hawks was emphatic in his insistence "that states, quasi states or dioceses, are alone competent to alter the instrument at all."[159] Consistently stressing the "rights of the dioceses," Hawks insisted on the interpretation that "made known to the several State Conventions" meant made known for their approval or disapproval, and if a majority of the diocesan conventions did not agree to the proposed amendment, it must then fail in General Convention. In such a case, the General Convention would be acting "unconstitutionally" to override the dioceses' disapproval.[160]

Also, the term "ratified in" he took to mean that General Convention is ratifying the diocesan decision, since "to ratify concerns some act which others, not themselves have performed."[161] And the Constitution says, further, "in" and not "by" General Convention.[162]

Murray Hoffman specifically refutes Hawks. Hoffman states that if the diocesan conventions had been called upon to act, the Constitution would

---

157. *Ibid.* There was no existing constitutional provision for a vote of this nature. A vote by orders did not require that a single diocese's deputies had to agree in both orders for that diocese's vote to be valid. The 1889 committee included in its report the statement "that the Convention is composed of independent dioceses that have adopted the Constitution, and that Constitution is declared unalterable unless in a majority of the dioceses that may have adopted the same" (*ibid.*).
158. Francis L. Hawks, *The Constitution and Canons of the Protestant Episcopal Church in the United States, Annotated* (New York: Stanford and Swords, 1841), 41–58.
159. *Ibid.*, 42.
160. *Ibid.*, 46–49, 51.
161. *Ibid.*, 42.
162. *Ibid.*

have so stated, as the framers had the United States Constitution before them.[163] He concludes that the only purpose of the "make known" phrase is to inform the diocesan conventions of proposed changes. The dioceses may then instruct the deputies how to vote, but both practice and logic show that the deputies are not then bound by their instructions. General Convention alone modifies the Constitution.[164]

Vinton, in his *Manual Commentary* here, as generally elsewhere, supports Hoffman's interpretation. The dioceses do not participate in the amending process in any formal way.[165]

William Seabury, endeavoring to show an analogy between ecclesiastical and civil polity in the United States, said that, regarding the church's article on amendment and that of the United States Constitution, "the two systems contemplate (though with a difference in the process) substantially the same thing, viz.: the concurrent consent, to such alterations, of two classes of actors; the one being the legislative body, the other being a fixed proportion of the constitutional elements of the Union represented in that body."[166]

Thus, in reply to the second question raised above, the conclusion is again reached that no authoritative decision can be made as to the intent of the 1789 Constitution in having proposed amendments "made known" to the diocesan conventions. In part, the word "ratify" was used by Hawks and Perry to demonstrate that the General Convention was to act upon the decisions of the diocesan conventions. What the subsequent General Convention was to "ratify" was the decision of the diocesan conventions. Yet it appears that the word could well be used to mean the action of the previous Convention. In any event, as Hoffman shows, the practice of the General Convention has not been to be bound by statements of diocesan conventions in the matter of constitutional amendments.

In 1901, in connection with the general revision of that year, Article IX was altered to read:

> No alteration or amendment of this Constitution shall be made unless the same shall be first proposed at one triennial meeting of the General Convention and by a resolve thereof be sent to the Secretary of the Convention of every Diocese, to be adopted by the General Convention at its next succeeding triennial meeting by a majority of the whole number of Bishops entitled to vote in the House of Bishops, and by a majority of the Clerical

---

163. Hoffman, *A Treatise on the Law,* 174.
164. *Ibid.,* 177–78.
165. Vinton, *A Manual Commentary,* 62–80, 184–86.
166. Seabury, *Ecclesiastical Polity,* 220.

and Lay deputies of all the Dioceses entitled to representation in the House of Deputies voting by orders.[167]

In this way, General Convention attempted to determine:

1. How the dioceses are to be made aware of the proposed amendment, something which had been a subject of some dispute before.[168]
2. That no necessary action is contemplated on the part of diocesan governments in the amending process.
3. General Convention "adopts" the amendment.
4. In the House of Bishops, voting is by a majority of all bishops entitled to vote, and not just a majority of those voting.
5. In the House of Deputies, it is necessary to secure a majority of both orders in the dioceses represented, and the vote is taken by orders and not by dioceses.

There have not been any essential modifications since 1901, although clauses have been added to allow missionary districts and their deputies to participate in the process, and retired bishops not present at the Convention are not counted in determining the figure necessary to have a majority of the House of Bishops.[169]

Conclusions

While it is difficult to distinguish nicely in the early period of the church's history between amorphous tendencies toward localism and the strict delegation of authority by governments to legal representatives, it appears to be a valid conclusion that while for a considerable time the movement toward the formation of the Protestant Episcopal Church in the United States was conducted by nonofficial representatives of the church in the states, the final draft of 1789 was accepted by deputies of the dioceses specifically authorized by their diocesan conventions to accept the Constitution on the conventions' behalf. Thus, while it is true that the Constitution was never submitted to the diocesan conventions for their approval *per se*, and while it is also true that the supremacy of the governing power of the diocesan conventions (especially without episcopal con-

---

167. *Journal of the General Convention* (1901), 250–51.
168. White and Dykman (1954), 1:136–38.
169. *Ibid.*, 1:130.

trol or guidance) may itself be subject to question,[170] the evidence up to 1789 shows that the approval of the conventions in the dioceses was obtained in establishing a government for the Protestant Episcopal Church in the United States of America.[171] However, as previously asserted, there was at no time any official statement, in either the diocesan or General Conventions, of a desire or intention to establish a federal or confederal government with the distribution of powers being between the dioceses and the central government, and with the dioceses thus possessing any "sovereign independence." The Constitution of 1789 reunited an unnaturally separated body, rather than fashioned a new religious organization. The former Church of England in the former American colonies—a naturally unified (and unitary) organism—was reconstituted as the Protestant Episcopal Church in the United States of America—a naturally unified (and unitary) organism. The Episcopal Church was not created by the federation or the confederation of ten sovereign churches.

Moreover, in the question of subsequent constitutional amendment, the role of the diocesan governments is somewhat different from what it was in 1789. At no point in the church's history has it been constitutionally necessary to secure the approval of the dioceses for constitutional changes. Constitutional amendments are made and enacted entirely by General Convention, although the requirement of a three-year wait between the proposal and its enactment, and the requirement for a vote by

---

170. Pennington, "Colonial Clergy Conventions," says about the colonial conventions of the Episcopal Church: "The conventions were more or less informal. This was to be expected, since the conventions lacked authority and remained voluntary meetings to the very end. No one was empowered to enforce their resolutions" (p. 217). See also Stowe, "The State or Diocesan Conventions of the War and Post War Period," 220–56.
171. It should be remembered that the Episcopal Church was formed, in 1789, from the church in only ten states. North Carolina and Georgia were too weak to participate. The Journal of the 1811 General Convention shows only one clergyman in Georgia (Perry, *Journals*, 1:397). Rhode Island had been aware of the previous plans of union in convention with Massachusetts and New Hampshire (Loveland, *The Critical Years*, 146–47). In the 1792 Convention, delegates from Connecticut accepted the constitution for Rhode Island being "vested by the said Church in Rhode Island with full powers to act in all things on their behalf" (Perry, *Journals*, 1:152). This General Convention also received a letter from a North Carolina diocesan convention indicating "their willingness to accede to the Constitution" of the Episcopal Church (*ibid.*, 1:154). However, North Carolina did not officially send a delegate or become a member of the Episcopal Church until the 1817 General Convention (*ibid.*, 1:457). For a description of the church in North Carolina, see *ibid.*, 1:475–76. Georgia did not enter the National Church until 1823 (*ibid.*, 2:14). For a description of the condition of the church in Georgia in 1823, see *ibid.*, 2:49–50. The ten dioceses were South Carolina, Virginia, Maryland, Delaware, Pennsylvania, New Jersey, New York, Connecticut, Massachusetts, and New Hampshire.

orders on its final passage, distinguish a constitutional amendment from a simple resolution or a canon.

While the method of constitutional change has been under considerable debate in the church's history, the only full-scale alteration of the article on amendment, done in 1901, resulted in strengthening the claim that constitutional amendment is entirely a process of the General Convention, in which the dioceses take no formal part. Consequently, it must be concluded that there is no evidence to lead to the conclusion that a federal or confederal government was intended in the adoption of the 1789 Constitution, as far as the process of enactment itself is concerned. The debate on the reconstitution of the Episcopal Church in both diocesan and General Conventions was at no time concerned with the question of a distribution of powers and the protection of diocesan rights. There was debate. Some diocesan conventions did object to particular features of various proposed constitutions. But the debate raged primarily over the adoption of an American Prayer Book, the function of the episcopate, and the role of the laity in the government of the church. None of these is a federal or confederal question.

The amending process, also, is neither federal nor confederal but rather unitary. Thus, the federal or confederal hypothesis about the church's structure is seriously challenged both by the amending process and the original method of constitutional enactment.[172]

Separation of Powers?

One of the claims most frequently made about the church's polity in defense of the federal hypothesis is that it is similar in structure to the government of the United States. Often it is claimed that General Convention is like the Congress, the Presiding Bishop like the President, and the courts like the regional judiciary. This claim finds interesting expression early in the church's history. An "observer" wrote in 1835:

> *The great leading principles of the science of government, are equally applicable to ecclesiastical and national affairs, and are the same in both.*

One of these principles, which can never be abandoned either with convenience or security is the following: *the three elementary powers* of which

---

172. See the Appendix for quotations from various sources that show the differences of opinion among students of the church's government as to whether the process of enactment was federal or confederal, on the one hand, or unitary, on the other.

every well organized administration is composed (the legislative, judicial, and executive) must always be placed in different hands.[173]

Is it true that the Constitution of the Protestant Episcopal Church in the United States of America outlines a threefold separation of powers? While a careful analysis of the General Convention, the Presiding Bishop, and the courts will be left to chapters 3 and 4, it may be absolutely denied here that there is a constitutional separation of powers in the Episcopal Church. No constitutional document considered in this book manifests an inclination toward a separation of powers. Indeed, from White's *Case* onward, the only form of government described has been one of parliamentary supremacy. Original constitutional documents, including the Constitution of 1789, described no system of courts at all, except those of the dioceses, and those that General Convention saw fit to establish and regulate. The office of Presiding Bishop was unknown in the written Constitution until 1901, and now is elected by the House of Bishops and ratified by the House of Deputies at General Convention.

In short, and while there is no necessary relationship between a separation of powers and a division of powers, it is informative to those who would draw too close an analogy between the polity of the Episcopal Church and that of the United States to suggest that there is no constitutional separation of powers in the church's government.

---

173. Observer, "On Church Government," *Gospel Messenger* 12 (1835): 24. Italics in source. This article is entirely an attempt to prove a tripartite separation of powers in the church.

CHAPTER THREE

THE STRUCTURE *of* GENERAL CONVENTION

Overview

William White's original plan of 1782 envisioned for the government of the church in the United States a unicameral, triennial convention, representative equally of the clergy and laity of the church. The "continental representative body" (as well as all other representative bodies, from the parish vestry up) was "to make such regulations, and receive such appeals in matters only, as shall be judged necessary for their continuing one religious communion."[1] But all governments were to govern minimally, because, White stated, the least government is the best.[2]

The "Fundamental Principles of 1784" were concerned only with the organization of a General Convention.[3] These principles provided that there should be a convention (Article I) composed of lay and clerical members from each state (Article II) or association of states (Article III), deliberating together but voting separately by orders, both orders concurring before a measure might be passed (Article IV). A bishop, if any, was an *ex officio* member of the convention (Article V), and the church should adhere to the doctrines and liturgy of the Church of England (Article IV).

---

1. William White, *The Case of the Episcopal Churches in the United States Considered*, ed. Richard G. Salomon (Philadelphia: Church Historical Society, 1954), 26.
2. *Ibid.*, 27.
3. Perry, *Journals*, 1:12–13.

"The General Ecclesiastical Constitution" of 1785 did not depart essentially from the plans of 1782 or 1784 as far as the organization and powers of the Convention were concerned.[4] The Convention was made triennial, but the chamber remained unicameral (Article I) with bishops still being merely *ex officio* members (Article V). Importantly, however, voting by orders was replaced with voting by dioceses.

The 1786 Constitution did not change the structure or powers of the Convention at all, except to permit a bishop, when present, to preside over the Convention.[5]

Not until the summer of 1789 did the Constitution provide for what appears to be a bicameral convention.[6] Article III provided that when there were three or more bishops in the church, they should "form a House of Revision; and when any proposed act shall have passed in the General Convention, the same shall be transmitted to the House of Revision for their concurrence."[7] It was possible to overrule the negative decision of the bishops by a three-fifths vote of the General Convention. Whether favoring or disapproving a proposal, the bishops were to "signify... within two days after the proposed act shall have been reported to them for concurrence, and in failure thereof it shall have the operation of a law."[8]

A more complicated voting system was provided for the clerical and lay delegates:

> When required by the Clerical or Lay representation from any state, each Order shall have one vote; and the majority of suffrages by States shall be conclusive in each Order, provided such majority comprehend a majority of the States represented in that Order. The concurrence of both Orders shall be necessary to constitute a vote of the Convention.[9]

Thus, for a measure to be enacted it was necessary to secure (1) a majority of both orders, (2) in a majority of all the dioceses in the church that had delegates to the Convention in either or both orders (not simply a majority of the orders-in-dioceses voting), and (3) the concurrence of both orders in the Convention.

A diocese was bound by the acts of the General Convention after the diocese had adopted the Constitution, even if no deputies were in attendance at the Convention from that diocese. However, if a diocese sent

---

4. *Ibid.*, 1:21–23.
5. *Ibid.*, 1:40–42.
6. *Ibid.*, 1:83–85.
7. *Ibid.*, 1:83, Article III.
8. *Ibid.*
9. *Ibid.*, 1:83, Article II.

deputies from one order only, the diocese was considered "duly represented."

The revised Constitution of October 1789 retained and strengthened the apparently bicameral Convention, and left unchanged Articles I and II.[10] However, in Article III, concerning the House of Bishops, the old "House of Revision" terminology was done away with and the House given the "right to originate and propose acts for the concurrence of the House of Deputies."[11] Moreover, the previous possibility of the House of Deputies overriding a disapproval of the Bishops by a three-fifths vote was changed to four-fifths. Bishops were given three instead of two days in which to give in writing their reasons for disapproval.

No substantial changes were made in the structure and powers of the House of Deputies from the 1789 Constitution until the major constitutional revision of 1901.

In 1901, a number of alternations were incorporated into the Constitution.[12] At this time, the previous material on the House of Deputies, Article II, was included as Section 4 of the new Article I:

1. The number of representatives from each diocese was not changed.
2. The definition of "laymen" eligible for membership in the House of Deputies was clarified.
3. Provision was made for the possibility of canonical proportional representation.
4. The method of electing deputies was left up to each diocese, continuing although modifying a constitutional change made in 1856. Since 1789 the Constitution had required that each deputy be "chosen by the Convention of the State."[13] After 1856, deputies were simply chosen in a manner prescribed by each diocese's convention.[14] From 1901, they were simply chosen in a manner prescribed by each diocese.
5. For a quorum of the House it was necessary to have at least one lay deputy from a majority of the dioceses and one clerical deputy from a majority of the dioceses.
6. The voting procedure was unchanged, but clarified considerably.

---

10. *Ibid.*, 1:99–100.
11. *Ibid.*, 1:99, Article III.
12. *Journal of the General Convention* (1901), 35–36, and White and Dykman (1954), 1:24–30.
13. Perry, *Journals*, 1:99, Article II.
14. *Journal of the General Convention* (1856), 179–80.

7. The requirement, found since 1789, that any diocese, once having been admitted into the Protestant Episcopal Church, was bound by the decisions of General Convention whether or not it had deputies at any General Convention, was not included in 1901. White and Dykman say this was "presumably because it was thought that so self-evident a truth required no constitutional provision."[15]

Since the revision in 1901, although a number of significant amendments have been proposed, the only significant change made in the structure of the House of Deputies up to 1959, the time of the original writing of this work, pertained to foreign and domestic missionary districts. In 1904 the Convention enacted a new Section 6 to Article I to allow each domestic missionary district to choose one lay and one clerical deputy with seats in the House of Deputies, but with no vote in a vote by orders.[16] In 1907 the Convocation of the American Churches in Europe was also allowed one lay and one clerical deputy under the same conditions.[17]

An amendment was adopted in 1931 that allowed domestic missionary districts to vote in a vote by orders, but with their vote counting only one quarter of a diocese's vote, in each order.[18] Deputies from foreign missionary districts and the American churches in Europe were still not allowed to vote in a vote by orders, and it was not until 1943 that these deputies were placed on a par with deputies from domestic missionary districts.[19]

Fuller discussion of the governing role of bishops in the American Episcopal Church is reserved for chapter 4. At the present time it is necessary, however, to describe briefly the structure and powers of the House of Bishops of the General Convention, as these have changed since 1789.

It was observed above that no provision was made for a House of Bishops until the first Constitution of 1789, at which time the bishops were to be a "House of Revision" that could, within a short time, limit, revise, or negate legislation of the "Convention."[20] Bishop Seabury and the New

---

15. White and Dykman (1954), 1:25.
16. *Journal of the General Convention* (1904), 31–32, 220, 228.
17. *Journal of the General Convention* (1907), 52, 91–92, 98–99, 284, 318.
18. *Journal of the General Convention* (1931), 33.
19. In 1970, the Constitution was amended to give foreign and domestic missionary dioceses equal representation with other dioceses (four clerical and four lay deputies) and to give them one vote in each order on a vote by orders. See White and Dykman (1981), 1:36–37. For a discussion of the implication of the governing role of missionary districts, see chapter 5.
20. The first Constitution of 1789 uniformly spoke of the House of Deputies as the "Convention" or the "General Convention" (see Perry, *Journals*, 1:83–84). The Bishops were almost an added, virtually nonessential feature in this Constitution (see the last two sentences of Article III, *ibid.*).

England clergy were able to secure a somewhat more strengthened House of Bishops in the second Constitution of 1789, as had been mentioned above. However, they were unable to obtain for the Bishops a "full negative," or, in other words, equal powers with the House of Deputies in lawmaking. But the October 1789 Convention did resolve "that it be made known to the several state conventions, that it is proposed to consider and determine, in the next General Convention, on the propriety of investing in the House of Bishops with a full negative upon proceedings of the other House."[21]

The proposed amendment was lost in 1792 when the Committee of the Whole of the House of Deputies refused to report it to the floor.[22] However, in 1808, an amendment was finally adopted with the affirmative vote of all dioceses and orders, save for the negative vote of the laity only of the Diocese of Pennsylvania, which "were in favour of the resolution, but voted in the negative, because they supposed it necessary that they should have received instructions on the subject from the convention of the State, which instructions they had not received."[23]

Thus, the provision that the rejection of a proposal of the Deputies by the Bishops could be overruled by a four-fifths vote of the House of Deputies was removed. However, until the constitutional revision of 1901, it was still necessary that the Bishops give their "approbation or disapprobation" in writing, in either case within three days, or an act by the Deputies would become law without the Bishops' concurrence.[24]

No further amendments were made in the structure of the House of Bishops until 1901. At that time, all legislative inequalities between the two houses of General Convention were removed.[25] Specifically, no longer did the Bishops have to act upon the legislation of the Deputies within three days, nor did they have to declare their reasons for disagreeing.[26]

---

21. *Ibid.*, 1:96.
22. *Ibid.*, 1:153. But the Convention resolved the next day to discuss the question at the next Convention.
23. *Ibid.*, 1:341, footnote 1.
24. Material for future research lies in seeking the answer as to how often and on what issues acts have passed General Convention because of the Bishops' failure to act within the time limit.
25. In the 1901 revision, the position in the Constitution of material referring to the two Houses was reversed. From 1789 to 1901, the House of Deputies was first considered (Article II) and the House of Bishops next (Article III). Since 1901, the Constitution has explained the House of Bishops first in Article I, Section 2, and the House of Deputies in Article I, Section 4.
26. *Journal of the General Convention* (1901), 35–36.

Who Are the Members?

Having summarized briefly the changing structure of General Convention from 1782 through the present time, it is now possible to evaluate that struggle in terms of the question of confederalism, federalism, or unitarism. Specifically, five questions will be raised: (1) What is the method of apportionment for the General Convention? (2) Of what are the members of General Convention representatives? (3) What are the implications of the method of voting in the General Convention? (4) Is General Convention bicameral? (5) What is the extent of General Convention's powers?

William White's *Case of the Episcopal Churches in the United States Considered* assumed that the General Convention would be formed from delegates from what would now be called the provinces, not from the dioceses. All subsequent constitutional documents of the church have provided that the church in each diocese should send delegates to General Convention. Thus, neither a lower group (the parishes or association of parishes) nor a higher one (the provinces or—with but the one exception of the "Fundamental Principles of 1784"—group of dioceses) sends deputies.

But what has been the method of apportionment? Has each diocese been permitted to send delegates proportionate to its church membership, or has every diocese been allotted the same number of deputies? White's *Case* does not specify a number: "The continental representative body may consist of a convenient number from each of the larger districts formed equally of clergy and laity, and among the clergy, formed equally of presiding ministers and others."[27] The "Fundamental Principles of 1784" stated simply "that the Episcopal Church in each State send deputies to the Convention, consisting of Clergy and Laity." However, "associated congregations in the two or more states may send Deputies jointly."[28] The Constitution both of 1785 and 1786 provided that "there shall be a representation of both Clergy and Laity of the Church in each state, which shall consist of one or more Deputies, not exceeding four of each Order."[29]

The division of the General Convention into a House of Bishops and a House of Deputies was first allowed in the Constitution of July 1789. Although differently worded, both Constitutions of 1789 retained the same substance regarding the House of Deputies as the two previous documents had regarding General Convention as a whole.[30] In 1856 the wording of

---

27. Salomon, in White, *Case,* 26.
28. Perry, *Journals,* 1:12.
29. *Ibid.,* 1:22, 41.
30. *Ibid.,* 1:83, 99.

the 1789 Constitution was changed, but still each diocese was allowed four deputies in each order in the House of Deputies.[31]

In 1901, the revision of that year retained the number four in each order, but allowed General Convention canonically to reduce the number to two.[32] General Convention has never implemented this provision, and there has been no constitutional revision regarding apportionment of the House of Deputies since 1901.

That there has been no constitutional change does not mean that there have been no suggestions for change. As noted above, Bishop White felt that the time would come when it was necessary to have deputies to the House of Deputies elected proportionate to the diocese's church membership.[33] This might be essential, he felt, both to keep General Convention from getting too large and to see that General Convention was truly representative and that the dioceses' disproportionate size did not mean minority, and hence unrepresentative, rule.

Thus, from an early time, there have been suggestions for proportionate representation in the House of Deputies. Those in favor of a system of apportionment on the basis of a diocese's numerical size have argued that:

1. The existing system allows General Convention to be unrepresentative of the will of the members of the church in the United States as a whole.
2. The smaller dioceses can and/or do unfairly limit the power of the larger dioceses.
3. One way to make General Convention smaller is to reduce the number of delegates that less-populous dioceses may send to General Convention.[34]

Those opposed to proportionate representation and in favor of retaining the present system allege that:

1. This is the way the church was originally established. They cite Bishop White to the effect that this is the only basis upon which the church could have been first formed.
2. It is unfair to the smaller dioceses to take away the legislative equality they now have with larger dioceses.

---

31. *Journal of the General Convention* (1856), 64–67, 179–80.
32. *Journal of the General Convention* (1901), 35–36.
33. See above.
34. For variations on these three positions, see Thomas L. Cole, "Three Questions and Their Relation," *Virginia Seminary Magazine* 2 (1889): 380–87, and Randolph H. McKim, "The Democratization of the Church," *Chronicle* 20 (1919): 29–33.

3. The present system helps prevent hasty, ill-considered decisions by the necessity of securing a wide consensus before action can be taken.
4. Proportionate representation would aid in destroying the principle of diocesan equality and independence that is "the very foundation upon which the church in the United States has been built up."[35]

Thus, in spite of several attempts in General Convention[36] and some agitation in the church press at various times, there has been no sufficient move toward proportionate representation for it to become part of the church's constitutional structure. The House of Deputies remains based upon the equality of each diocese, and within each diocese, each order, as far as apportionment is concerned. Each diocese, regardless of its size, can have up to four delegates in both orders in the House of Deputies, depending upon how many are chosen by the diocese and how many actually attend the Convention.

The status of missionary districts, both foreign and domestic, in the church's polity has been mentioned above and will be described in more detail in chapter 5. However, regarding apportionment, each missionary district, while for a considerable time denied any representation in General Convention, after 1943 has been allowed not more than one delegate in each order in the House of Deputies. Hence, while not equal to a diocese in the number of delegates that it may send, the principle of equality-regardless-of-size is retained. Each missionary district is allowed only a total of two deputies, without reference to the comparison of its size with other dioceses or missionary districts.[37]

From 1789 until 1901 there was no clear constitutional statement as to which bishops were to be allowed to attend and vote in General Convention. This is in part because the original Constitution assumed only one kind of bishop—a bishop who was head of a diocese; a bishop, in short, who had "jurisdiction." There had arisen, however, a need for "assistant"

---

35. The quotation is from White and Dykman (1954), 1:5, but it is not their position (see 1:37). Also Francis L. Hawks, *The Constitution and Canons of the Protestant Episcopal Church in the United States, Annotated* (New York: Stanford and Swords, 1841), 20; John W. Andrews, *Church Law* (New York: T. Whittaker, 1883), 66–69; and William J. Seabury, *An Introduction to the Study of Ecclesiastical Polity* (New York: Crothers and Korth, 1894), 223–55. See also his "The System of Representation in the General Convention," *Church Eclectic* 17 (1889): 579–92, and W. T. Gibson, "Proportionate Representation," *Church Eclectic* 17 (1889): 523–27.
36. See White and Dykman (1954), 1:35–38, and White and Dykman (1981), 1:34.
37. Since 1970, missionary districts have had the same number of deputies as dioceses. See White and Dykman (1981), 1:36–37.

bishops in some dioceses who are called "bishops coadjutor," if they possess the right automatically to succeed the "ordinary" or "diocesan" (*i.e.*, a bishop who is head of a diocese) upon the ordinary's death, resignation, or deposition. "Bishops suffragan," though fully consecrated to the episcopal office, are simply delegated some functions by the ordinary and are not allowed to succeed him unless specifically chosen by the diocese.[38]

Moreover, during the years before 1901, some bishops had resigned their jurisdictions because of age or other reasons, but still retained the episcopal order. Should such persons be allowed seats and equal rights with other bishops in the House of Bishops?

Whereas the Constitution from 1789 until 1901 had not defined which bishops were allowed seats in the House of Bishops, the 1901 revision remedied the deficiency. Article I states:

> Every Bishop of this church having jurisdiction, every Bishop Coadjutor, and every Bishop who by reasons of advanced age and bodily infirmity arising therefore has resigned his jurisdiction, shall have a seat and a vote in the House of Bishops. A majority of all Bishops entitled to vote, exclusive of foreign Missionary Bishops and Bishops who have resigned their jurisdictions, shall be necessary to constitute a quorum for the transaction of business.[39]

In 1904 the word "and" between "advanced age" and "bodily infirmity" was changed to "or."[40] In 1919, provision was made for a bishop who resigned his jurisdiction in order to accept an office created by General Convention to retain his full powers in the House.[41] Not until 1943 were bishops suffragan allowed equal powers in the house.[42] And attempts have

---

38. See chapter 4 for a fuller explanation of the different types of bishops in the American Episcopal Church and the implications thereof. See also Seabury, *Ecclesiastical Polity*, 249-50, and Francis Vinton, *A Manual Commentary on the General Canon Law and the Constitution of the Protestant Episcopal Church in the United States* (New York: E. P. Dutton, 1870), 138-41.
39. *Journal of the General Convention* (1901), 35.
40. *Journal of the General Convention* (1904), 45-47, 240, 245.
41. *Journal of the General Convention* (1919), 48, 275, 318. In 1970, the words "or for reasons of missionary strategy determined by action of the General Convention or the House of Bishops" were added after "bodily infirmity" (*Journal of the General Convention* [1967], 390). The result is that bishops who resign other than due to advanced age, bodily infirmity, to take an office created by the General Convention, or for reasons of missionary strategy do not have a vote.
42. *Journal of the General Convention* (1943), 185-86. In 1982, the position of assistant bishop was added and those bishops also have a vote (*Journal of the General Convention* [1982], C-21). See White and Dykman (1981), 1:18-19.

subsequently been made to remove their voting privileges, along with those of retired bishops.[43]

While in the House of Deputies each diocese is allowed four delegates in each order, there is no constitutional limit to the number of bishops that may be in the House of Bishops from each diocese. To the extent that larger dioceses tend to have more bishops than do smaller ones to aid the ordinaries in the exercise of their episcopal duties, semblances of proportionate representation may be found in the House of Bishops that may not be found in the House of Deputies. The possibility that smaller dioceses may send fewer representatives to the House of Deputies than do larger, and thus in this way achieve proportionate representation, is offset by the provision of a vote by orders (and thus by diocese on an equal basis) in this House.

As far as the method of apportionment alone is concerned, the organization of General Convention, at least in the House of Deputies, tends toward confederalism or federalism. That each diocese is equal to every other diocese regardless of size in the number of deputies it may have in the House of Deputies—with no formal provision for a more proportionate representation—trends strongly in the direction of a federal, if not a confederal, structure.

Within the House of Bishops, the situation is different. Each bishop of the Episcopal Church is entitled to a seat, a voice, and a vote in the House of Bishops. It is not a question of apportionment, as such. Bishops are entitled to places in the House of Bishops by virtue of their office, not on the basis of diocesan apportionment. Thus several bishops may be from one diocese, and some—retired bishops—from no diocese, strictly speaking, at all.

Whom Do They Represent?

Of what are the members of General Convention representatives: do they represent their orders and/or their orders in their dioceses, their diocesan conventions, or the church in their dioceses? In seeking to answer these questions, five further problems must first be explored:

1. What have the church's constitutional documents said regarding representation?

---

43. See White and Dykman (1954), 1:15–17; *Journal of the General Convention* (1955), 190–92; *Journal of the General Convention* (1958). See also White and Dykman (1981), 1:21–22; *Journal of the General Convention* (2003), 669; and *Journal of the General Convention* (2006), 567.

2. What qualifications have the church's constitutions placed upon the deputies?
3. How and by whom are the lay and clerical deputies elected?
4. What have been the opinions of leading commentators on the church's polity regarding the problem of representation?
5. What is the distinction between the houses of General Convention regarding representation?

The "Fundamental Principles of 1784" stated "that the Episcopal Church in each State send Deputies to the Convention, consisting of Clergy and Laity."[44] And "that in every State where there shall be a Bishop duly consecrated and settled, he shall be considered as a member of the Convention ex officio."[45]

The 1785 Convention uses the following language in reference to the 1784 meeting and the question of representation:

> And, whereas, at a meeting of Clerical and Lay Deputies of the said Church, in sundry of the said States..., held in the city of New York... it was recommended to this Church in the said States represented as aforesaid, and proposed to this Church in the States not represented, that they should send Deputies to a convention to be held in the city of Philadelphia....
>
> And whereas, in consequence of the said recommendation and proposal, Clerical and Lay deputies have been duly appointed from the said Church in the said States....
>
> This Church, in a majority of the States, aforesaid, shall be represented before they proceed to business, except that the representation of the Church from two States shall be sufficient to adjourn....
>
> There shall be a representation of both Clergy and Laity in each State.... In the said Church in every State represented in this convention.

Bishops were still members *ex officio*.[46]

The Constitutions of 1786 and 1789[47] use almost exactly the same language regarding the House of Deputies. The article creating a House of Bishops did not change the position either regarding episcopal representation. The terminology for both houses was unchanged until the 1901 revision, except for the substitution of "diocese" for "state" in 1835 wher-

---

44. Perry, *Journals*, 1:12, Articles II and V.
45. *Ibid.*, 1:21–22.
46. *Ibid.*
47. *Ibid.*, 1:40–42 and 1:83–84, 99–100, respectively.

ever the word appeared in the Constitution. In 1901, though reworded and reorganized extensively, the principle of representation of the church in the dioceses was retained in the House of Deputies:

> The Church in each Diocese which has been admitted to union with the General Convention shall be entitled to representation in the House of Deputies....
>
> To constitute a quorum for the transaction of business, the Clerical Order shall be represented by at least one Deputy in each of a majority of the Dioceses entitled to representation, and the Lay Order... likewise.[48]

In 1943, the foreign and domestic missionary districts and the Convocation of the American Churches in Europe were declared "entitled to representation in the House of Deputies."[49] While the article on bishops was extensively altered in other regards, no change was made in reference to the problem of representation. Thus, the church's constitutional documents uniformly refer to the lay and clerical deputies as being deputies from the church in the states or dioceses. Careful attention shows that the wording always refers to the "church" (singular) rather than "churches" (plural), affording the connotation that the deputies are not representatives of the dioceses or of diocesan conventions, but rather deputies of the Episcopal Church in (and not "of") the state or diocese.

The first instance of a Constitution of the church proscribing qualifications for diocesan representative to the House of Deputies of the General Convention (save that each diocese should—later, might—have clerical and lay representatives) was in 1856 when the Constitution was amended to require that all lay deputies must be "communicants of this Church" and "residents in the Dioceses" from which they were chosen.[50]

In 1901, this was altered to require that clerical deputies be "canonically resident in the Diocese" and the lay deputies be "communicants of this Church, having domicile in the Diocese" that they represent.[51] To have "canonical residence" means that a clerical deputy can only represent a diocese to whose canons and episcopal discipline he is subject, regardless of where, at the moment, he may actually have his home. The contrary is true of a layperson, whose eligibility for election to General Convention is

---

48. *Journal of the General Convention* (1901), 35–36.
49. *Journal of the General Convention* (1942), 186–88.
50. *Journal of the General Convention* (1856), 64, 67, 179–80.
51. *Journal of the General Convention* (1901), 35.

dependent upon the location of his or her home.[52] No constitutional change was made in the qualifications of persons to the House of Deputies from 1901 until 1970, at which time the first woman lay deputy was seated.[53]

Not until 1786 did a constitutional document of the American Episcopal Church state by whom lay and clerical deputies were to be elected.[54] In conjunction with the first establishment of deputy qualifications in 1856, the Constitution was amended to read that deputies were to be "chosen in the manner prescribed by the Convention" of the deputies' diocese.[55]

Still further change was made in the 1901 revision, which stated, "each Diocese shall prescribe the manners in which its Deputies shall be chosen."[56] No change has been made in this provision.

Thus, since the first requirement of 1786, each change has apparently been a gradual relaxation of General Convention's control over who should be elected to the House of Deputies. At first, all deputies were to be elected by the diocesan convention. Then they were simply elected as the diocesan convention required. Finally, election was as each diocese prescribed—although this was in effect simply another way of leaving it up to the diocesan convention, unless a diocese were to be organized without a convention, perhaps leaving all government in the hands of its bishop or with the deputies being chosen popularly in a diocese-wide election.

What is the pattern of practice for the dioceses in the election of representatives to the House of Deputies? Hoffman in his *Law of the Church* examined the practices of several dioceses of his time (ca. 1850) and ob-

---

52. See Vinton, *A Manual Commentary*, 102–18, for a more complete discussion of the meaning of "residence" in the Constitution before 1901. For the meaning of "communicant" see *ibid.*, 102, and White and Dykman (1954), 1:338–354. Since 1979, lay deputies no longer have to be domiciled within the diocese and must be "in good standing" (*Journal of the General Convention* [1979], B–48).

53. In the Episcopal Church, women did not receive Holy Orders until they began being ordained as deacons in 1970 and as priests in 1974. Women were not seated as lay deputies until 1970. Frequent attempts were made to allow women to become deputies—they served on many parish vestries, as wardens, as deputies to diocesan conventions and provincial synods—but with no success until the General Convention of 1970 (see White and Dykman [1954], 1:25, 29, 653). A requirement that lay deputies be "in good standing" was added in 1976 (see *Journal of the General Convention* [1976], C–76). Since 1982, deacons have been able to serve as clerical deputies (see *Journal of the General Convention* [1982], C–21–22). In 1988 the requirement that lay deputies be "confirmed adult" members was added (see *Journal of the General Convention* [1988], 612).

54. Compare Perry, *Journals*, 1:12 (1784) with 1:21–23 (1785) and 1:41 (1786). In 1786 it was decided that deputies were to be "chosen by the Convention of each State." The wording is identical in 1789 (*ibid.*, 1:83, 99).

55. *Journal of the General Convention* (1856), 179.

56. *Journal of the General Convention* (1901), 36.

served that the normal practice was for the entire diocesan convention to have final approval on the election of its deputies to General Convention.[57] In some dioceses, the lay and clerical deputies might first be nominated and/or elected by their own orders alone, but at the time he was writing, the Constitution of the church required that deputies be "chosen by the Convention of the Dioceses." While this was uniformly the practice for a diocese's primary delegates, some dioceses allowed the bishop or standing committee to appoint alternates in the event that convention-chosen deputies could not attend. While General Convention recognized these deputies as validly chosen, Hoffman felt the method used by some dioceses—the choosing by the diocesan convention of alternates—was superior and more nearly according to the church's Constitution.[58]

However, the manner of choosing deputies to General Convention is now left up to each diocese. While there are at the present time different methods of balloting and counting ballots, diocesan conventions themselves still elect lay and clerical deputies to the House of Deputies of General Convention. Again, while some dioceses may make an initial selection by orders, they nonetheless provide some method for having both orders jointly in Convention, rather than either order exclusively, decide finally upon both clerical and lay deputies.

The evidence of the constitutions of the church in its national and diocesan organizations leads to the conclusion that the lay and clerical deputies to the House of Deputies of the General Convention are deputies of the church in their dioceses and representatives of their orders in their dioceses, and not simply representatives of their orders or of their diocesan governments alone. The major writers on the church's government all agree that the deputies are representatives of the church in the dioceses, although they often draw different inferences from their common conclusions. Hoffman, White and Dykman, and especially Vinton stress that this means that it is the *church,* only incidentally organized into dioceses, that is represented.[59] Perry, Seabury, Andrews, and Hawks assert that it is the dioceses-as-the-basis-of-the-church that is represented.[60]

---

57. Murray Hoffman, *A Treatise on the Law of the Protestant Episcopal Church in the United States* (New York: Stanford and Swords, 1850), 144–49.
58. *Ibid.,* 148–49.
59. Hoffman, *A Treatise on the Law,* 149; White and Dykman (1954), 1:35; Vinton, *A Manual Commentary,* 93–95.
60. Seabury, *Ecclesiastical Polity,* 242–46; William S. Perry, *History of the Constitution of the American Church* (New York: T. Whittaker, 1891), 104–5; Hawks, *Constitution and Canons,* 20–21; Andrews, *Church Law,* 66–69.

As of the time of the original writing of this work, no major commentator of the church's polity has maintained that the deputies were solely representatives of their orders—although some stress this as of significant importance—or of their diocesan conventions. The members of the House of Clerical and Lay Deputies, then, are chosen as representatives of the church and their orders in their dioceses. Persons in the House of Bishops, however, hold their membership by virtue of their office. Indeed, episcopal attendance in General Convention even before the creation of a House of Bishops—from 1784 to 1786—was *ex officio*. In July 1789, bishops, when three or more in number, were to form a House of Revision during General Convention. In October 1789, they were simply to form a "Separate House."

In 1901, the specific classes of bishops who were entitled to a seat and a vote in the House of Bishops were enumerated. Bishops, then, do not represent their dioceses nor their orders. Part of being a bishop in the American Episcopal Church is, now, the privilege of attending and participation fully in the proceedings of General Convention through the House of Bishops.

Consequently, there is no evidence sufficiently strong to lead to the conclusion that members of General Convention are representatives of the dioceses of the church. While membership in the House of Clerical and Lay Deputies is apportioned on an equal basis to the diocese, and, on a reduced but proportionate basis, to missionary districts, members of the House of Deputies are representatives of the church "in" the dioceses, not "of" the dioceses. It is the church, in two orders, which is being represented in the House of Deputies, not the dioceses.

In the House of Bishops there is no problem about representation. Since all bishops of the church are permitted full privileges in the House of Bishops, there is no question of whom they represent. The House of Bishops "represents nothing." It is composed of all the bishops of the church, holding their membership by virtue of their office.

Since there is nothing in the membership of General Convention to demonstrate that the Episcopal Church has a federal or confederal government, although the basis of apportionment to the House of Deputies does show federal or confederal characteristics, toward what conclusion does the voting procedure of General Convention seem to lead?

How Do They Vote?

The method of voting in the House of Bishops has always been relatively simple, though not explicit in the Constitution until 1901.[61] Each bishop who is qualified for a vote at all in the House is entitled to one vote only. Before this time, the only constitutional mention of voting procedure for bishops was in the last sentence of Article III of the October 1789 Constitution. There it was provided that when there were not enough bishops to form a separate house (*i.e.*, only one or two), they should vote with the clerical deputies of the diocese to which they belonged. A bishop, voting as an *ex officio* member of the Convention, has never been required to vote either in concert with other bishops from his diocese (if there are any), or with his diocese's delegates in the House of Deputies.

Voting procedure in the House of Deputies is somewhat more complicated than that of the House of Bishops, and has had an interesting history of constitutional development. Article VI of the "Fundamental Principles of 1784" provided "that the Clergy and Laity assembled in Convention shall deliberate in one body, but shall vote separately. And the concurrence of both shall be necessary to give validity to every measure."[62] For a measure to pass the proposed unicameral convention, then, it had to be accepted by two orders, clerical (including bishops) and lay, though voting was to be counted by dioceses.[63]

Article II of the 1785 Constitution considerably modified this principle: "In all questions, the said Church in each State shall have one vote; and a majority of suffrages shall be conclusive."[64] No longer were votes to be taken by orders. The basis was to be the diocese, each having one vote. It was not necessary to have the concurrence of the orders. This procedure was retained in Article II of the 1786 Constitution.[65]

With the August Constitution of 1789, the requirement of a vote both by orders and dioceses was combined into one of two voting alternatives, the second alternative being a simple majority vote of members present.[66] This feature was retained in all subsequent constitutional revisions, although the section was reworded and clarified in 1901.[67]

---

61. *Journal of the General Convention* (1901), 35, Article I, Section 2.
62. Perry, *Journals*, 1:13.
63. The decision that voting should be taken by dioceses and not by the mere count of clergy and laity irrespective of their dioceses was made in regard to the 1784 "Fundamental Principles" by the 1785 Convention. It was not clearly stated in the principles themselves (*ibid.*, 1:18).
64. *Ibid.*, 1:22.
65. *Ibid.*, 1:41.
66. *Ibid.*, 1:83.
67. *Journal of the General Convention* (1901), 36.

As of the 1958 General Convention, the last paragraph of Article I, Section 4 of the Constitution, pertaining to voting in the House of Deputies, could be outlined this way:

1. All questions carry by a simple majority of delegates present unless:
    a) The Constitution specifically requires another method as, for example, it does in the case of constitutional amendments and Prayer Book alterations.
    b) The canons require a different method.

2. A vote by orders (really a vote by dioceses and orders) is taken in this way:
    a) The two orders (clerical and lay) vote by dioceses. The vote of the four lay deputies is counted together, and the vote of the four clerical deputies of a diocese is counted together.
    b) Each diocese has but one vote in each order.
    c) Each missionary district has only one-quarter vote in each order.
    d) It is not necessary that the two orders in each diocese concur for a question to pass, but it is essential that both orders of the House of Deputies as a whole concur in a majority of their votes by dioceses for a question to pass.
    e) Because each diocese is allowed four deputies in each order, it is possible that one or both orders in any or all dioceses might be split equally (*i.e.,* two for and two against). This is a "divided vote," and is construed to count as a vote in the negative, since "no action of either Order shall pass in the affirmative unless it receives the majority of all votes cast."[68]
    f) Missionary districts are given one-quarter vote in each order, but no question passes unless "the sum of all the affirmative votes shall exceed the sum of other votes by at least one whole vote."[69]

"The government of the Protestant Episcopal Church is so organized as not to render it necessary for its ecclesiastical assemblies to transact a great deal of business."[70] Many others have agreed with this early observation. The voting method in General Convention does not encourage the hasty

---

68. See the Appendix for a brief discussion on the implications of counting a divided vote in the negative, instead of either as a blank vote or as half affirmative and half negative.
69. As of 1970, on a vote by orders each missionary district (now "missionary diocese") has one full vote in each order (*Journal of the General Convention* [1970], 260).
70. "The General Convention of the Protestant Episcopal Church," *Christian Journal* 1 (1817): 175.

passage of ill-considered questions by a mere majority vote.[71] Rather, legislation is possible only by the joint action of a number of concurrent majorities. General Convention has disadvantageous aspects that may cause the passage of unfortunate legislation, or prevent the adoption of needed measures. But the voting method itself presents a formidable hurdle over which all measures must jump, and should act as a considerable deterrent to unusual or new legislation.[72]

The voting method since 1789 appears to be a compromise between theories of diocesan representation and orders representation in the House of Deputies. While the two orders vote by dioceses and as dioceses, it is significant that the two orders in each diocese do not themselves have to concur for a bill to be enacted. A divided vote does not mean a division *between* the orders of a diocese, but an equal division of the deputies within one (or both) orders in a diocese.

Nonetheless, that the provision for a vote by orders and by dioceses was included in the Constitution, that it was retained, even in the 1901 revision, and that the provision has in practice been frequently used in General Convention is sufficient to enable this conclusion to be reached. The voting procedure of General Convention, at least in one alternative in the House of Deputies, has attributes that indicate the possibility of a federal or confederal government.[73]

On the other hand, voting normally proceeds in the House of Deputies on the basis of majority rule in the House regardless of orders or dioceses. The vote by orders procedure may be requested by the members of either order of a diocese's deputies or may be constitutionally or canonically required on special measures.[74] There is no requirement for a vote to be taken

---

71. See "The Value of the Vote by Orders," *Virginia Seminary Magazine* 3 (1889): 91: "One of the most ingenious checks to hasty and inconsiderate legislation that was ever devised is the system of voting by Orders that obtains in our... Conventions." See also Seabury, *Ecclesiastical Polity*, 230–31.
72. It has been complained that the Convention is too large, meets too infrequently, the delegates are mostly uninformed before they reach the Convention, committees and "experts" do all the work, etc. See, for example, "Is General Convention Obsolete?" *Living Church* 131 (October 2, 1955): 23–25; and John Cotton Smith, "The General Convention of 1880 and the Organization of the Church," *Church Review* 33 (1881): 65–75. On the other hand, it is contended with some force that the ancient councils did "no law-making in advance—no hunting after new statutes." Rather, "the truth was protected against none but actual assailants." See "The Divine Role of the Church's Legislation," *Church Review* 4 (1851): 404. It is there contended that this should be the "rule" for the Episcopal Church also.
73. See William J. Seabury, *Notes on the Constitution of 1901* (New York: T. Whittaker, 1902), 38–42.
74. The rule of majority vote was confirmed in 1976, but that provision was amended to provide that a vote by orders must be requested by three clerical or lay deputations rather than one (*Journal of the General Convention* [1976], C–74).

by dioceses in the House of Bishops. Consequently, while the vote by orders does appear federal or confederal, it is not a mandatory method in all instances, and the alternate voting procedures are not essentially connected with the federal, confederal, or unitary questions.

Is General Convention Bicameral?

General Convention would appear to be bicameral. Says one church historian of the General Convention:

> These representatives are divided into two houses, the one being the House of Bishops (corresponding, except in tenure of office, with the United States Senate) and the other the House of Clerical and Lay Deputies (corresponding to the House of Representatives).[75]

Superficially, it is accurate to call General Convention "bicameral." There are two houses. However, the composition and apportionment of these two houses and the differences in their voting procedure is sufficiently unusual to merit special mention.

It was noted in chapter 1 that some persons considered a bicameral legislature essential to federal government, not to mention good government in any form. Marriott wrote "that whatever be the case with unitary states, the bicameral system is essential to the successful working of a genuinely federal system.... The second chamber embodies and enshrines the federal principle of the Constitution."[76]

Whether or not this is the case—and this writer believes that, while perhaps having other merits, a bicameral legislature is not essential for federalism—a bicameral legislature in a federal system should emphasize the federal principle by allowing one house, the "lower," to include representatives of the "people," the nation, or the association as a whole. The "upper" house, or second chamber, incorporates representatives of the member governments to the federation.

The bicameralism of General Convention, as such, appears in no way to have been meant to emphasize a federal structure. The second chamber or upper house—the House of Bishops in the church—which, in federal states, is to embody the federal principle, does not serve this function at all in General Convention. Bishops have, since 1786, been members of General Convention *virtute officii,* not as representatives of the dioceses or diocesan governments. In fact, insofar as federalism or confederalism is evidenced at

---

75. George Hodges, *The Episcopal Church* (New York: T. Whittaker, 1892), 48.
76. John A. R. Marriott, *Second Chambers* (Oxford: Clarendon, 1910), 241.

all in the membership of General Convention, it is in the House of Deputies, the lower house, rather than in the House of Bishops. The bishops are present as an order, not as representatives of any temporal territory.[77]

Moreover, within the House of Deputies, the voting-by-orders provision, which is frequently used, results in a system that is almost tri-cameral in its operation. Bills often not only pass two houses, but also within those two houses, three orders.[78]

Finally, though when voting by orders the tally is taken by orders-in-dioceses rather than by the aggregate count of orders alone, the lack of a requirement that both orders in a single diocese must agree for a diocese's vote to count, coupled with the basis of apportionment in the House of Bishops, strongly suggests that General Convention, considered as both houses together, might actually be representative more of orders than of dioceses. Such a bicameral system would be unique for a federal system.

Conclusions

In a federal, or confederal, government, the power of the central government must be constitutionally limited in certain of the significant areas of governance, and protected for exercise by the member governments. If the governmental institutions of the central government are constitutionally unlimited or only self-limited, the government is unitary. The division of powers is the essence of the federal principles.

Since the General Convention is the major governing body of the American Episcopal Church, what is the extent of General Convention's powers? Are they—or have they ever been—limited by the retention of specified or residual powers within the dioceses?

In only one constitutional document has there been any specific inclination to limit the governing power of General Convention. The exception is White's *Case* in 1782. White, however, wished to limit the power of all parts of the church, favoring that the bulk of the political power should lie in the local parish. In no subsequent document has there been as express or implicit limit to the Convention's powers.

Thus, there appears to be no limit to the power of General Convention but its own self-limitations.[79] Specifically, there is no evidence in the Con-

---

77. See Vinton, *A Manual Commentary*, 94, and Hawks, *Constitution and Canons*, 217. See Seabury, *Ecclesiastical Polity*, 165, 248–355, to the contrary.
78. But see White and Dykman (1954), 1:80.
79. There is considerable controversy within the American Episcopal Church as to whether the so-called "Ancient Canons" and the canons of the Church of England in force before 1776 are now legally applicable and restraining upon the power of General Convention and the American Episcopal Church. This controversy is described and evaluated in the Appendix.

stitution that the power of the General Convention was to be in any way limited in favor of diocesan conventions, nor that the two were to have mutually exclusive powers in any particular area.[80]

The General Convention exhibits two structural characteristics that are reminiscent of federal, and especially confederal, governments in its basis of apportionment to, and vote by orders provision in, the House of Deputies of the General Convention. However, these features are placed within a legislative framework that otherwise appears to be unitary in design and intent. Although deputy apportionment is by dioceses on an equal footing, the basis of representation is the church in the diocese and not the churches of the dioceses. The voting scheme also emphasizes more an intention to secure the approval of the three orders within the church as a whole than of the dioceses.

Most importantly, the governing powers of General Convention are not fundamentally limited by the Constitution. Especially is there no expression of a division of powers or a limitation to the powers of General Convention in favor of the dioceses. In consequence, General Convention does not exhibit essentially federal or confederal structure, but rather a unitary one. Its powers are virtually unlimited.

---

80. The extent of General Convention's powers has been the subject of considerable dispute between persons writing about the church's government. See the quotations given in the Appendix.

CHAPTER FOUR

EXECUTIVE, ADMINISTRATIVE, *and* JUDICIAL POWERS

What Are Bishops?

At no point in the church's polity is there greater confusion than that surrounding the episcopate. There is no authoritative common agreement as to the purpose, function, role, rationale, or calling of bishops in the American Episcopal Church. Various groups, especially adherents of one or other of the great ecclesiastical "parties," have definite—and often mutually exclusive—understandings of what bishops are and should be. There can be distinguished, however, three broad theories of the episcopate, described as *esse, bene esse,* and *plene esse.*

The first theory, *esse,* states that bishops are essential for the very "being" of the church: no bishops, no church—and vice versa. Following the doctrine of apostolic succession, adherents to the *esse* theory believe that bishops are directly in the line of those persons commanded by Christ to be his witnesses and officers. It is the responsibility of the bishop, above all others, to keep pure the faith once committed to the saints, committed to her or him at consecration. The way the church must be governed to be truly a church is by validly consecrated bishops. Episcopacy is not just a convenient—or inconvenient—device that grew out of the socio-political structure of the second- and third-century Roman Empire. It is the way Christ himself caused his church to be governed, so that, led by the Holy

Spirit, his witness might be continued for all time in the living body of Christ, the church.

The tendency of this theory is to stress strongly the power and position of the episcopate. Bishops are to rule according to an express mandate from God. Bishops ought to have, as shepherds of souls, considerable disciplinary and other governing powers, and ought not to be too severely circumscribed by human rules and conventions. Thus, there is a tendency to feel that the governing power of bishops should be virtually unlimited because of their special calling.

This theory finds an excellent expression in this statement made in the late nineteenth century by one of the church's most devoted laymen:

> In the State, under our form and theory of government, power *ascends* from the people whereas, in the Church, it *descends* from above to the Bishops, and, in some respects, *through* the Bishops, into the subordinate ministry. The Bishops are the *governing* order.
>
> ......
>
> Neither priest nor layman posses any inherent power of legislation. Their counsel and advice is taken by the Bishops, as was the case in the Primitive Church; and in "this Church" the Bishops have granted to them, as represented in national synod, the constitutional right of initiating and vetoing measures, in other words, the Bishops have consented and in legal form agreed not to *exercise* certain of their inherent functions, except so far as advised and approved by the House of Deputies in General Convention.
>
> ......
>
> The powers of a Bishop in his Diocese are not merely and only those flowing from his individual functions, but those flowing from the authority and functions of the College of Bishops, or the Bishops of the Province, through whom his individual functions are derived.... There can be no such thing as an "independent" Church or Diocese.
>
> ......
>
> The National Church is not a Church of delegated powers at all, but one possessing in and through the Bishops, or College of Apostles, inherent authority of government and discipline, the Constitution of the National Church being simply an instrument under the terms and conditions of which *organisation* was effected and jurisdiction recognized, and not conferring or attempting to confer any law-making or governing power.
>
> ......
>
> The fact is known to all that, nevertheless, the General Convention legislates in ecclesiastical matters without reserve or hindrance, except so far as

restrained by the limitations of the Constitution, and in subordination to Divine and Catholic Law.[1]

The *bene esse* theory states that bishops are simply desirable for the "well-being" of the church. They are not essential, but merely historical or desirable, if strongly so. The strict theory of apostolic succession might or might not be true—it probably is not—and has mainly token or symbolic value.[2] Bishops are primarily, then, persons chosen simply to be the "presiding clergy," superintendent of an area, elected leader, or overseer. They have no special ecclesiastical functions, except as others are willing to grant them, save confirmation and ordination. In this latter duty they play their chief role. They are persons responsible for the continuation of the priesthood. They do not embody and "continue" in themselves the church.[3]

There is no mysticism in this theory, only the hard-headed, realistic view that people need some sort of leadership, and since it appears that, insofar as bishops have served "from the earliest time," they should be had now. "The history of the early church proves that bishops are not necessary to its *being*, though practical experience has indicated that they are helpful to its *well* being."[4]

Bishops, however, should not be autocratic or unrestricted in their rule. Indeed, their rule should be carefully defined and subject to the review of the church:

> It is dangerous to elect anyone to an office with wide administrative powers. But we repeat that the episcopal form of church government is the most practical and the most efficient which has ever been attempted—if

---

1. S. Corning Judd, "By What Laws the American Church Is Governed and Herein Chiefly, How Far, If at All, English Ecclesiastical Law Is of Force as Such, in This Church [Reply to Mr. Burgwin]," *Church Review* 37 (1882): 194–97. See also Hill Burgwin, "The National Church and the Diocese," *Church Review* 45 (1885): 438. A writer in 1837 observed, "In a word, if our Blessed Lord gave to the one grade alone, distinguished as that of Bishops, the right of legislation, then can acts of legislation solely take place by their permission" (Caesariensis, "The Episcopal Veto," *Protestant Episcopalian* 8 [1837]: 207). The best and most scholarly modern statement of the *esse* theory is found in Kenneth E. Kirk, ed., *The Apostolic Ministry* (London: Hodder and Stoughton, 1946).
2. In 1919, the Rev. John H. Melish, speaking as one of three lecturers on the subject "The Functions of the Episcopate in a Democracy," published by the 1919 Episcopal Church Congress, said: "None but the ecclesiastical caveman believes any longer in apostolic succession" (p. 220). Interestingly, the speaker who had preceded Melish, Bishop Irving P. Johnson, had spoken of his understanding of the episcopate as naturally following from "The Theory of Apostolic Succession" (p. 208). See Protestant Episcopal Church Congress, *The Church and Its American Opportunity* (New York: Macmillan, 1919), 207–35.
3. See Walter Ayrault, "Proper Place of Episcopacy in the Church," *Church Eclectic* 10 (1883): 961–68.
4. "In Defense of Episcopacy," *Chronicle* 47 (1947): 82.

the bishop does not forget that he is an elected officer of the church whose powers are restricted by its canons.[5]

Thus the *bene esse* theory tends to stress a limited, defined, pragmatic episcopacy, subject to considerable control by the church and the object of no particular honor or reverence—ecclesiastical or otherwise. It favors rule primarily by the members of the church itself. Hence, persons of this view favor conventions of clergy and laity, and otherwise representative government, with the bishop serving as little more than the presiding officer.

The *plene esse* theory, attempting to be a *via media* or middle way, is a refinement and emphasis of an aspect of *bene esse*. It evidences the feeling that bishops are necessary for the "full being" (or "fullness") of the church, for its more nearly perfect being.[6] To have bishops is to have one mark necessary for a true church. Bishops, however, may be present, and heresy still abound. The mere presence of even validly consecrated bishops does not mean a true church by definition. No church can be perfect in its organization without valid bishops, but some churches at some times, wholly without bishops, have more nearly been true to the faith than churches with bishops. One must look to more than merely the presence of bishops for the true church. Bishops are necessary for the fullness of perfection, it is true. But more than that cannot be said for episcopacy, *per se*. Thus, some adherents to this theory are willing to grant considerable governing powers to bishops as long as the church as a whole holds the ultimate check, probably in representative assemblies. They do not fear the power of the episcopate as such, because they have an affectionate view of the office; but they do deplore unrestrained power for bishops.

This, in only the barest outline, sketches some essential features of the three theories of the episcopate in the American Episcopal Church today.[7] The relevance to the problem of the church's constitutional structure is this: Is it believed that bishops are essentially "the church," or are they no more than elected administrative officers? Does ecclesiastical government flow from the House of Bishops as a whole to the clergy and laity? Or does it lie substantially perfect in each diocese with its bishop, clergy, and laity? A unitary structure is suggested if governing power is derived from the as-

---

5. *Ibid.*, 83.
6. One of the best-known statements of *plene esse* appears in a book edited by Kenneth M. Carey, *The Historic Episcopate* (London: Dacre Press, 1954). It was written in opposition to Kirk's *Apostolic Ministry*. See especially the article by H. W. Montefiore, pp. 105–27.
7. The contrast between *esse* and *bene esse* is excellently illuminated in Samuel A. Wallis, *Synopsis of Lectures on Church Polity in the Theological Seminary of Virginia* (Alexandria, Va.: R. Bell's Sons, 1904), 54–55.

sembled bishops. A federal or confederal one seems evidenced if each diocese is complete.

The theological justification for bishops is a subject of debate within the Episcopal Church. Thus, the point here is only to stress that there is no monolithic attitude toward bishops, but rather at least two or three widespread and popular differences of opinion. These beliefs are both reflected in constitutional and canonical statements about the episcopate, and help to determine how constitutional and canonical provisions are interpreted in their operation. In order to understand the governing role of bishops in the Episcopal Church in the United States more fully, the following points are also important to note.

Bishops' Jurisdiction, Mission, Selection, and the General Church

Every bishop at the time of consecration receives both *mission* and *jurisdiction*: the power to perform the acts that are peculiar to a bishop, and a particular place and/or people over which to exercise that mission. Moreover, while he may be deprived of office, insofar as he may be removed from jurisdiction by certain canonical procedures, that mission may never be obliterated.

Thus, once a bishop, always a bishop, as far as the power of ordination, confirmation, and other episcopal powers are concerned. No bishop is allowed, in the canon law of the Episcopal Church following what is believed to be the practice of the ancient church, to exercise mission except in his jurisdiction, and according to the canons of the church. A bishop's mission, therefore, is restricted to the jurisdiction to which he is appointed. Save for exceptions specifically provided for in canon law, he cannot exercise episcopal powers outside his jurisdiction. To be sure, if a bishop were to perform an ordination, for example, outside of his jurisdiction, it would be a "real" ordination, because a bishop's power to ordain does not depend essentially upon his jurisdiction but upon the validity of his own consecration, his mission, the intent of his act in ordaining another, and the intent of the person receiving Holy Orders. It would be a defective ordination insofar as it was performed outside his jurisdictional sphere. The defect could only be removed by the power that established the canon whose contravention resulted in the defective ordination.[8]

---

8. See William J. Seabury, *An Introduction to the Study of Ecclesiastical Polity* (New York: Crothers and Korth, 1894), 124–42; and White and Dykman (1954), 2:107–9. For an earlier interesting statement, see Caesariensis, "On Episcopal Jurisdiction," *Protestant Episcopalian* 3 (1832): 233.

Following logically from the strict definition of jurisdiction is the principle of episcopal co-equality, which is part of the theory of episcopacy of the Protestant Episcopal Church in the United States. While there are different types of bishops, and while bishops may be from weak or strong, large or small, rich or poor areas, each bishop is completely equal to every other in his mission.

In the American Episcopal Church, moreover, there is no archbishop, metropolitan, primus, or pope. Instead, there is a "Presiding Bishop," whose title was chosen originally because it accurately described his duties and has been retained partly because of the relative minuteness of authority manifest in the designation. This makes him or her unusual among catholic bishops, and while the powers of the office have gradually grown since 1789,[9] the Presiding Bishop still has few of the powers of bishops of other churches who bear the titles mentioned above. In fact, he or she possesses few powers different from any other bishop in the American Church, although her or his activities are different and manifold.

There are, however, certain types of bishops in the Episcopal Church who may be distinguished by their jurisdictional duties.

1. *Ordinary, or Diocesan, Bishops.* An ordinary is a bishop who is given control, according to the national and diocesan canons, of a particular diocese.[10] He or she[11] is superior, governmentally and under the canons, to any other bishops which a diocese may have. The ordinary's mission, however, is restricted to her or his own diocese only. He or she has no power outside of it, save under certain strictly canonical exceptions.

2. *Assistant Bishops.* A bishop who is responsible to an ordinary is an assistant bishop.[12] He or she is chosen by a diocese to aid the ordinary in the exercise of certain specifically assigned duties. Assistant bishops are not usually designated as such in the American Church today, being rather called:

---

9. More recent Presiding Bishops have added the designation "Primate." In 1967, the designation "Chief Pastor" was added and the status and duties of the Presiding Bishop were stated in more detail. See White and Dykman (1981), 1:202.
10. A diocese is always geographically defined in the Episcopal Church.
11. The first woman elected as bishop in the Episcopal Church—indeed, in the Anglican Communion—was the Rev. Barbara C. Harris, elected as bishop suffragan in the Diocese of Massachusetts in 1988.
12. See White and Dykman (1954), 2:27–31.

a) *Coadjutor.* This is an assistant bishop who has the right automatically to succeed to the diocesan episcopacy upon the ordinary's death, resignation, or deposition.
b) *Suffragan.* A suffragan is an assistant bishop without the right of automatic succession to the ordinary's position. Generally, also, suffragans have been chosen to perform episcopal work over certain groups of people,[13] while coadjutors have a more general assignment of jurisdiction within the diocese.[14]

3. *Missionary Bishops.* Both foreign and domestic missionary bishops are assigned to their jurisdictions by the church in General Convention.[15]

4. *Retired Bishops.* Retired bishops fully retain the episcopal mission but have resigned from their jurisdiction. They may exercise their office upon request, or may be assigned as priests to local parishes or missions. However, they retain certain prerogatives, such as that of co-equal participation in the House of Bishops of General Convention.

5. *Provincial President.* The bishop elected by a provincial synod to be head of a province is called a Provincial President. She or he retains, however, jurisdiction as ordinary (or whatever he may be) and does not devote her or his time exclusively to provincial duties. In recent years, lay people have served as Provincial Presidents.

6. *Presiding Bishop.* There is only one Presiding Bishop, elected by the General Convention, and acting mainly as the executive and administrative head of the national church. A bishop resigns from her or his old jurisdiction to take over the duties of Presiding Bishop.

While the method of choosing bishops shall be mentioned in a different context below, it seems necessary to note at present that bishops are now elected to their office in one of two six-stage procedures:

1. a) A diocese, destitute of a bishop, chooses, at its diocesan convention, and according to diocesan and national canons, a person it wishes to have as its bishop. He or she does not have to

---

13. For example, the Bishop Suffragan for Federal Ministries.
14. White and Dykman (1954), 1:50–54; 2:57–69. See also John H. Hopkins, "Assistant Bishops," *Church Review* 42 (1883): 226–50. In reply, see William P. Orrick, "Assistant Bishops: A Rejoinder," *Church Review* 43 (1883): 376–90.
15. See Thomas H. Vail, "Our American Episcopate: Comments on Title I, Canon 15 of Digest," *Church Review* 41 (1883): 301–30, especially 313–14 regarding missionary bishops.

be a resident of the diocese, or to have had any previous connection with it.

b) The House of Deputies then consents to the election.

c) The House of Bishops subsequently consents to the election.

d) The Presiding Bishop notifies the diocese and the bishop-elect of General Convention's approval.

e) The bishop-elect accepts his or her election.

f) The Presiding Bishop and two other bishops of his or her[16] choosing, or three bishops appointed by the Presiding Bishop, consecrate the person bishop. If the person is already a bishop (if he or she is a bishop suffragan or a missionary bishop), he or she is not re-consecrated. Only suffragans and missionary bishops are "translated," however. That is, only they may be moved from one jurisdiction to another. Ordinaries and coadjutors by custom have not been translated in the Episcopal Church, although there is nothing in the Constitution or Canons specifically to prevent this.[17]

2. If the election of a bishop is within three months of a meeting of General Convention, the above procedure is used. If not, then steps "b" and "c" are replaced with:

a) The approval of a majority of all the Standing Committees of every diocese in the church.

b) The approval of a majority of all the bishops having jurisdiction in the United States; that is, all diocesan bishops.

Thus, election to an episcopal office is a procedure requiring the intimate participation of diocesan and national church personnel.[18] It should especially be noted that the laity are a part of the procedure of election on both the diocesan and national level.[19] Finally, the process is marked by the elec-

---

16. The first woman elected as Presiding Bishop of the Episcopal Church was the Rt. Rev. Katharine Jefferts Schori, elected in 2006.

17. See two articles by Joseph Beale and John R. Crosby on "Should the Church Allow the Election of Bishops from One Diocese to Another?" in Harold A. Prichard, ed., *The Hartford Papers* (Spencer, Mass.: Heffernan Press, 1932), 101–36. Since 1967, the Constitution has explicitly provided for the translation of a diocesan or coadjutor to another diocese as long as he or she has served at least five years prior to his or her translation (see White and Dykman [1981], 1:66–70). There are at least two recent instances of translation: one cited in White and Dykman (1981) on page 70 and that of the Rt. Rev. Don A. Wimberley, who was diocesan bishop of the Diocese of Lexington from 1985–1999 and was then elected and served as diocesan bishop of the Diocese of Texas from 2003–2009.

18. See Murray Hoffman, "Bishops Elect: The Office of the House of Deputies, and Standing Committees in the Election of a Bishop," *Church Review* 28 (1876): 235–51.

19. G. MacLaren Brydon, "New Light on the Origins of the Method of Electing Bishops Adopted by the American Episcopal Church," *Historical Magazine of the Protestant Episcopal Church* 19 (1950): 202–13.

tion by the convention of the diocese over which the bishop is to serve, not by cooptation by other bishops, on the one hand, or, except in the case of missionary bishops (as shall be seen) by General Convention, on the other. This election, nonetheless, must subsequently be approved by a majority of persons acting as representatives of the clergy and laity of the dioceses of the church in the United States. This is not expected procedure for confederal governments and would be unusual for a federal one, but not exceptional for a decentralized unitary government.

Thus, in the manner of election and in many other ways, the episcopate of the Episcopal Church is "constitutional." While it is not unique for the catholic episcopate to be canonically defined, it is unusual to find the canons subjecting bishops to such considerable control (both in the election and continuance in office) by lesser clergy and the laity. Not only are decisions for the general church made by a representative convention of which the bishops are only one part of three, but also, in their diocesan office, bishops have been required since the earliest canons to maintain Standing Committees.[20] Bishops thus perform both their ecclesiastical (for example, ordination and confirmation) and administrative duties under canons that provide for the approval or dissent of representative bodies of clergy and laity.[21]

Finally, since Samuel Seabury, the first American bishop, bishops in the American Episcopal Church have been non-civil personnel. Under the

---

20. Perry, *Journals*, 1:81. A Standing Committee is a group of lay and clerical persons, chosen according to both diocesan and national canons, to serve as the ordinary's Council of Advice, to act as the ecclesiastical authority for the diocese when the ordinary is disabled and there is no coadjutor or suffragan empowered to act, and to perform other duties assigned to it by diocesan and national canons.

One other institutional feature concerning the American episcopate that merits intensive study is the "cathedral system." Cathedrals—that is, churches built exclusively or primarily as the ecclesiastical seats for diocesan bishops—were a new and controversial feature in the American Church beginning during the latter part of the nineteenth century (and continuing to some extent today). See Thomas Duncan, "Cathedrals and the Cathedral System in the Light of Church History," *Protestant Episcopal Review* 10 (1887): 568–87; Carl E. Grammer, "Cathedrals and Representative Government," *Southern Churchman* 85 (February 14, 1920): 4–5 (see a reply to this article on page 8, July 17, 1920); Francis Granger, "Primitive Cathedrals: Reasons and Hints for Adopting Them," *Church Review* 29 (1877): 283–301; John E. Egar, "Cathedrals and Parishes," *Church Review* 29 (1877): 16–42; William Adams, "The Cathedral," *Churchman* 33 (1876): 488, 516; and Walter H. Stowe, "The Cathedral in America," *Historical Magazine of the Protestant Episcopal Church* 19 (1950): 324–39.
21. Suggestions have occasionally been made that the election of bishops should be for only a few years and that bishops should be more inclusively subject to recall. For example, it was affirmed "if bishops were elected for a definite term of years, it would be a great incentive for them to so 'make good' that their re-election *might* be reasonably sure" (Alpha Centauri, "Quis Custodiet Custodes?" *Chronicle* 18 [1918]: 296).

American system of church-state relations, bishops officially exercise duties pertaining to the ecclesiastical and administrative affairs of the church only. They are not state officials by virtue of their episcopal office.[22]

What is the significance of these attributes of the American episcopacy to the question of the constitutional structure of the church's government? These three points seem especially distinctive.

Bishops are elected by the dioceses, but confirmed in that election by other bishops and by representatives of the clergy and laity in the dioceses of the American Church as a whole. They are not appointed by General Convention or the House of Bishops alone (which would be a distinctly unitary method) nor by the dioceses alone (which would be a distinctly confederal method). Since bishops play both a diocesan and national role, the present method of election (which perhaps could, by itself, be considered federal or decentralized unitary) seems justified.

That bishops must restrict the exercise of their mission to the jurisdiction to which they were elected (almost always a diocese, although the Presiding Bishop and the Constitution's provision for a bishop for the U.S. Armed Forces seem to be exceptions), and that the mission of all bishops is equal, although their jurisdiction may vary in importance and the specificities of their governmental powers differ, may seem to tend toward either confederalism or federalism. If each bishop is equal, it may by argued, then each diocese must be equal. If each bishop must restrict the exercise of his mission to his own diocese, then there must be something "sovereign" in each diocese upon which no other diocese (nor combinations of dioceses through General Convention) may impinge.

These arrangements of ecclesiastical government, however, are offset by the fact that General Convention determines them, often by canon without constitutional authorization. In any event, the Constitution itself is amended solely by General Convention and this scheme may be abolished or altered. Consequently the episcopal system may not be federal or confederal at all, but rather a form of decentralization decided by what is ultimately a unitary government.

It is now possible to describe the constitutional and canonical position of bishops in relation to the general church. Such a consideration of the episcopate should be examined especially at three points: (1) the House of Bishops, (2) the Presiding Bishop, (3) other considerations of the episcopate in the Constitution and Canons.

---

22. Neither are priests or deacons, although the line is somewhat blurred when clergy are permitted to sign marriage licenses on behalf of state governments.

EXECUTIVE, ADMINISTRATIVE, AND JUDICIAL POWERS   85

At the present time the Constitution defines the role of the episcopate on these ten points, apart from the provisions regarding the House of Bishops and the Presiding Bishop:

1. Method of choosing bishops
2. Limits on a bishop's jurisdiction and mission
3. Ecclesiastical trials of a bishop[23]
4. Ordination by bishops
5. Assistant bishops: coadjutors and suffragans
6. Missionary bishops
7. Suffragan bishop for the Armed Forces
8. Resignation of a bishop
9. Standing Committees and bishops
10. New dioceses and bishops.

The "Fundamental Principles of 1784" were silent on all points concerning bishops except their right of attendance at General Convention. The 1785 Constitution added three other items regarding their mode of election, their jurisdiction, and their trials. In 1786, there were added the first mention of the right of a bishop to preside at General Convention, the possibility of more than one bishop per diocese, and the diocesan's duty to examine candidates for Holy Orders. The role of bishops in the creation of new dioceses was explained in 1838, and an "assistant bishop" was specifically mentioned for the first time.

Besides reorganizing and restating all previous constitutional sections pertaining to the episcopate, the 1901 revision first stipulated the relationship between bishops and Standing Committees, prohibited bishops from resigning their jurisdictions without permission of the House of Bishops, and defined how missionary bishops were to be chosen.

Dioceses were allowed to choose bishops suffragan in 1910, although they were not given equal privileges in the House of Bishops until 1943.[24] In 1940, bishops were required to retire at age seventy-two, and provision for a bishop suffragan for the Armed Forces was made in 1949.[25]

---

23. Since 2003, the Constitution has provided that only the Court of Review for the Trial of a Bishop must be made up of bishops only (*Journal of the General Convention* [2003], 571).
24. In 1955, the General Convention voted to amend the Constitution to deprive the retired bishops of their voting rights. This failed to secure the necessary reconcurrence of the 1958 Convention, however. See note 43 in chapter 3 on attempts to take the vote away from retired bishops.
25. The bishop suffragan for the Armed Forces is under the direction of the Presiding Bishop and the General Convention. The office was first filled in 1964 and has been held by five bishops; the office's current title is Bishop Suffragan for Federal Ministries.

Article VI of the 1785 Constitution stated, "The Bishops or Bishops in every State shall be chosen agreeably to such rules as shall be fixed by the respective Conventions."[26] Article VI of the 1786 Constitution clarified this by concluding instead, "by the Convention of that State,"[27] and this language was retained in the 1789 Constitution and up until 1901, except when, in 1838, "state" was changed to "diocese" throughout the Constitution.[28]

In 1901, the Constitution was reworded to read, "In every diocese the Bishop or Bishop Coadjutor shall be chosen agreeably to rules prescribed by the Convention of that Dioceses. Missionary Bishops shall be chosen in accordance with the canons of the General Convention."[29] However, Section 2 of Article I at the same time added that no one could be consecrated bishop unless:

1. He was thirty years of age.
2. He had the consent of a majority of all the Standing Committees in the dioceses.
3. He had the consents of a majority of all the bishops exercising jurisdiction.
4. Consecration was performed by no fewer than three bishops.

Provision was made, however, to allow consent by the House of Deputies to replace that of Standing Committees if a bishop's election occurred within three months of a meeting of General Convention.

Moreover, in 1901, bishops were specifically forbidden by the Constitution to resign their jurisdictions without consent of the House of Bishops. This was designed to end a number of unhappy incidents regarding bishops who had resigned with unfortunate repercussions.[30] In 1940, the Constitution was amended to require a bishop to tender his resignation at age seventy-two.[31]

Dioceses prior to 1910 had been prohibited from electing bishops suffragan. In that year, the Constitution was amended to allow a diocese to choose, with the ordinary's consent, one or more suffragans, with a seat but no vote in the House of Bishops.[32] In 1919, amendment was made to allow diocesan constitutions to provide that a diocese's suffragan could be-

---

26. Perry, *Journals*, 1:22.
27. *Ibid.*, 1:41.
28. *Journal of the General Convention* (1838), 24–25, 93, 96.
29. *Journal of the General Convention* (1901), 36.
30. See White and Dykman (1954), 1:54–57.
31. *Journal of the General Convention* (1940), 256.
32. *Journal of the General Convention* (1910), 231–32, 306.

come temporary ecclesiastical authority for the diocese upon the ordinary's death or incapacity.[33]

Thus, although the Constitution states that bishops shall be chosen according to the dioceses' rules, General Convention has, itself and by the Constitution and Canons, defined an increasingly large number of rules. There appears to be nothing on the face of the Constitution, at any point, to prevent General Convention from preempting the field entirely and determining all the rules for the election of bishops.

Since 1785, the church's constitutions have limited a bishop's exercise of his office to his own jurisdiction, or, in other words, to his own diocese. Article VI of 1785 states that "every Bishop of this Church shall confine the exercise of his Episcopal Office to his proper jurisdiction, unless requested to ordain and confirm by any Church destitute of a Bishop."[34] The Constitution added, "or perform any other act of the Episcopal office," in addition to confirmation and ordination.[35] In the first Constitution of 1789, this section, rearranged as Article IV, was reworded to replace "his proper jurisdiction" with "his proper Diocese or District."[36] It remained in this form until 1838, when the words "or district" were removed.

Inasmuch as no provision was made for the proper calling of a bishop to perform episcopal acts in a bishopless diocese prior to 1874, in that year the Constitution was amended to have the ecclesiastical authority (generally, the Standing Committee of the diocese) issue the request.[37]

The 1901 revision did not significantly alter this section except to change it to Article II, to include missionary bishops and districts in the provision above, and to allow the House of Bishops to permit a bishop to operate in ecclesiastically unorganized territory.[38] There have been no subsequent changes to date.

It has been shown that while the Constitution states at one point that the dioceses over which the bishop is to exercise his office provides for his mode of election, the Constitution still provides a number of significant rules itself. General Convention has revealed even less reluctance toward defining the role of the episcopate through canonical legislation than by constitutional amendment.

---

33. *Journal of the General Convention* (1919), 48, 221. Also see sources cited above regarding the struggle for bishops suffragan in the American Church.
34. Perry, *Journals*, 1:22.
35. *Ibid.*, 1:41.
36. *Ibid.*, 1:84.
37. *Journal of the General Convention* (1874), 82, 96, 161, 164.
38. *Journal of the General Convention* (1901), 36–37.

Indeed, of the ten canons enacted by the first Convention of 1789 (and, interestingly, adopted before the Constitution of 1789 itself was adopted),[39] every one of them mentions, pertains to, or otherwise defines the role of bishops in the American Church. Moreover, they do not refrain from directing the bishops' activities not only at the national and diocesan level, but also at the parochial level. Thus, for example, Canon 2 of 1789 stated that a bishop-elect must receive from his diocesan convention and from the General Convention a certificate of their approval for his election. Canon 3 required that the ordinary should visit the parishes in his diocese "for the purposes of examining the state of his Church, inspecting the behaviour of the Clergy, and administering the Apostolic Rite of Confirmation."[40] Canon 8 forbade a bishop from ordaining a candidate until he had examined and been satisfied with the candidate's knowledge of "the New Testament in the original Greek, and can give an account of his faith in the Latin tongue, either in writing or otherwise, as may be required."[41]

Since August 1784 the body of canonical legislation of the Episcopal Church has grown. Many items regarding the episcopate, once governed by canons only, have been incorporated into the Constitution. Thus, the conclusion must be reached on the basis both of precedent and the analysis of the written Constitution and Canons that while in the absence of legislation by General Convention to the contrary the dioceses may define the roles of their bishops, there is no legal basis upon which General Convention can be kept from enacting its own all-inclusive canons for the election and conduct of the episcopate and from overriding all diocesan canons to the contrary.

Once again, it must be mentioned that loyalty to tradition, the faith, and/or the ancient canons may restrain or prevent General Convention from acting outside what it considers to be the catholic tradition on the matter of episcopacy. Political realities necessitating heavy reliance upon diocesan and parochial support—and other factors—also may be limiting. But it seems that there is no legal barrier, within the church's polity itself as defined by the Constitution and Canons, to prevent legislation on the episcopate.[42]

---

39. Perry, *Journals*, vol. 1; compare 79–82 with 83–85.
40. *Ibid.*, 1:79–80.
41. *Ibid.*, 1:81.
42. The preceding discussion concerned bishops and the general church alone. There does not exist a good analytical study of the governing role of bishops in their diocesan situation. Bishop Lewis Bliss Whittemore's interesting book, *The Care of All the Churches* (Greenwich, Conn.: Seabury, 1955), is designed in its homey way to aid new bishops in understanding their office more clearly, and it does the job adequately. But there still are lacking adequate

The Presiding Bishop

The Presiding Bishop now stands as the "chief executive" of the American Episcopal Church, although the development of the office was slow, and, as shall be seen, largely extraconstitutional. While the analogy is undoubtedly incorrect, the Presiding Bishop has frequently been likened to the President of the United States. Consequently, it is important to the purposes of this work to describe in some detail the office of the Presiding Bishop, including the Executive Council, in order to see whether it embodies federal, confederal, or unitary characteristics.

The first constitutional mention of a Presiding Bishop was made in the 1786 General Constitution, Article V. Here, assuming a unicameral General Convention, it was stated that "a Bishop shall always preside in the General Convention, if any of the Episcopal order be present."[43] The provision for a Presiding Bishop in a unicameral Convention was retained in both Constitutions of 1789. Although these Constitutions also mentioned for the first time a bicameral Convention, if there were not enough bishops in the church to form a separate house, then a bishop was to preside at General Convention. Otherwise, there was no constitutional mention of a Presiding Bishop.

Until 1901 there were only two places in the Constitution where the Presiding Bishop was mentioned. In 1823, the Constitution was amended to allow the "Presiding Bishop" to have the power to appoint an alternate place for General Convention to meet if some "good cause" made it necessary not to meet in the chosen place.[44] In 1844, Article X was added to the Constitution, which, in part, allowed the "Presiding Bishop" under certain circumstances to take order for the consecration of bishops for foreign countries.[45]

Section 3 of the new Article I, in 1901, was finally written in an effort to attempt to define constitutionally the office of the Presiding Bishop. The office was to be determined by seniority from the point of consecra-

---

careful studies of diocesan constitutions, canons, and conventions, the operation and composition of Standing Committees and their actual relations to the episcopate, and their interaction, from a governmental view, between the bishops and the clergy and laity. On this last point, for one example, it would be interesting to test Thomas Vail's hypothesis in *The Comprehensive Church,* second edition (New York: D. Appleton, 1879), 113, that there is a wider gap between the bishops and their clergy than between the bishops and the laity. Vail feels that the laity are more willing to give political power to the bishops than are the clergy (who, instead, are trying to restrict this power) because the power of the bishops is more immediately and effectively felt over the clergy than over the laity.

43. Perry, *Journals,* 1:41.
44. Perry, *Journals,* 2:17, 19, 66, 95.
45. *Journal of the General Convention* (1844), 26, 36, 71, 73, 128.

tion among bishops having jurisdiction in the United States. He was to "discharge such duties as may be prescribed by the Constitution and Canons of the General Convention."[46]

After a struggle that had officially begun in 1887, the House of Deputies amended the Constitution in 1919 to make the office of Presiding Bishop elective by the House of Bishops and subject to confirmation.[47] There has been no subsequent constitutional amendment on the subject.

Actually, however, most of the regulation concerning the Presiding Bishop has been by Rules of Order of the House of Bishops, or by canons. In August 1789, Bishop White presided over the Convention that was being held according to the provisions of the 1786 Constitution. He signed the minutes as the "President of the Convention."[48] White, moreover, presided at the adjourned 1789 Convention that opened without the number of bishops requisite for forming a separate House.[49] When Bishop Seabury and the New England clergy joined the Convention, the body immediately became bicameral.

The very first business of the newly formed House of Bishops was to provide three rules for the government of the House, one of which was: "The senior Bishop present shall be the President; seniority to be reckoned from the dates of the Letters of Consecration."[50] Samuel Seabury twice in the records of this Convention suffixed his name with the word "President."[51]

The seniority rule for choosing a Presiding Bishop was changed in the next General Convention by the House of Bishops. In 1792, it was decided that:

> The office of President of this House shall be held in rotation, beginning from the North; reference being had to the presidency of this House in the last Convention.
>
> In consequence of the above rule, the Right Rev. Dr. Provoost took the chair.[52]

---

46. *Journal of the General Convention* (1901), 35.
47. See White and Dykman (1954), 1:18–22, for a summary of this struggle. See also C. Rankin Barnes, "The Office of Presiding Bishop: An Evolution," *Pan Anglican* 8 (1957): 21–24.
48. Perry, *Journals*, 1:86.
49. *Ibid.*, 1:93.
50. *Ibid.*, 1:115.
51. *Ibid.*, 1:123 and 130.
52. *Ibid.*, 1:162.

The first use in the journals of General Convention of the words "Presiding Bishop" was in 1795 when Bishop White signed his name as such in two places.[53] The first use of the term in the canons was in 1799 when it was provided that special meetings of General Convention could be called "by the Presiding Bishop, or, in case of his death, by the Bishop who, according to the rules of the House of Bishops, is to preside at the next General Convention."[54]

The House of Bishops readopted the seniority rule as the first action of business in 1804.[55] In 1820, Canon 6 of that year was added to require the Presiding Bishop to perform consecrations in conjunction with two other bishops; or any three bishops the Presiding Bishop should designate could perform consecrations.[56] At the same Convention, "the Presiding Bishop of this Church" was made the President of the Church's Missionary Society.[57]

As noted before, in 1823 the Constitution for the first time mentioned the office of Presiding Bishop. Since that time, the duties assigned to him by the Constitution and Canons have continued to grow. The following is a summary of those provisions relating to the office in the American Episcopal Church since 1832. The purpose of the summary is to show the extent of Presiding Bishop's powers and responsibilities in order that the office may be analyzed in relation to the question concerning the constitutional structure of the church.

The "Presiding Bishop" was, in 1832, canonically required to announce when the House of Bishops had accepted an episcopal resignation.[58] A canon of 1841 required that presentments in the trial of a bishop be sent to the "Presiding Bishop of the Church" and that he notify all bishops in the American Church.[59] The canon on episcopal resignation was amended in 1844 to allow a bishop wishing to resign his jurisdiction when the House of Bishops was not in session to notify the Presiding Bishop, who in turn was to notify all other bishops.[60] The Presiding Bishop was required by a

---

53. *Ibid.*, 1:206, 210.
54. *Ibid.*, 1:249. William J. Seabury, in his *Memoir of Bishop Seabury* (New York: E. S. Gorham, 1908), 351, says that the first time the phrase "Presiding Bishop" officially occurred was in the Prayer Book rubric for the Office of Consecration as adopted in 1792. See C. Rankin Barnes, *The General Convention: Offices and Officers 1785–1950* (Philadelphia: Church Historical Society, 1951), 5.
55. Perry, *Journals*, 1:305.
56. *Ibid.*, 1:567.
57. *Ibid.*, 1:589.
58. *Ibid.*, 2:456–57, 539.
59. *Journal of the General Convention* (1841), 118.
60. *Journal of the General Convention* (1844), 54–55, 157–58.

canon of 1853 to pronounce sentence of deposition on a bishop who abandoned his ministry.[61]

The Presiding Bishop was given a single five hundred dollar appropriation for expenses in 1871. This was made a regular appropriation of two hundred and fifty dollars annually in 1874.[62]

A "Chairman of the House of Bishops" and "Assessor to the Presiding Bishop," elected by the House, was provided by a Rule of Order of the House of Bishops in 1886. He was to be the presiding officer of the House in the absence or at the request of the Presiding Bishop and to aid the Presiding Bishop between meetings of the General Convention.[63] In 1889, the Assessor was allowed take on any of the duties of the office of Presiding Bishop that that person might wish to devolve to him.[64] In order further to lighten the load of the Presiding Bishop, the House of Bishops in 1892 resolved that the Presiding Bishop might devolve all his duties upon the Assessor, or decline to accept the office in the first place, or resign it later at his discretion. It also enabled the bishops of the seven dioceses adjoining that of the Presiding Bishop to call a special meeting of the House of Bishops if they felt the Presiding Bishop was incompetent and mentally unable to resign.[65]

The first standing rule of the House of Bishops was amended and reworded in a special meeting of the House of Bishops in 1896:

> The Senior Bishop of the Church, in the order of consecration, having jurisdiction within the United States, is the Presiding Officer of the House of Bishops. He shall discharge such duties as may be prescribed by the Constitution or Canons of the General Convention, or for its own needs by the House of Bishops; and shall hold office for life, unless he resign or be relieved from that office by a vote of a majority of the Bishops entitled to vote in the House of Bishops.[66]

In 1919, the office was for the first time made elective, under the Constitution, and a canon was written providing for a term of six years. Election

---

61. *Journal of the General Convention* (1853), 37, 42, 60–61, 160, 173. The Presiding Bishop's role in the discipline of bishops has been expanded by a number of amendments to the canons, including the authority to temporarily inhibit a bishop from functioning while allegations of misconduct are investigated (*Journal of the General Convention* [1997], 769–79 and 811–71).
62. *Journal of the General Convention* (1871), 79–80 and *Journal of the General Convention* (1874), 179–80, respectively.
63. *Journal of the General Convention* (1883), 633.
64. *Journal of the General Convention* (1889), 10–13.
65. *Journal of the General Convention* (1892), 12, 88.
66. Contained in *Journal of the General Convention* (1898), 427.

was by the House of Bishops, subject to confirmation by the House of Deputies.[67]

The Presiding Bishop was also made executive head of the National Council in 1919.[68] In 1922 he was made administrative head of that body as well.[69]

A new resolution of General Convention in 1931 allowed an assistant to the Presiding Bishop to be nominated by the Presiding Bishop and approved by the Convention to serve as the Presiding Bishop saw fit, and to have the right to temporary succession.[70] The Presiding Bishop was made *ex officio* Chairman of the National Council in 1934.[71] In 1937, the General Convention made the Presiding Bishop the President of the National Council, removed the six-years limit to the term of the office, and made tenure last until sixty-eight years old, and finally required the Presiding Bishop to relinquish the administration of his diocesan office.[72] Not until 1943, however, was it impossible for the Presiding Bishop to retain his position as bishop of the diocese and also be Presiding Bishop. He was required to resign his previous jurisdiction entirely.[73]

The Executive Council

The canon that established the National Council [which is now called "Executive Council" and will be referred to as such for the remainder of this work] has been extravagantly called, by the foremost annotators of the church's Constitution and Canons, "one of the greatest pieces of constructive legislation, if not the greatest, ever enacted by [General Convention] since the First General Convention of 1789."[74] Until 1919, the "executive branch" of the Episcopal Church had comprised the Presiding Bishop, a few relatively uncoordinated boards and joint commissions established by General Convention to handle particular affairs (the most important of which was the Domestic and Foreign Mission Society), and several specifically chosen officers. Indeed, the persons who served to execute the legislation of General Convention were, for the most part, extra-constitutional officials responsible only to the Convention and not

---

67. *Journal of the General Convention* (1919), 32, 48, 275, 318.
68. *Ibid.*, 165–70.
69. See Canon 61, Section 1, 1, 159, in *Journal of the General Convention* (1922).
70. *Journal of the General Convention* (1931), 87, 326.
71. *Journal of the General Convention* (1934), 233–39.
72. *Journal of the General Convention* (1937), 178–81, 196–208.
73. *Journal of the General Convention* (1943).
74. White and Dykman (1954), 1:176–77.

formally coordinate in their work with other executive officers. Thus, there was no "executive branch" in any sense analogous to a body of such designation in the usual tripartite separation of powers theory.

By and large, until the latter part of the nineteenth century, the legislation of General Convention could be satisfactorily carried out by a few national officers and boards, and by the dioceses. But, just as the duties of the Presiding Bishop came to be more nearly those of a true executive and leader of the church, so also it became necessary to combine and coordinate the persons and groups executing the policy of General Convention.

The creation of the Executive Council in 1919 was a piece with the movement toward election of the Presiding Bishop and the abolition of mere seniority in the choice of a chief executive, and the greater obligation of the general church for the development and presentation of church policy. Canon 69 of 1919, "Of the Presiding Bishop and Council," as the Executive Council was then titled, began, "The Presiding Bishop and Council, as hereinafter constituted, shall administer and carry on the missionary, educational, and social work of the church, of which work the Presiding Bishop shall be executive head."[75] The remainder of the canon spelled out in considerable detail of whom the Council was to be composed, how its officers were to be chosen, how its internal departments were to be organized, how it was to develop and present the budget for the church, and various other related matters.[76]

In short, while the canon was rather revolutionary in its scope and purpose, it was a culmination and continuation of a slow movement toward somewhat greater centralization of power that has characterized the history of the polity of the American Church.[77]

The canon was revised considerably in 1922, generally in the direction of strengthening and streamlining the Executive Council. For example, the Presiding Bishop was declared to be not only the executive but also the administrative head of the church's work.[78] Also, the officers of the Council were given greater leeway in appointing their own subordinates, instead of having them chosen by the Council as a whole.[79]

---

75. *Journal of the General Convention* (1919), 165.
76. *Ibid.*, 165–69.
77. See C. Rankin Barnes, "The General Convention of 1919," *Historical Magazine of the Protestant Episcopal Church* 21 (1952): 238–42, for a discussion of the enactment of the original canon on the National Council.
78. *Journal of the General Convention* (1922), 194.
79. *Ibid.*, 140–47, 162, 189–90, 195–96, 345–49, 369–72.

Since 1922, there have been a number of important changes, but none has significantly altered the original concept of the Executive Council.[80] Consequently, a summary of the Executive Council will explain its role. The Council has "charge of the unification, development, and prosecution of the Missionary, Educational and Social work of the Church." The powers and duties may be outlined as follows according to the canon on the Executive Council:

1. Enact its own by-laws.
2. Dispose of money and property of the Missionary Society.
3. Initiate and develop new work between sessions of General Convention.
4. Prepare and submit to General Convention a detailed administrative budget.
5. Recommend a plan of fiscal apportionment to General Convention and check on its fulfillment by the dioceses.
6. Publish a detailed annual account of its work, receipts, and disbursements.

At the time of the original writing of this work, the Executive Council was composed of persons chosen by three groups. The General Convention chose sixteen members. Four were chosen by the House of Bishops and confirmed by the House of Deputies; four clergy and eight laypersons were chosen by the House of Deputies and confirmed by the House of Bishops. These sixteen held their office for six years. One person of any order was chosen by each of the eight provincial synods. Finally, four members of the General Division of Women's Work (formally the Woman's Auxiliary to the Council) were nominated by the Division and elected by the General Convention. Terms of office were limited for all members to six consecutive years. The President of the Council, being the Presiding Bishop, the Vice Presidents (nominated by the Presiding Bishop and elected by the Executive Council), and the Treasurer who is elected by the General Convention as Treasurer of the Domestic and Foreign Missionary Society for three years, are *ex officio* members of the Council. In 1967, the composition and selection of members and officers of Executive Council was changed significantly, with twenty members elected by General Convention and eighteen members elected by the (now nine) provincial synods.[81]

---

80. White and Dykman (1954), 1:220–46, traces the canonical development of the National Council from 1919. White and Dykman (1981), 1:268–74, discusses the developments from the time of the original publication of this work through the 1979 General Convention. The 1991 Supplement to White and Dykman (1991), 24–25, tracks the developments through the 1991 General Convention. See also *Journal of the General Convention* (1997), 193–94 and 284.
81. *Journal of the General Convention* (1976), C–38.

Finances

The nature of the budgeting and appropriation system in relation to the problem of the question of the structure of the church's government should be mentioned at this time insofar as it is a major part of the Executive Council's responsibilities.

Without analyzing the totality of the church's system of finances from the parish level to the General Convention, and without describing the history of the church's fiscal system from its original basis on pew rents to its present reliance on "free will" offerings and pledges, the way in which the general church's budget is determined and apportioned is significant to the question about the church's constitutional structure.[82]

According to Canon 4, as of 1958, the Executive Council submits to the General Convention at each regular meeting of the General Convention, an itemized budget of its program for the next three years. The Council is required to have submitted to the presidents of the provinces and then to diocesan and missionary bishops, for their consideration and report back to the Council, a statement of existing and proposed appropriations within their respective jurisdictions. The Executive Council is also required to submit to the General Convention a plan suggesting how much money each diocese and/or missionary district should be requested to provide toward the total budget.

When General Convention has passed the budget and plan, as necessarily amended, the Council advises each diocese and missionary district of its allotted share, or "objectives." The dioceses then are required to allot proportionate "objectives" to their parishes, and the parishes then request their members to meet the quota. The general church thus is dependent in large part upon a "trickle-up" system of financing from the individual church member through his parish church, and his diocese, to the Executive Council. In terms both of theory and practice, this method does not work very satisfactorily as far as the Executive Council is concerned, because of the considerable uncertainty as to the amount of money that will actually be received; the lack of any kind of legal control over the dioceses or parishes or individuals, by Executive Council, to force, coerce, or make

---

82. A study of the history of the church's financial system, reasons for and implications of change, is badly needed. The ramification of the change from the "pew rent" system to the "free will" system, and the fights surrounding the alteration should be significant to the subsequent development of the church. See W. C. Winslow, "Some Financial Considerations," *Church Eclectic* 10 (1883): 1132–37. Also, James Craik, "The Financial Question in the Church," *Church Review* 38 (1882): 57–66. In reply see Samuel Wagner, "Another Aspect of the Financial Question in the Church," *Church Review* 39 (1882): 19–32.

it legally mandatory that they meet their respective quotas;[83] and the quite indirect way in which money rises to the Executive Council. Instead of having each member pay, or pledge to pay, or directly be assessed, a fixed amount of money per week or year to the general church, the parishioner pays directly to his parish, which in turn is supposed to pay a certain amount to the diocese, which is then to turn over a fixed proportion to the general church.

The general church has relatively few independent sources of funds, and is thus exceedingly reliant in the exercise of its programs upon the dioceses and, in turn, upon the parishes; it is felt that this budgeting method alone greatly restricts the church's programs,[84] and causes many to feel that the Protestant Episcopal Church is a loosely knit confederation of independent dioceses.

It should be observed, however, that the idea of diocesan equality, found in many other features of the church's polity, is absent in the actual method of fiscal apportionment. The budget is allotted to the dioceses and districts in large part on the basis of the number of clergy in them. Therefore, larger dioceses and districts pay a larger share of the church's expenses.[85]

Finally, there is nothing in the church's Constitution to make such a method of financing mandatory. While it may at present be politically difficult for General Convention to adopt a general fund or some other direct system of finances, there certainly is no constitutional reason why it could not. This is the test for the question about the legal extent of General Convention's powers. Is there a reasonably implicit or explicit constitutional restraint upon General Convention in the matter? Regarding finances, there definitely is not. In fact, there is no mention in the Constitution of budgeting and financing methods at all. While the present system may cause members of the Executive Council, frustrated in their plans by recalcitrant

---

83. It should be noted, however, that Canon 4, Section 6 (D) requires that all funds received by the dioceses from the parishes shall be divided between the diocese and the Executive Council "strictly in accordance with the proportion which the total proposed budget of the Diocese or Missionary District bears to the total objective presented on behalf of the [Executive] Council." Section 6 (E) states that "the National Council shall approve a standard form for the use in Dioceses and Missionary Districts for all purpose of showing receipts and the distribution of receipts for all purposes. Each Diocese and Missionary District shall annually report to the National Council all receipts and the distribution of such receipts on the standard form."
84. See William C. Langdon, "Reform in Church Finance," *Church Review* 42 (1883): 364–75.
85. Powel Mills Dawley, *The Episcopal Church and Its Work* (Greenwich, Conn.: Seabury, 1955), 102. Also see pp. 244–53 regarding the system of budgeting and financing. More recently, the budget is allocated to the dioceses based on a percentage of diocesan net income. *Journal of the General Convention* (1979), C–16; *Journal of the General Convention* (1985), 246; *Journal of the General Convention* (2006), 332–35.

dioceses over whom they have no canonical control, to feel the church's polity is confederal (or at least federal), there is actually no constitutional basis for this belief, and mere canonical legislation, coupled of course with the necessary political consent, would relieve the frustration.[86]

Sufficient data have been arrayed to demonstrate that the development of a separate executive and administrative branch has only had a beginning. The Presiding Bishop and the Executive Council are both highly reliant upon General Convention, and, ultimately, the dioceses and parishes. It is in this reliance, especially in its financial aspects, that the government of the church takes on in practice the character of a confederacy.

The executive and administrative sector of the church, consequently, may at first seem to exhibit what might be taken to be more nearly confederal than federal attributes. Yet it appears that a case can instead better be made for a unitary method. The Presiding Bishop, the church's "chief executive," has never been in any way governmentally responsible to the dioceses. Instead, the Presiding Bishop was originally responsible (if at all) only to the House of Bishops, and, especially more recently, to the General Convention as a whole. The dioceses do not participate in the Presiding Bishop's selection at all.

The same is also true of the Executive Council, an agency wholly extraconstitutional in its creation and continuation, whose members are mainly elected by General Convention, although the provincial synods also elect members to the Council. The significant point for the question of the church's constitutional structure, however, is that the dioceses do not participate in the election of the Executive Council at all.

Thus, it is too much to say with White and Dykman that the first canons on the Executive Council "erected a strong form of centralized government"[87] even though protests occur frequently in the church press about the "bureaucracy at 281."[88] The church has still not achieved a strong, relatively independent executive. The Executive Council remains very con-

---

86. It should be noted that the expenses of General Convention itself have been taken care of in a number of ways. In 1832, a canon was passed assessing each diocese triennially seventy-five cents per diocesan clergyman. In 1835 this was changed to fifty cents annually (Perry, *Journals*, 2:548, 611, 712). By 1959, the amount has risen to "not more than twenty-two dollars annually" (Canon 1, Section 6, 1958).
87. White and Dykman (1954), 1:285.
88. The address of the offices of the Executive Council, until 1962, was 281 Fourth Avenue, New York; at that time the offices were moved to a newly built building at 815 Second Avenue, the Episcopal Church Center. The Council was colloquially called "281," and the Church Center is now often referred to as "815." The methods, techniques, and successes of administration of the Executive Council should be very interesting to the student of public and private administration, considering especially the fragmented and hypercritical environment in which the Council must work.

siderably under the control of General Convention, and in the execution of its programs, upon the pleasure of the dioceses and parishes. But this political weakness should not be interpreted as evidence of federalism or confederalism.

The Judicial System

The church's judicial arrangement may appear at first glance to evidence a confederal structure. The general church possesses no primary system of courts for the trial of the lower clergy, and must rely on the diocesan courts. Courts in the provinces hear appeals on questions of doctrine, faith, or worship. There is, moreover, no final court of appeal for the general church.

Also significant for the question of the structure of the church's government is the absence of a body specifically empowered to determine authoritatively questions of constitutional interpretation. In this connection, it is necessary to appreciate the role of the civil courts in the United States in resolving intrachurch disputes.

Does the judicial scheme of the church, then, tend toward a confederal, federal, or unitary hypotheses concerning the church's constitutional structure? The following account will enable a conclusion to be reached about the church's system of courts.

The first mention in a constitutional document of the courts was Article VIII of the 1785 Constitution, which stated:

> Every clergyman, whether bishop, or presbyter, or deacon, shall be amenable to the authority of the Convention in the State to which he belongs, so far as relates to the suspension or removal from office; and the Convention in each state shall institute rules for their conduct, and an equitable made of trial.[89]

To this was added in 1786:

> And at every trial of a Bishop, there shall be one or more of the Episcopal Order present, and none but a Bishop shall pronounce sentence of deposition or degradation from the ministry on any clergyman, whether Bishop, or Presbyter, or Deacon.[90]

In August 1789, the addition of 1786 was retained in full, but the 1785 provision was shortened to read, "in every State, the mode of trying cler-

---

89. Perry, *Journals*, 1:22.
90. *Ibid.*, 1:41.

gymen shall be instituted by the Convention of the church therein."⁹¹ This was unaltered in October 1789.⁹²

The first significant change after 1789 was in 1841 when the Constitution was amended so that "the mode of trying Bishops shall be provided by General Convention. The Court appointed for that purpose shall be composed of Bishops only." Also the word "shall" was changed to "may" in the sentence regarding trials of clergy so that clergy trials "might" instead of "must be" provided for by dioceses.⁹³

Attempts were made from 1853 until 1901 to establish either a national system of courts or at least a general court of appeals. In 1853, for example, the Convention agreed to amend the Constitution to read that diocesan courts should operate "until the General Convention shall provide a uniform mode of trial."⁹⁴ However, the 1856 Convention did not ratify the 1853 decision because the laity refused to concur with the bishops and clergy.⁹⁵

In 1901, the former Article VI was made Article IX of the revision and changed to read substantially as it does at present. In summary, Article IX provides that General Convention may establish a court for the trial of bishops, composed of bishops only, and for a court to review the decision of this court, also composed of bishops only. Since 2003, the Constitution has provided that only the court of review for the trial of a bishop must be made up of bishops only.⁹⁶ The House of Deputies elected priests and laypersons to the Court for the Trial of a Bishop for the first time at the 2009 General Convention.⁹⁷ It continues to allow priests and deacons to be tried by diocesan courts, but allows General Convention to establish a court of review over these courts. Even more importantly, it allows General Convention to establish "an ultimate Court of Appeal, solely for the review of the determination of any Court of Review on questions of doctrine, faith, or worship."⁹⁸ As before, none but a bishop can pronounce sentence, and a sentence of suspension must specifically state when and how suspension may be removed.

---

91. *Ibid.*, 1:84, Article VI.
92. *Ibid.*, 1:100.
93. *Journal of the General Convention* (1841), 23.
94. *Journal of the General Convention* (1853), 101. See also 27, 59, 100–1, 107, 141, 193, 229.
95. *Journal of the General Convention* (1856), 36–43, 163–64. White and Dykman (1954), 2:310, observes: "It is a singular fact that efforts to establish such courts... were usually defeated by the vote of the laity."
96. *Journal of the General Convention* (2003), 571.
97. *Journal of the General Convention* (2009), publication still in progress.
98. *Journal of the General Convention* (1901), 313–14.

The Canons of August 1789 did not discuss the matter of ecclesiastical courts and discipline. However, two of those of October 1789 were to the point and shall be quoted in full:

> If any persons within this Church offend their brethren by any wickedness of life, such persons shall be repelled from the Holy Communion, agreeably to the rubric, and may be further proceeded against to the depriving of them of all privileges of church membership, according to such rules or process as may be provided, either by the General Convention or by the Conventions in the different States.
>
> No ecclesiastical persons shall, other than for their honest necessities, resort to taverns or other places most liable to be abuses to licentiousness. Further, they shall not give themselves to any base or servile labour, or to drinking or riot, or to the spending of their time idly. And if any offend in the above, they shall be liable to the censure of admonition, or suspension, or degradation, as the nature of the case may require, and according to such rules or process as may be provided, either by the General Convention or by the Conventions in the different States.[99]

Since 1789, the legislation by General Convention on the subject of ecclesiastical discipline has increased considerably. The disciplinary canons underwent a major revision at the General Convention in 1994 and again in 2009. The list of offenses in the 1994 revision can be found at Title IV, Canon 4.1 (1997 Canons). The proposed 2009 revision, which was adopted with only minor amendments, can be found in the *Report to the 76th General Convention, Otherwise Known as The Blue Book*.[100] At the present time, the list is as follows:

a) Crime.
b) Immorality.
c) Holding and teaching publicly or privately, and advisedly, any doctrine contrary to that held by this Church.
d) Violation of the Rubrics of the Book of Common Prayer.
e) Violation of the Constitution or Canons of the General Convention.
f) Violation of the Constitution or Canons of the Diocese in which the person is canonically resident.
g) Violation of the Constitution or Canons of a Diocese of this Church wherein the person may have been located temporarily.

---

99. Perry, *Journals*, 1:128, Canons XII and XIII.
100. *Report to the 76th General Convention, Otherwise Known as The Blue Book* (2009), 766–95.

h) Any act which involves a violation of Ordination vows.
i) Habitual neglect of the exercise of the Ministerial Office, without cause; or habitual neglect of Public Worship, and of the Holy Communion, according to the order and use of this Church.
j) Conduct Unbecoming a Member of the Clergy.[101]

For these offenses, a priest or deacon may be presented for trial if three-fourths of all the members of the Standing Committee of the accused's diocese consent to it. A bishop may be presented, by any ten bishops exercising jurisdiction, for holding and teaching publicly or privately and advisedly doctrine contrary to that held by this church. A bishop also may be presented similarly, under certain qualifications, for the other offenses listed above.

While ten offenses are specifically enumerated, they are quite broad, and almost no act or belief seems beyond presentment, although the requirement of the consent of the Standing Committee may minimize frivolous and irrelevant charges being filed. In actuality, while the chance of "crime" is frequent, recourse to ecclesiastical trials is rather infrequent. For example, an article reporting the results of a questionnaire on the use of the Episcopal *Book of Common Prayer* in the service of Holy Communion by 255 priests in five dioceses showed that in the five dioceses only 5 percent of the clergy said that they invariably followed the directions of the Prayer Book rubrics. Thus, the remaining 95 percent were guilty of at least the third and seventh offense mentioned above, if not guilty of all of them.[102] It is unusual, however, though not unheard of, for a priest to be presented to an ecclesiastical court for his failure to adhere strictly to the rubrics of the Prayer Book. Hence, the fragmented nature of the church's judiciary is of concern to many churchmen.[103]

What can be said in summary about the church's judicial system? These points seem significant. First, since 1804, clergymen have been tried only in the dioceses to which they canonically belong, regardless of where the offense was committed.[104]

Moreover, the general church operates through diocesan courts for courts of first instance in the trial of a priest and deacon. This reliance upon courts not directly established and regulated by the general govern-

---

101. *Constitution and Canons,* Title IV, Canon 4.1 (2006); http://www.churchpublishing.org/general convention/index.cfm?fuseaction=constitutionCanons.
102. Forrest E. Vaughan, "How Obedient Are the Clergy?" *Living Church* 128 (May 9, 1954): 12–13, 18–20.
103. See John W. Andrews, *Church Law* (New York: T. Whittaker, 1883), 69–72; and Dawley, *The Episcopal Church and Its Work,* 87–88.
104. See White and Dykman (1981), 2:1057–62, for a discussion of whether the canon providing for trial in the diocese where the offense was committed is constitutional.

ing authority may be unusual for either a unitary or a federal government, and more in line with the practice of confederation.

Nevertheless, there is some significant historical precedent for such an alteration. The Convention of October 1789, in Canon 13 of that year, stated that clergy accused of specific offenses might be tried "according to such rules or processes as may be provided, either by General Convention, or by the Conventions in the different States."[105] Even more interestingly, Canon 37 of 1832 stated that ministers were triable according to the canons of the diocese in which the trial takes place, "until otherwise provided for by the General Convention."[106]

It would take a constitutional amendment for General Convention to set up its own primary courts because Article IX has stated since 1901 that priests and deacons shall be tried in diocesan courts. But there seems to be little in the earlier history of the Episcopal Church as a precedent for forbidding an amendment in this direction. Indeed, there is evidence to the contrary, that it was expected that General Convention would fully develop its own system of courts. Moreover, at the present time, even though canonically stating that the "procedure in Diocesan Courts shall be provided by the canons of the respective Diocese or Missionary district," the very same canon also outlines in some detail a number of prerequisites of procedure.[107]

It may be argued, nonetheless, that the utilization of diocesan courts by the general church is a device more in keeping with a confederal than with either a federal or unitary government, especially since the system is made constitutionally mandatory. On the other hand, depending upon the essential relation of the dioceses to the general church, this feature of the church's polity may be evidence of the church's decentralized unitary structure. At the crucial points the Constitution is unitary, and the precedents indicate that General Convention is simply using diocesan courts in lieu of setting up specific courts of its own. Finally, and most importantly, insofar as the dioceses are not independent *loci* of power, but are legally subservient to General Convention, the diocesan courts in a very real sense are the courts of the General Convention.

There is no body, established by the Constitution or subsequent by canon, whose duty it is to render an authoritative opinion on the meaning of the Constitution and Canons of the Episcopal Church, either in a

---

105. See above.
106. Perry, *Journals*, 2:542.
107. Canon 55 (f), Sections 20–24 (1958). The 1994 revisions of the disciplinary canons set out extensive requirements for the composition and functioning of diocesan courts (*Journal of the General Convention* [1994], 845–90).

real case or controversy, or as an advisory opinion. Attempts have been made to establish a permanent "Commission on Canon Law" whose reports were either to be taken as official and final, or only advisory, but none has yet been established.[108] Thus, the interpretation of the Constitution and Canons rests formally and legally upon the General Convention.

Although the Constitution since 1901 has allowed General Convention to establish a "Final Court of Appeal on matters of Doctrine, Faith, or Worship," none have thus far been established.[109] Consequently, just as there is no body specifically empowered to interpret the Constitution and Canons, neither is there one finally to determine what the doctrine, faith, or worship of the church is (save General Convention itself), in spite of the fact that it is possible to bring suit against a minister of the church for believing or acting contrary to these.

The Constitution in 1901 was amended also to allow the establishment of courts of review over diocesan courts. A canon toward this end was enacted in 1904, which, in 1913, made the courts coterminous with the eight provinces into which the Episcopal Church was at that time divided.[110] Now, instead of each diocese and missionary district being a first and final court of canonical offenses with each possibly reaching contradictory conclusions on similar matters, it is now possible to have only nine conflicting opinions.[111]

An understanding of the role of the civil courts in the United States in adjudicating intrachurch disputes is necessary for a full appreciation of the judicial system of the Episcopal Church. This understanding is especially important because there is no final court of appeals or constitutional interpreter in the church's formal constitutional structure.

Briefly, in matters of dispute within a church, the civil courts will seek to discover what the decision of the highest adjudicatory body in the church was, and, if its decision was in accordance with the procedural law

---

108. See White and Dykman (1954), 1:113–19.
109. For two articles containing arguments against such a court and one article for, see Prichard, *Hartford Papers*, 199–252. George H. Bates, "Courts of Appeal and the General Convention," *Church Review* 48 (1886): 113–30, contains an excellent historical survey of the struggle for courts of appeal up to 1883. See also Stephen P. Nash, "The Constitution of Ecclesiastical Courts," *Church Review* 48 (1886): 284–92. For an opposite view, see Joseph Packard, Jr., "Ecclesiastical Courts of Appeal," *Virginia Seminary Magazine* 2 (1888): 8–16.
110. *Journal of the General Convention* (1904), 107–12, 319–23; *Journal of the General Convention* (1913), 273.
111. At the time of the original writing of this work, there were eight provinces in the Episcopal Church. Province IX of the Episcopal Church comprises the non-domestic dioceses of Colombia, Dominican Republic, Ecuador Central, Ecuador Litoral, Honduras, Puerto Rico, and Venezuela.

of the church and does not violate the general laws of society, the decision of the church court will tend to be affirmed by the civil courts.

> If questions of property rights or of discipline, or of faith, or ecclesiastical rule, custom, or law have been decided by the highest church judicatory to which the particular congregation is subject, and to which the matter has been carried, the legal tribunals must accept such decisions as final and binding on them in their application to the case before them.[112]

This is the statement of the Supreme Court of the United States in *Watson vs. Jones,* the leading case in the matter. In 1952, in *Kedroff vs. St. Nicholas Cathedral,* the Court substantially reaffirmed this decision.

> There are occasions when civil courts must draw lines between the responsibility of Church and State for the disposition or use of property. Even in these cases when the right follows as an incident from decisions of the church custom or law on ecclesiastical issues, the church rule controls.[113]

From the *Watson* case the proposition has developed that the civil courts will hear only intrachurch disputes involving property and civil rights, and not those of a purely theological nature.

> The civil courts have no power, under the Constitutions by which they exist, in this country, to intermeddle with religious matters purely as such, or to assume to settle discipline, or organization. These things are wholly apart and aside from the paths to which civil courts are accustomed, and the fields in which they are wont to work. But when church organizations buy and take title to property, then they enter the domain wherein civil courts control. In case any questions arise between contending parties or individuals as to such property, the title, right of possession, or use, the civil court must decide that question. It must be decided like any other question, according to the contract on which the right is based. In order to ascertain the terms of that contract, and its true construction, it may become necessary to decide ecclesiastical or theological questions. If any tribunal within the church organization has not previously decided such question, the civil court will decide it according to the best lights attainable. If it has been already decided by any tribunal of the church appropriate for its decision under the contract, before the controversy arose on

---

112. *Watson vs. Jones, Wall* 13 (1871): 727.
113. *Kedroff vs. St. Nicholas Cathedral, U.S.* 344 (1952): 120–21.

which the subsequent litigation was based, the civil court will give that decision very great, if not controlling, weight.[114]

Generally, then, the civil courts will not hear a church dispute unless it somehow involves property or civil rights.[115] The decision will rest upon the church's own law and judicial procedure. Though the *Watson* case involved a dispute in the Presbyterian Church, the Court stated in that case that this procedure would also determine the decision in a case involving a dispute within the Protestant Episcopal Church.[116] There have been other cases, moreover, involving disputes within the Episcopal Church in which the *Watson* decision has been reaffirmed. For example:

> The civil courts will not revise the decisions of churches or religious associations upon ecclesiastical matters; but they will interfere with such associations when rights of property or civil rights are involved.[117]

> Before the civil law, religious organizations are merely voluntary associations, and members uniting themselves to such organizations impliedly consent to and are bound to obey the laws which they thus make for themselves; and the decision of the tribunals established by such bodies concerning any question of doctrine, *discipline,* or worship, are final, when properly rendered, and the civil courts will not undertake to review such decision.[118]

> The Supreme Court has no right to order the specific performance of a canon of the Episcopal Church or to supervise the action of the proper officer thereunder.
>
> Where a person voluntarily enters the ministry of the Episcopal Church he thereby becomes subject to the rules and canons of the church, and in case of any dissatisfaction with the manner in which the ecclesiastical affairs of the church are administered, he must accept the benefits or burdens of whatever remedies are provided for him within the church.[119]

The Episcopal Church, therefore, cannot expect the civil courts to serve as the "supreme court" on every dispute. If the civil courts, however, can be convinced that property or civil rights are at stake, they may take jurisdic-

---

114. *Landrith vs. Hudgins,* Tennessee 121 (1908): 556. Cited in Anson Phelps Stokes, *Church and State in the United States,* vol. 3 (New York: Harper, 1950), 388–89.
115. See also the Iowa (1895) and New York (1897) cases quoted by Stokes, *Church and State,* 3:387–38.
116. *Watson vs. Jones,* 729.
117. *Bird vs. St. Mark's Church of Waterloo, Iowa Reports* 62 (1883): 573.
118. *Bartlett vs. Hipkins,* Maryland 76 (1892): 14.
119. *Rector, et al of St. James' Church etc. vs. Huntington,* (New York) *Hun* 82 (1894): 125.

tion. If they do, they will attempt to enforce the decisions of the church's courts or otherwise to settle the dispute by what they feel to be the law of the church.

Hill Burgwin made this same point forcefully in an article written to demonstrate the supremacy of General Convention over the dioceses. In the event of a dispute within the Episcopal Church between a diocese and the general church, Burgwin stated:

> All the property in the Dioceses held in trust for Church purposes, whether by the Diocese at large, by Parishes, or by any other corporations or individuals, would remain for the use and benefit of those whom the law held to be, though a minority, yet members of the Protestant Episcopal Church in the United States of America, and her lawful representatives in the Dioceses concerned.
>
> And in determining this question, the [civil] courts would confine their examination within very narrow bounds. They would not inquire as to the abstract right or wrong of the particular matter in controversy... but merely whether the National Church had therein violated her own fundamental law or exceeded her own powers. Hence, if the authority of the National Church and her relations be as I have sought to prove them [nothing] would in the eyes of the law suffice to justify or legalize a separation, and the faithful few adhering to the Old Church, and recognized by her, would retain all the Church's civil and ecclesiastical rights, while the Separatists would be told to depart in peace.[120]

The ramifications of this attitude by the courts are these. Unless property or civil rights are at stake, the church is given relatively free rein in allowing justice—or injustice—to flourish in its judicial proceedings. Even when property and civil rights are involved, the decisions of church courts probably have controlling effect upon the civil courts. Thus, the civil courts will be lending the coercive power of the state to the decisions of diocesan or provincial courts. The absence of a final court of appeal in the church may be very significant here.

Because of the canonical statement of the jurisdiction of the church's courts, however, most decisions reached by the church's courts probably do not include property rights in a way sufficient to change the civil court's consideration in ecclesiastical matters. Most disputes over property or civil rights will therefore arise as the result of decisions by clergy, vestry, bishops, or diocesan or General Conventions—that is, decisions by persons or groups not purely judicial in scope and purpose—rather than as the result

---

120. Burgwin, "The National Church and the Diocese," 455.

of a decision by a final court of appeal or constitutional interpreter. Thus, any argument to the effect that augmentation and clarification of the church's judiciary is unnecessary seems to be subject to question. It may be of some concern to Episcopalians whether a civil court, probably composed of non-Episcopalians, is making a decision on its own reading of the church's law or whether the Court is following the decisions of a competent judicial body within the church.[121]

---

121. See the Bibliography for a list of sources consulted for this section on civil courts. Also see the Appendix for a list of some of the cases heard by civil courts involving disputes within the Episcopal Church.

CHAPTER FIVE

PROVINCES, DIOCESES, *and the* GENERAL CHURCH

Provinces

The dioceses and missionary districts of the Episcopal Church are now arranged into provinces embracing the states and territories of the United States, as well as certain foreign countries. What is the relation of the provinces, which have been and still remain a controversial feature of the church, to the general church?

Although the organization of the American Episcopal Church into provinces was not constitutionally permissible until 1901 nor canonically effectuated until 1913, it has frequently been suggested that Bishop White's *Case of the Episcopal Churches in the United States Considered* first envisioned the necessity of them.[1] It is true that White did suggest four different progressions of representative bodies from the local parish to the continental assembly, but there really is no more structural similarity between the provinces and the "three larger districts" than there is between the General Convention and the "continental representative body."[2]

---

1. See, for example, Louis C. Sanford, *The Province of the Pacific* (Philadelphia: Church Historical Society, 1949), 10.
2. See the excerpt from White's *Case* cited earlier.

The unification of the dioceses into provinces was first suggested in General Convention in 1850.³ At this time, the bishop of Western New York suggested that the dioceses of the church be grouped into four provinces under a General Convention which would meet but once every twenty years and have "exclusive control over the Prayer Book, Articles, Offices and Homilies of this Church."⁴ Although this suggestion failed, recommendations were made in almost every ensuing Convention to form similar governmental organizations to serve between the dioceses and the General Convention. Several recommendations prayed for no more than a canon permitting and implementing the "federation" of the dioceses in any state having within its boundaries more than one diocese. A canon permitting the formation of "federate councils" was adopted in 1868. The idea of a confederation of dioceses within a single state was perhaps considered to be a compromise between no provinces at all and a complete system of them.⁵ In 1880, the dioceses in the State of Illinois formed themselves into a "federated Council."⁶

In connection with the general revision of the Constitution completed in 1901, Article VII of the Constitution stated for the first time a positive official position on the provincial idea:

> Dioceses and Missionary Districts may be united into provinces in such a manner, under such conditions, and with such powers as shall be provided by Canon of the General Convention; *provided, however,* that no diocese shall be included in a province without its own consent.⁷

This article was not changed since it was first included into the Constitution until 1982, when the article was amended by deleting references to missionary districts [now called missionary dioceses].⁸ The adoption of this article did not indicate an especial willingness on the part of the General Convention quickly to implement the provincial idea. Indeed, in spite of

---

3. For good coverage of the struggle for provinces within General Convention, see Sanford, *The Province of the Pacific,* 1–71, and White and Dykman (1954), 1:97–101 and 285–304. For earlier surveys, see "Review," *Protestant Episcopalian* 6 (1835): 281–95; and Thaddeus A. Snively, "The Need of the Provincial System," *Church Eclectic* 17 (1890): 978–84.
4. *Journal of the General Convention* (1850), 146.
5. These were really "confederations." For a clear explanation of them, see "The Provincial System," *Church Review* 15 (1863): 193–218.
6. See John H. Hopkins, "Federate Council of the Province of Illinois, Established A.D. 1880," *Church Review* 39 (1882): 167–87.
7. *Journal of the General Convention* (1901), 38. See also Louis C. Sanford, "The General Convention of 1901," *Historical Magazine of the Protestant Episcopal Church* 15 (1946): 98–99.
8. *Journal of the General Convention* (1982), C–17.

the continual insistence from some quarters, it was not until 1913 that the first canon supporting provinces was enacted. That canon grouped the dioceses of the church into eight provinces. Provision was made for a provincial synod within each province, composed of all bishops within the province having seats in the House of Bishops of the General Convention, and of clerical and lay deputies chosen by the dioceses and missionary districts in a manner prescribed by them. One bishop of each province was elected president of the synod.

The powers allowed each province were very modest. In summary, each province had power to:

1. Enact ordinances for its own governance.
2. Act as, and/or provide for a Board of Missions, Board of Religious Education, and Board of Social Service for these matters within the province, and as auxiliaries to similar bodies of the general church, in the Executive Council.
3. Elect the judges of a court of review within the province.
4. Deal with all matters within the province, so long as it does not try to regulate or control the policy or internal affairs of any constituent diocese or district, subject to the approval of General Convention, and in conformity with the Constitution and Canons of the church.
5. Perform the duties assigned to it by General Convention or other agencies of the general church and to create a Provincial Council to aid in the carrying out of these duties.[9]

The passage of this canon on provinces had been made possible in part by the failure in the reorganization of the church's Missionary Society that had taken place in 1907. In that year, the dioceses had been grouped into eight departments, each of which was to have a representative body called a Missionary Council for the purpose of prosecuting missionary activity within the dioceses and districts of the department, and encouraging support of the missionary effort of the church as a whole.

These missionary councils were not successful as "they were soon recognized, especially by the layman, as more or less interesting debating assemblies, and were but slimly attended."[10] Their lack of success enabled proponents of the provincial organization to persuade General Convention to adopt a canon on provinces in 1913, with missionary activity being a major part of the provinces' entire work. Since 1913, the canon on

---

9. *Journal of the General Convention* (1913), 89.
10. White and Dykman (1954), 1:214.

provinces has been frequently amended, originally in the direction of allowing the provincial synod itself, rather than the dioceses, to have greater latitude in determining its governmental structure.[11] Later changes, however, seem to have altered this tendency.[12] Still, the present Canon 8 is essentially the same as that enacted in 1913 as far as the relationship of provinces to the general church is concerned.

Provinces continue to be a controversial feature of the church's polity, as they have been for over one hundred fifty years. Bishop Sanford, in his interesting little book on the Province of the Pacific and the provincial movement in general, summarizes the three main reasons why provinces have been viewed with suspicion.

First, the concept of "diocesan sovereignty" has made the dioceses jealous of their powers and reluctant to give any of them to the provinces. Secondly, there has been a fear of the danger of sectionalism and the splitting of the church into eight or more separate and potentially antagonistic Episcopal Churches.[13] Finally, there has been a fear of a return to disliked features of Roman Catholic polity, especially since many early advocates of provinces were "High Churchmen."[14]

A number of arguments for the provincial system may also be summarized both as reasons for its adoption in the first instance and for its continuance and strengthening. It has been said that the American Episcopal Church is now the largest "province" in the world, as the church in America is really organized as one big province. As such, it is too big and unwieldy. Thus, General Convention's load could be eased by allowing the provinces to enact more general legislation, subject to General Conven-

---

11. See, for example, *Journal of the General Convention* (1922), 189–90, 192, 200, 293, 397, and Canon 54.
12. *Journal of the General Convention* (1937), 614, Canon 52.
13. On the other hand, the adoption of provinces was considered by some Northern churchmen during the Civil War as a way of achieving close harmony with the church in the South if the Confederacy won, or at least in enabling the Southern church more easily to return to the general church if the South were defeated. This comment was made in an article on the 1862 Convention in *Church Review* 15 (1863): 124. A Tennessee priest wrote anonymously in the *Church Journal* during the Civil War that "if we could have had Provincial Councils before the War, without any division of the Church and without destroying the Church's unity, then there might have been a Convention of the Southern States or dioceses without breaking that unity." This is cited by Edgar L. Pennington, "The Organization of the Protestant Episcopal Church in the Confederate States of America," *Historical Magazine of the Protestant Episcopal Church* 17 (1948): 323.
14. Sanford, "The General Convention of 1901," 18–23. But one of the leading advocates for provinces pointed out 130 years ago that the Episcopal system of provinces was more like the Presbyterian synod than Roman Catholic provinces; see William E. McLaren, "The Diocese and the Province," *Church Eclectic* 5 (1877): 386.

tion's review, or at least to debate relevant important issues in the synods, prior to meetings of General Convention.[15]

Provinces, also, can lessen the centralizing and bureaucratic tendencies in the activities of the Executive Council. Granted genuine legislative powers as well, they can gradually supplant the dioceses and overcome the faults and weaknesses of diocesan localism.[16] They should have greater encouragement in the formation and prosecution of missionary, educational, and social work.

Finally, provinces should enable bishops to exercise a more positive governmental role, on the one hand, by making possible the removal of current restrictive canons on bishops, and yet, on the other hand, provinces could end the "lawless" aspect of episcopal jurisdiction by making bishops responsible to the provincial synod. The province can exercise more effective control than the bishops' own dioceses and more immediate control than General Convention.[17]

Provinces, according to Article VII of the Constitution, which allows their existence, and Canon 8, which describes their constitution, are structurally similar to General Convention, inasmuch as each province may have a bicameral synod consisting of a House of Bishops and a House of Deputies. Each diocese may send to the synod four (or six, if the synod so decide) presbyters and four (or six) laypersons. Each missionary district in the province may send two (or three) presbyters and laypersons. A bishop is elected president of the province.[18]

---

15. For an enlightening analysis of provinces, including the points made here, see Albert J. duBois, "The Provinces: Groupings of Weakness Under a Canon of Straw," *Living Church* 136 (June 15, 1958): 14–17. See also L. H. Bristol, Jr., "Those Provinces," *Living Church* 135 (August 11, 1957): 17; also his "Those Provinces Again," *Living Church* 135 (November 10, 1957): 20; and Frederick Sontag, "Many Suggestions on Provinces," *Witness* 44 (November 14, 1957): 3–4, and "Commission Urges Expansion of System of Provinces," *Witness* 45 (February 20, 1958): 4–5.

16. Anti-diocesan supremacy comments are frequently found in early suggestions for provinces. For example, "The first *muddle* we have fallen into is mistaking *the Dioceses* to be the ultimate ecclesiastical *unit*—inherently possessed of *all* ecclesiastical power except what it has voluntarily ceded to the General Convention. Unless we can correct this primary blunder, we shall never get straight" (Hopkins, "Federate Council," 169). See also W. E. Wilson, *Papal Supremacy and the Provincial System* (New York: James Pott, 1889), chapters on the American system.

17. This final point is made by William E. McLaren, "On the Provincial System," *Church Eclectic* 9 (1881): 693–97, as well as by duBois, "The Provinces." See also W. T. Gibson, et al., "Report on Federate Councils and the Provincial System," *Church Eclectic* 17 (1889): 422–32. In the fifty years since the initial writing of this work, bishops remain accountable to their own dioceses and to the General Convention, not to provincial synods.

18. The current constitutional citation is Article VII. The synod decides the number of deputies to which each diocese or area mission is entitled (*Journal of the General Convention* [1967], 64). The president need not be a bishop (*Journal of the General Convention* [1979], C–152).

The powers of the province remain substantially similar to those outlined for the canon passed 1913.[19] Provinces do not appear to be like provinces in any other branch of the Anglican Communion, or within Roman Catholicism. They surely do not play the role for the Episcopal Church that the provinces of Canterbury and York, under their respective archbishops, do in the Church of England.[20] Provinces, then, are strictly the creation of General Convention. General Convention grants their powers, and they were not in existence until General Convention formed them. Even though they are groupings of dioceses and not formations composed without regard to diocesan boundaries, a diocese may refuse to participate in a province, and, even though diocesan initiative actually implements the canon, they are designed to act primarily as agents of the general church, and not as clearing house or secretariat for associated dioceses. As such, they are like subdivisions of a unitary government. Nonetheless, the provinces are expected to concern themselves with the peculiarities of their particular regions and, thus, often do act for the dioceses on many matters. But their creation, definition, and continuation are dependent upon General Convention and not upon the dioceses.[21]

Dioceses

Unlike provinces, there is not, nor has there ever been, a constitutional article or clause devoted to dioceses, save that on the admission of new dioceses. Further, there is not and has not been a canon "on dioceses" as such. It would be wrong, however, to interpret this absence as evidencing the unimportance of dioceses in the church's polity. To the contrary, it probably demonstrates the very fundamental nature of dioceses to the being of the American Episcopal Church.

---

19. There is divided opinion as to whether provinces are at present too weak under the existing canons to be effective, and thus are virtually useless, or rather can be effective units of governance if the dioceses and persons in the provinces desire to make them so. See duBois, "The Provinces," *passim*; White and Dykman (1954), 1:302; George E. DeMille, *The Episcopal Church Since 1900* (New York: Morehouse-Gorham, 1955), 31; Powel Mills Dawley, *The Episcopal Church and Its Work* (Greenwich, Conn.: Seabury, 1955), 141. But see Sanford, *The Province of the Pacific*, 136 and *passim*, and James Thayer Addison, *The Episcopal Church in the United States, 1789–1931* (New York: Charles Scribner's Sons, 1951), 300–1.
20. See Edward L. Parsons, "Provinces: Ancient and Modern," in Sanford, *The Province of the Pacific*, 1–9.
21. This not only stresses General Convention's legislative supremacy in the matter of provinces, but also evidences the reluctance of the dioceses to join with other dioceses in a common body that would have legislative power over the dioceses' internal affairs.

One does not find, for example, a constitutional or canonical statement dividing the United States into a number of dioceses, each within a definite boundary or including certain people as is found to some extent in Canon 8 on provinces. Rather, the organization of the church in the United States into dioceses is and always has been assumed by the church's Constitution and Canons as a given fact. In chapter 2 it was indicated that the Constitution was developed and finally adopted on a diocesan basis and that every feature of the Constitution is now grounded on an assumption of the existence of dioceses. Thus, dioceses are essential to the church as it is now organized.

The organization of and procedure in General Convention; the election and jurisdiction of bishops and standing committees; the forming and operation of provinces; the ordering of the ministry; and the basis of ecclesiastical discipline are now all dependent upon the dioceses. Is this relationship between the dioceses and General Convention on a confederal, federal, or unitary basis? Do the dioceses have any "sovereign" rights upon which General Convention cannot impinge, or are all the cited arrangements subject to the pleasure of General Convention?

The dioceses within the American Episcopal Church have written constitutions similar in design to that of the general church. Indeed, the governmental organization of dioceses is quite analogous to that of the general church in nearly every relevant detail.[22] Each diocese has a convention (or council) usually meeting yearly, composed of all the diocesan clergy and representative laity from each parish and mission in the diocese. While diocesan conventions are generally not bicameral, most have some provision for a vote by orders. Some require equality of the franchise of each parish, regardless of the relative size or wealth, while in other dioceses, individuals vote separately and not by parishes.[23] The diocesan bishop is generally the presiding officer of the convention. The courts of each diocese are used by the general church and the dioceses alike for the trial of priests and deacons accused of violating national or diocesan canons.

---

22. On diocesan constitutions and governments, see, in addition to the constitutions of each diocese, and the various diocesan histories, Murray Hoffman, *A Treatise on the Law of the Protestant Episcopal Church in the United States* (New York: Stanford and Swords, 1850), 179–223; Francis Vinton, *A Manual Commentary on the General Canon Law and the Constitution of the Protestant Episcopal Church in the United States* (New York: E. P. Dutton, 1870), 131–41; and more recently but more briefly, Dawley, *The Episcopal Church and Its Work*, 135–38.
23. See the Appendix for a brief explanation of parish government.

The diocesan convention possesses legislative powers for the diocese similar to those of General Convention for the entire church.[24] That is, the conventions determine diocesan policy. However, each diocese has a Standing Committee, and many have another grouping that is similar to the Executive Council of the Episcopal Church, often called the Diocesan Council.

The Standing Committee at the present time is a body of probably three or four laypeople and an equal number of clergy who serve as a council of advice to the ordinary and can act as the ecclesiastical authority for the diocese in the bishop's absence. Standing Committees were first mentioned in Canon 6 and 7 of August 1789. Canon 7 required that "in every State in which there is no Standing Committee, such Committee shall be appointed at its next ensuing Convention."[25] Canon 6 required that every candidate for Holy Orders secure a recommendation to the bishop from "a Standing Committee of the Convention of the State wherein he resides."[26] This was originally the only duty specifically assigned to a Standing Committee by General Convention.

In 1808, however, a canon was passed causing the Standing Committee to serve as "a council of advice to the bishop," capable of being summoned either by the bishop or, on its own accord, by its own president, whenever it felt "disposed to advise the bishop."[27] In 1832, the canon on Standing Committees was amended to allow that their "duties, except so far as provided for by the Canons of the General Convention, may be prescribed by the canons of the respective dioceses."[28] Also, provision was made for the Standing Committee to act as the ecclesiastical authority of the diocese when the diocese was without a bishop.[29]

Since that time, no substantial change has been made in the duties and powers of Standing Committees as far as the present discussion is concerned.[30] In summary, the role of Standing Committees is as follows. The

---

24. It has been suggested, however, that the canons of General Convention are so extensive that even though General Convention has often not been constitutionally empowered to act in any spheres, it has legislated to such an extent that very few significant questions are left to the dioceses. To the extent that this is true—and there is considerable evidence to validate the contention—a federal or confederal structure is very questionable. See Hill Burgwin, "The National Church and the Diocese," *Church Review* 45 (1885): 423–55.
25. Perry, *Journals*, 1:80–81.
26. *Ibid.*, 1:81.
27. See White and Dykman (1954), 1:64.
28. Perry, *Journals*, 2:464.
29. *Ibid.*
30. For a summary of the constitutional and canonical development of Standing Committees, see White and Dykman (1954), 1:63–70, 311–17.

canons of General Convention first provided for Standing Committees to be a group, representative of the church in a diocese, to recommend to the bishop candidates for Holy Orders. Now, however, the Standing Committees are also meant to be councils of advice for diocesan bishops and, though not so required by General Convention, are composed equally of clerical and lay members.

Regarding the subject of this book, the main feature of Standing Committees is that they appear at first to be strictly diocesan bodies, and, in the main, are regulated in their particulars by diocesan constitutions and canons. But they have been required for all dioceses by the general canons since 1789, and General Convention specifically reserved, by Article IV of the Constitution, the right to legislate for them to the exclusion of diocesan canons, if it wishes. The ability of the General Convention to legislate for this important diocesan institution is more in keeping with unitary than with federal or confederal government.

May Dioceses Nullify or Secede?

Do the dioceses possess the right to nullify or otherwise declare of no effect (and make that declaration effective) legislation by General Convention? May any diocese secede from the church for cause or at will?

There has never been anything in the Constitution of the church which allowed, or reasonably could be inferred to allow, a diocese either to nullify acts of General Convention or to secede from the church against General Convention's will, either to become an independent church itself or to join with other dioceses to form a separate church, or to unite with an existing church.

As to the matter in practice, until the twenty-first century, there appears to have been no instance in the church's history when a diocese declared an act of General Convention of no effect within that diocese's boundaries. Until recently, no diocese has ever attempted to nullify an act of General Convention.[31] Thus, in answer to the first question raised above,

---

31. Following the 2003 election of the Rev. V. Gene Robinson, an openly gay man in a committed long-term relationship, as bishop of New Hampshire, the Diocese of San Joaquin in 2006 voted to amend its diocesan constitution's second article in such a way as to make the diocese accede not to the Constitution of the Episcopal Church but to the "faith, order and practice of a province of the one, holy, catholic and apostolic church known as the Anglican Communion" (Mary Frances Schjonberg, "San Joaquin Diocese to Consider Constitutional Amendments Severing Relationship with the Episcopal Church," Episcopal News Service [October 2, 2006], http://www.episcopalchurch.org/3577_78309_ENG_HTM.htm). The dioceses of Pittsburgh and Fort Worth followed suit with similar resolutions a year later (Mary Frances Schjonberg, "Pittsburgh Convention Approves First Reading of Constitutional

it may be stated that dioceses do not possess the right of nullification over General Convention's actions, but, rather, must obey them. There being no other body within the church to interpret the church's Constitution and Canons save the General Convention, a diocese disagreeing with these documents legally can only seek to have remedial legislation passed by the Convention itself.

THE CHURCH IN THE CONFEDERATE STATES

In regard to the second question, however, the answer is more involved.[32] While the Constitution and Canons do not allow for secession *per se,* there has been one major act of separation within the Protestant Episcopal Church in the United States. This act of separation was the result of the formation of the Protestant Episcopal Church in the Confederate States of America.

The American Civil War, with the attempt of the Southern states to secede from the United States, and, subsequently, to form a new nation, the Confederate States of America, raised the question of what the relation of the dioceses within the seceding Southern states should be to the Protestant Episcopal Church in the United States of America.

The several dioceses of the South did not possess identical opinions regarding the Protestant Episcopal Church in the United States of America when the Civil War broke out. Three different positions can be discerned.

The first statement on the relation of the Southern dioceses to the American Episcopal Church was by Bishop Leonidas Polk of Louisiana. Bishop Polk believed, along with many churchmen,[33] that the "Church must follow nationality"[34]; that, in other words, the organization of the

---

Changes," Episcopal News Service [November 2, 2007], http://www.episcopalchurch.org/79901_91563_ENG_HTM.htm; Matthew Davies and Jan Nunley, "Fort Worth Convention Approves First Reading of Constitutional Changes," Episcopal News Service [November 17, 2007], http://www.episcopalchurch.org/79901_91941_ENG_HTM.htm).

32. A report on diocesan-general church relations to the Virginia Convention of 1877 stated: "Having voluntarily, as a scripturally constituted diocese, entered into a limited confederation—of delegated powers, and of delegated power only—it would be clearly competent for Virginia to withdraw upon sufficient cause, given and shown, and in the exercise of her godly discretion. Nay, it might even become her sad and solemn duty to withdraw, e.g., upon a departure from some essential of the faith, or the imposition of a sinful term of communion" (J. S. Hanckel, "Report on Diocesan Autonomy and Federal Relations," in *Journal of the 83rd Annual Council of the Protestant Episcopal Church in Virginia,* [Richmond, Va.: Clemmitt and Jones, 1878], 68). The report did not recommend secession, however.

33. See G. MacLaren Brydon, "The Diocese of Virginia and the Southern Confederacy," *Historical Magazine of the Protestant Episcopal Church* 17 (1948): 395–96.

34. Joseph B. Cheshire, *The Church in the Confederate States* (New York: Longmans, Green, 1912), 13–17, 20, 26.

church was dependent upon the government of the territory in which it was located. Thus, when Louisiana seceded from the Union in January of 1861, Polk issued a Pastoral Letter stating that the Diocese of Louisiana was necessarily independent from the Protestant Episcopal Church in the United States of America, and from all other dioceses of that church.

> We have, therefore, an independent diocesan existence....
>
> Our separation from the brethren of the "Protestant Episcopal Church in the United States of America" has been effected because we must follow our nationality; not because there has been any difference of opinion as to Christian doctrine or Catholic usage. Upon these points we are still one....
>
> Our relations to each other hereafter will be the relations we both now hold to the men of our Mother-Church of England.[35]

Cheshire states that "none of the other leaders in the South ever took exactly Bishop Polk's position. They endeavored to reach the same conclusions by different arguments."[36] Polk, however, had correctly stated the fact if not the theory of the situation. That is, the split between North and South affected the church's organization as well as the state's, and the popular feeling was that a separate ecclesiastical administration should be formed.

The bishops of Alabama, Georgia, and South Carolina argued variations on the thought that the Constitution of the American Episcopal Church itself applied only to those dioceses "in the United States" (Article I) or "in any of the United States" (Article V). Since the dioceses in the South were no longer "in the United States," they could not constitutionally be part of the American Episcopal Church. But the point was that the church's Constitution itself determined membership, not merely the activity of the civil government.[37] If the Constitution had not made separation mandatory, the secession of the Southern states alone would not have meant the necessity of the formation of the Southern church.

Bishop Atkinson of North Carolina and, apparently, Bishop Otey of Tennessee[38] took a third, completely different view. Though both participated fully in the organization of the Confederate church, Bishop Atkinson declared that the secession of the Southern states from the United

---

35. William M. Polk, *Leonidas Polk: Bishop and General*, vol. 1, second edition (New York: Longmans, Green, 1915), 304, 306.
36. Cheshire, *The Church in the Confederate States*, 16.
37. *Ibid.*, 20–25.
38. *Ibid.*, 34–35.

States had no effect whatever on the organization of the American Episcopal Church, and the Southern dioceses were still within the American Episcopal Church unless they were allowed or forced to separate by an act of General Convention, or they chose, for any reason, at any time, to withdraw from the church.[39]

> We do not lose our rights and interests, then, in that Church by ceasing to be citizens of the United States, but only when we voluntarily withdraw from that Ecclesiastical organization, and establish another for ourselves. This, I conceive, we had the right to do, even if the United States had not been divided, were there sufficient causes for it; and that division does itself furnish sufficient cause.[40]

Before the war, probably there were among the Northern churchmen some persons who supported the position of the Southern states in relation to the correctness of slavery or of states' rights and secession. But the bulk of the Northern Episcopalians supported the Northern position. However, when the war actually commenced and the Southern dioceses began the work of setting up an organization independent from the Episcopal Church in the United States of America, the members of the church in the North agreed officially that this action was illegal. There were two general variations within this common agreement of sufficient importance to merit delineation.

One group, of whom Murray Hoffman is the most eloquent and well-known representative, held that the Southern dioceses were acting schismatically in removing themselves from the church without its permission.[41] This group also attempted to have the church go on record as officially stating that the Southern dioceses were schismatic and worthy of the church's full condemnation and censure.[42] While they were completely unsuccessful in this venture, they were instrumental in having the General Convention adopt a lengthy and weighty resolution more mildly criticizing the Southern states.[43]

The bulk of the church, however, felt that the action of the Southern dioceses, while wrong and "unconstitutional," was nonetheless logical from the Southern point of view. That is, the Southern states had seceded, and

---

39. *Ibid.*, 28–35, 261–62, and Pennington, "Organization," 316–18.
40. Cheshire, *The Church in the Confederate States,* 34. It is generally assumed that Atkinson was stating that the dioceses possess by right the ability to secede from the church at will. See Brydon, "The Diocese of Virginia and the Southern Confederacy," 395.
41. Murray Hoffman, *What Is Schism? According to the Law of the Protestant Episcopal Church in the United States of America* (New York: E. Jones, 1863).
42. See this group's resolution introduced into the 1862 General Convention, but not accepted by the Convention, in *Journal of the General Convention* (1862), 37–40.
43. *Ibid.,* 51–54, 92–94.

inasmuch as intercourse between the North and the South was almost impossible, the formation of a church in the South was not inconceivable. Just as the United States civil government, however, refused to accept the possibility of secession, and continued to act officially as though the Southern states were still in the Union, the Episcopal Church continued to consider the Southern dioceses as still being within the church. For example, in the only General Convention held during the war, every roll call included the Southern dioceses.[44] In actions in which the approval of the dioceses were required outside of General Convention—for example, the acceptance of the election of a bishop—the Southern dioceses were notified and their action solicited.[45] The church acted as though the Southern dioceses were only temporarily absent.

When the war was over and the Southern political rationale militarily contradicted, it became necessary for the dioceses within the Southern states to reconsider their position. There were four attitudes taken by leading Southern churchmen toward reunion with the Episcopal Church in the United States.[46]

One attitude, adopted only by the Diocese of Texas,[47] was that the end of the war automatically effectuated the end of the Confederate church. Inasmuch as the Southern church had been formed because of the formation of the Confederate States, the reunion of the states reunited the church. The Diocese of Texas, on the insistence of its bishop, took immediate action to be represented at the church's General Convention to meet in 1865, and to resume normal relations within the church.

Bishop Atkinson and the Diocese of North Carolina, as well as the now-bishopless Diocese of Tennessee, and Bishop Lay of Arkansas (then resid-

---

44. See Addison, *The Episcopal Church in the United States,* 198.
45. In this connection it is significant to know that the Diocese of Tennessee and the Diocese of North Carolina both acted favorably upon the election of William Bacon Stevens as coadjutor of the Diocese of Pennsylvania. The other Southern dioceses took no official notice at all of the election. Even more interestingly, Tennessee and North Carolina also refused to recognize—either by accepting or rejecting—the election of W. J. Wilmer to the Diocese of Alabama. The other Southern dioceses did accept it, and Wilmer was consecrated to that see. When the war was over, one of the important factors effecting a happy reunion of the churches was the acceptance by General Convention of Bishop Wilmer's election even though it was, strictly speaking, unconstitutional, inasmuch as it did not have the approval of a majority of the bishops and Standing Committees in the church. See *Journal of the General Convention* (1865), 45, 56–57, 167–68.
46. DuBose Murphy, "The Spirit of a Primitive Fellowship: The Reunion of the Church," *Historical Magazine of the Protestant Episcopal Church* 17 (1948): 435–48. See also Henry T. Shanks, "The Reunion of the Episcopal Church, 1865," *Church History* 9 (1940): 120–40.
47. Cheshire, *The Church in the Confederate States,* 182–83, and DuBose Murphy, "The Protestant Episcopal Church in Texas During the Civil War," *Historical Magazine of the Protestant Episcopal Church* 1 (1932): 98–100.

ing in North Carolina, his diocese having been devastated) felt that just as it had been up to each diocese to make up its own mind at the outset of the war, so each diocese could decide what course to take. On this premise, Atkinson recommended immediate reunion with the church.[48] He and Bishop Lay, with lay and clerical deputies from the Dioceses of North Carolina and Tennessee, attended the 1865 General Convention.[49] Most of the rest of the churchmen in the South felt that while reunion was probably desirable, the members of the Confederate church should meet in General Council as regularly planned[50] and there decide what action should be taken. For fear that the North might injure the sensitivities of the Southern churchmen, and also might deem the action of the South as schismatic or otherwise unacceptable, these persons recommended a cautious and watchful policy on the part of the South.[51]

There was, however, strong pressure to retain the Southern church independent of the Episcopal Church of the United States, either as such or as separate dioceses under no ecclesiastical formation. This was the position taken initially by Bishop Davis of South Carolina[52] and by the clergy and laity of the Diocese of Virginia at their first postwar convention.[53]

The General Convention of 1865 came shortly after the end of the Civil War. Present from the South were the bishops of North Carolina and Arkansas. Deputies from Texas, Tennessee, and North Carolina took their places in the House of Deputies. Most of the Southern churchmen felt it best not to attend, but to see if the church in the North would make a sincere and nonacrimonious solicitation for the return of the Southern dioceses.

The developments of the 1865 General Convention could not have been more gracious to the Southern action. In spite of considerable pressure upon the Convention from the public at large, and a small group within, to demonstrate their patriotism by censuring the Southern church, the Convention accepted the Southerners warmly, and officially, as if they

---

48. Actually, North Carolina and Tennessee had been active in the affairs of both Northern and Southern churches to some extent during the war.
49. Murphy, "The Spirit of a Primitive Fellowship," 438. Also, Henry C. Lay, "The Return of the Southern Bishops to the General Convention of 1865," *Churchman* 87 (1883): 421–22, 478–79, 534–35, 591–92, 646–47.
50. The Southern General Council was to meet a short time after the Northern General Convention.
51. Murphy, "The Spirit of a Primitive Fellowship," 438; Cheshire, *The Church in the Confederate States*, 210–14.
52. Murphy, "The Spirit of a Primitive Fellowship," 439; Cheshire, *The Church in the Confederate States*, 231–34.
53. Brydon, "The Diocese of Virginia and the Southern Confederacy," 409.

had never been absent.[54] Even those who had wished to hold the Southern church schismatic in 1862 endeavored to make the Southerners feel welcome back in the church again.[55]

The last General Council of the Protestant Episcopal Church in the Confederate States of America met on November 8, 1865, and resolved, in part:

> That in the judgment of this council it is perfectly consistent with the good faith which she owes the Bishops and dioceses with which she has been in union since 1862, for any diocese to decide for herself whether she shall any longer continue in union with this Council.[56]

By May 16, 1866, all the dioceses of the Confederate church had "renewed their connection with the Church in the United States."[57]

Why was the separation—and reunion—or the Episcopal Church during and after the Civil War so easily realized? How was it possible for the Episcopal Church, unlike other major Protestant denominations, not to continue and perpetuate the sectional strife between North and South that resulted in the Civil War? These following factors seem to have been controlling.

The Protestant Episcopal Church in the United States had taken no official or quasiofficial stand on slavery or states' rights before the war. During the war, the church in the North did not take censorious or condemnatory actions against the church in the South.[58]

Many of the Southern dioceses were still young, small, and dependent upon older dioceses, and without a long history of relative self-sufficiency. Moreover, the church in the Confederacy itself did not become fully or-

---

54. Cheshire, *The Church in the Confederate States*, 246–48; Murphy, "The Spirit of a Primitive Fellowship," 443–46.
55. For example, Murray Hoffman wrote to the Presiding Bishop of the Southern church, Bishop Elliott, expressing his hope for the speedy return of all the Southern dioceses (Murphy, "The Spirit of a Primitive Fellowship," 447).
56. Quoted in Pennington, "Organization," 335.
57. Cheshire, *The Church in the Confederate States*, 252.
58. The fact that the 1862 General Convention did not take a strong anti-Southern position was generally severely criticized at the time, both within and without the church. An editorial in *Church Review* 15 (1863): 118, quotes this conversation between two Methodist churchmen about the 1862 Convention when it was in progress: "They are a set of stupid asses; of miserable dolts; of moral imbeciles; they are living in an age, when oppressed humanity calls on them for relief, and yet though they have discussed this question for a week, they haven't said one word about *Slavery*." Addison, *The Episcopal Church in the United States*, 196, quotes the famous Episcopal minister Phillips Brooks: "It was ludicrous, if not sad, to see those old gentlemen sitting there for fourteen days, trying to make out whether there was a war going on or not, and whether if there was it would be safe for them to say so."

ganized. Some of the dioceses located in the South never did become official members of the Episcopal Church in the Confederate States. The Southern church met only on few occasions also, and was unable fully to develop a lasting *esprit* of its own.

Importantly also was that the Southern church had consistently declared itself at every point as not desiring to be schismatic or otherwise out of communion with the church in the North. There never was a bitter word uttered officially by any responsible Southern churchmen against the Episcopal Church in the United States.

Finally, the General Convention of 1865 came very shortly after the war and before Reconstruction and other factors mutually embittered the North and South. It came at a time when the desire of the country was more one of relief and a wish for normalcy than for recrimination. Thus, by the next Convention, of 1868, the difficulties of the Civil War period were insignificant among the problems of the church.

What is the import of the Southern church for the problem concerning the church's constitutional structure? There is not a great deal, although it definitely does not show an element of diocesan sovereignty or independence as far as the American Episcopal Church and its General Convention are concerned. The church in the North generally refused to recognize the legality of the South's action and, though accepting some ecclesiastical operations by the Southern dioceses, in so doing it specifically endeavored to show that it was recognizing them in spite of their illegality and as a general desire to forget the unhappy period.[59]

The Southern dioceses, on the other hand, felt impelled to form a new church by virtue of the formation of what they felt was a new nation. If each state in the South were to be sovereign and independent, then each diocese could be also. If the South were to form a common, if confederate, government, then the church could form one also. When the Union was restored, that the Protestant Episcopal Church in the Confederate States of America allowed each diocese to decide for itself whether or not it would return to the church in the United States may tell a great deal about the polity of the church in the South, but nothing about the American Episcopal Church, especially inasmuch as all dioceses returned within less than a year, and one diocese—Texas—felt the Southern defeat automatically reunited the dioceses to the church.[60]

The test would have come if one or more dioceses had refused to return to the General Convention. Could the church in the United States have se-

---

59. For example, see the *Journal of the General Convention* (1865), 45, 56–58.
60. See a discussion of the constitution of the Confederate Episcopal Church in the Appendix.

cured a judgment in civil courts recovering church property in these dioceses? Inasmuch as civil courts in the United States tend to make their decisions on the basis of the church's own government, it seems that it could be expected that the Northern church could anticipate a decision in its favor.[61] But there was no test. Therefore, if the period of the Civil War is informative of the church's polity at all, it seems to indicate unitary or perhaps federal, but definitely not confederal features.[62]

Dioceses do not govern themselves with extensive autonomy. There are a few constitutional and canonical pronouncements specifically concerning diocesan governments. But General Convention does not hesitate to legislate with impunity on diocesan matters when it desires. This has been demonstrated at various points in this thesis.

The right of dioceses to secede from the American Episcopal Church was asserted by most Southern dioceses during the American Civil War. This assertion was denied by the American Church, and the evidence leads to the conclusion that a diocese can not secede without the permission of General Convention, although the "National Church Theory"[63] and sociopolitical factors that are not part of the church's constitutional structure, similar to those of the Civil War, may alter the constitutional situation independently of General Convention's wishes.[64]

Admitting New Dioceses

Three final problems are of importance to the question of the constitutional structure of the church: the method of admission of new dioceses into the American Episcopal Church, the governmental responsibility of missionary districts, and the question of whether membership in the Epis-

---

61. The problem would have been even more interestingly complicated if the Diocese of Virginia had refused to return to the church in the United States. The diocese had an inclination in that direction (see Brydon, "The Diocese of Virginia and the Southern Confederacy," 409). The creation of West Virginia from the State of Virginia would have effected the complication because the Diocese of Virginia included the State of West Virginia until the creation of the Diocese of West Virginia in 1877. Thus, from one point of view, the Episcopal churches in a part of the United States were governed from 1863 until 1865 by an ecclesiastical organization whose loyalty lay in an enemy government.
62. Burgwin, "The Diocese of Virginia and the Southern Confederacy," 453–55, argues that the civil courts would protect the general church's property if any diocese tried to secede. A. S. Richardson, "Can the General Convention Prescribe the Qualifications of Members of Diocesan Conventions?" *Church Review* 48 (1886): 139–42, argues for the right of secession, but admits Burgwin's claim.
63. See earlier discussion.
64. The Constitution of the Reformed Episcopal Church, which resulted in a schism from the Protestant Episcopal Church in 1873, is discussed in the Appendix.

copal Church is determined by the parish, diocese, or national church, particularly whether or not a person has dual membership in both the dioceses and general church.

The Constitution of 1785 stated that "a Protestant Episcopal Church in any of the United States not now represented, may at any time hereafter by admitted, on acceding to the articles of this union."[65] Almost identical wording was retained in subsequent constitutions, including that of 1789. In 1838, upon the request of New York, a new article was adopted to allow the division of a diocese into two or more dioceses, or the junction of two or more dioceses into one.[66] At the same time, the division and junction was made subject to the approval of the bishops and conventions of the dioceses involved, and of the General Convention. Moreover, no new dioceses could be formed by these methods that had less than eight thousand square miles of territory and thirty ministers.[67]

Since 1838 the Constitution has been modified several times toward the relaxation of requirements for the formation of new dioceses. At the present time, a new diocese must contain at least six parishes and six priests. New dioceses may be formed

1. by the election into a diocese of the whole or of any part of one or more missionary districts
2. by the division of any existing diocese
3. by the junction of two or more dioceses or of parts of two or more dioceses
4. by the junction of the whole or part of a missionary district with a diocese, or any part of one or more dioceses.[68]

---

65. Perry, *Journals*, 1:22, Article VII.
66. *Journal of the General Convention* (1838), 23–26.
67. This article, as finally passed in 1838, probably represents General Convention's reluctant concession to New York's plea. It was the first time General Convention had recognized that a diocese might not have its boundaries coextensive with those of a state. This article caused an alteration in many other articles and canons because it was necessary to change the word "state" to "diocese" throughout the church's Constitution and Canons. The church at the present time is still reluctant to allow a diocese to encompass parts of more than one state. There are some "interstate" dioceses at present, however. For example, the Diocese of Rio Grande is interstate, and the Diocese of Spokane covers parts of eastern Washington and northern Idaho. See the article on "Diocese" in Angelo Ames Benton, *The Church Cyclopaedia: A Dictionary of Church Doctrine, History, Organization and Ritual... for the Laity of the Protestant Episcopal Church in the United States of America* (Philadelphia: L. R. Hamersly, 1884). See also Kinloch Nelson, "Diocesan Growth and Diocesan Division," *Virginia Seminary Magazine* 5 (1892): 266–76.
68. Article V of the Constitution (1958).

Action toward the founding of new dioceses must be approved by the bishops and the dioceses or missionary districts involved, and by General Convention. Interestingly, the suggestion was made in 1940 to amend the Constitution to allow new dioceses to be formed when General Convention was not in session by the approval of submitted plans by Standing Committees and bishops having jurisdiction. The suggestion was not enacted.[69] Thus, as Article V begins, "A new diocese may be formed with the consent of the General Convention, and under such conditions as the General Convention shall prescribe by General Canon or Canons." The new dioceses must accede to the church's Constitution and Canons also. Although General Convention has final authority to accept or reject a diocese, each new diocese has the power to adopt its own Constitution and Canons.

The missionary endeavor of the Episcopal Church developed slowly. The Domestic and Foreign Missionary Society was begun in 1820,[70] although the real missionary activity of the church probably dates from 1835, when Jackson Kemper was chosen the first missionary bishop of the church. Prior to Kemper's consecration, it had been necessary for the church to plant itself in new areas and grow to the condition whereby it could elect a bishop and request to be admitted into the general church. With Kemper, the church was recognizing its obligation to send its highest officers into the mission field to guide and encourage the growth of the church.[71]

The first constitutional article on missionary districts was enacted as Article VI in the General Revision of 1901.[72] This article, which remains substantially unchanged today, allows General Convention to establish missionary districts in areas where there are no diocesan governments in existence. It also allows a diocese to cede to General Convention portions of the diocese for General Convention's complete control as a missionary district. General Convention also makes provision for the retrocession to a diocese of a missionary district so received.

White and Dykman use their discussion of this article to illustrate their belief that General Convention's powers are plenary, and that General Convention may do anything that is not specifically forbidden by the Consti-

---

69. *Journal of the General Convention* (1940), 257–58; and see the *Journal of the General Convention* (1943), 199–200.
70. Perry, *Journals*, 1:588–90.
71. See Walter H. Stowe, "A Turning Point: The General Convention of 1835," *Historical Magazine of the Protestant Episcopal Church* 4 (1935): 152–79. The remainder of this issue of the *Historical Magazine* is composed of articles about Kemper.
72. *Journal of the General Convention* (1901), 38.

tution. Further, since the General Convention itself originally wrote the Constitution and amends it as well, the Constitution is nothing more than a self-limitation for General Convention.[73] General Convention had been creating missionary districts for many years before the adoption of this article. Indeed, an attempt in 1877 to amend the Constitution to allow General Convention to create missionary districts was defeated partly because it was argued that General Convention already possessed this power.[74]

In any event, surely since 1901 it can be understood that missionary districts are entirely under the control of General Convention. Whatever the inherent "rights" of dioceses may be alleged to be against the power of General Convention, missionary districts have only the rights and duties assigned to them by General Convention, primarily through the House of Bishops and the Presiding Bishop.

At the present time (and since 1835), missionary districts do not elect their own bishops as dioceses do.[75] Instead they are elected by the House of Bishops, subject to the consent of the House of Deputies or of the dioceses' Standing Committee. Missionary bishops are also exceptional in that they may be translated,[76] and their participation in the House of Bishops has not always been equal to that of ordinaries.

Missionary districts also at the present are represented in the House of Deputies by only one person in each order—rather than four, as diocese are—and a missionary district's vote in a vote by orders counts only one-fourth, instead of one in each order. Before 1904, missionary districts were allowed to send informal representation to General Convention. After that date, domestic districts only were permitted to send one deputy in each order with all deputy privileges except the right to vote in a vote by orders.[77] In 1907, the Convocation of the American Churches in Europe was given similar privileges.[78]

The formula allowing domestic districts to have one-fourth vote was added to the Constitution in 1931.[79] At the same time, foreign missionary districts, as well as the European Convocation, were allowed seats with no vote. Finally, in 1943, General Convention amended the Constitution

---

73. White and Dykman (1954), 1:93.
74. *Journal of the General Convention* (1877), 246, 253. See also Edward Henry Ward, "The Government of Missionary Jurisdictions," *Church Journal* 1 (1878): 303–4.
75. See White and Dykman (1954), 2:32–57, for the development of the canon on missionary bishops.
76. That is, a missionary bishop may be transferred from his district to a diocese or another district.
77. *Journal of the General Convention* (1904), 31–32.
78. *Journal of the General Convention* (1907), 69, 91–92, 98–99.
79. *Journal of the General Convention* (1931), 33–34, 226–27.

to allow all missionary districts, foreign and domestic, and the convocation of the American Churches in Europe, to have all the rights of other deputies.[80] In a vote by orders, however, being represented by only two instead of eight deputies, missionary districts were counted as one-fourth a diocese's vote. As of 1970, on a vote by orders each missionary diocese has one full vote in each order.[81]

It is evident, therefore, from the Constitution and Canons of the church that missionary districts are subject to General Convention in a way in which dioceses are not. If the church is a federation or confederation, the missionary districts, like the provinces, are not part of the federation except as creations of the central government, the General Convention.[82]

WHO IS A MEMBER OF THE CHURCH?

A statement of what constitutes lay membership in the Episcopal Church had not authoritatively been made until such statements were adopted in the Canons beginning in 1961.[83] Indeed, in the first set of canons, of October 1789, Canon 12, already quoted in a different instance, stated "persons within this Church" who "offend their brethren by any wickedness of life" could, among other things, be deprived "of all privileges of church membership."[84] But, just as the extent and degree of "wickedness" was not elaborated for more exact implementation of the canon, neither were the "privileges of church membership."

Since 1789, a number of different canons respecting the laity have been introduced and adopted by General Convention.[85] The bulk of the church's legislation regarding the laity has to do with marriage,[86] although there is now one canon that includes an implementation of the Prayer Book rubric prohibiting an "evil liver" from receiving Holy Communion,[87] and a section that imposes an obligation upon a communicant moving from one parish to another, that he himself, his old minister, and his new one see that

---

80. *Journal of the General Convention* (1943), 186–88.
81. *Journal of the General Convention* (1970), 260.
82. For a discussion of the different uses of the word "mission" in the Episcopal Church, see the Appendix.
83. See White and Dykman (1991 Supplement), 32–37.
84. Perry, *Journals*, 1:128.
85. For examples, see White and Dykman (1954), 1:338–89.
86. *Ibid.,* 339–87.
87. See the "General Rubrics" at the end of the Communion Office and Section 2 of Canon 16 (1958). A new *Book of Common Prayer* was adopted in 1979 and it allows a priest to deny communion to a person "living a notoriously evil life." See the Disciplinary Rubric in the Additional Directions, *Book of Common Prayer,* 489, and Canon I.17.6 (2006).

his certificate be removed from his old parish to his new. This certificate states "that he or she is duly registered or enrolled as a communicant or baptized member in the Parish."[88]

There have been several attempts to secure canonical legislation from General Convention that would more expressly define the term "baptized person," "communicant," and "communicant in good standing." For example, in 1952, the House of Bishops passed a resolution defining these terms that was not concurred in by the House of Deputies.[89] Hence, there was until 1961 no authoritative statement regarding what constitutes lay membership in the Episcopal Church—whether it is occasional attendance at an Episcopal parish, baptism recognized by the church, valid confirmation, and/or support of the church of money and/or service.[90]

It is therefore difficult to ascertain precisely what is the relation of lay membership to the question of the constitutional structure of the church. While it is clear that an individual has responsibilities to and receives benefit from three areas of ecclesiastical governance—the parish, the diocese, and the general church—it is uncertain whether this be triple membership, dual membership, or simply single membership in three aspects.

The individual no doubt feels primary allegiance to his parish, for it is there that he comes directly into contact with the church. Moreover, the laity generally make the contribution of money and services to the parish. The financial aspect is especially important, because individuals give most of their money to the parish, as has been seen, from which a certain amount goes to the dioceses and thence to the general church. The individual, significantly, generally has no direct financial obligation to the general church.

The layperson is, however, in some areas, also ultimately responsible to the bishop of his diocese. In the few matters of discipline relevant to the laity, while it may initially be the parish minister that administers the discipline, cases of lay discipline are ultimately adjudicative at no higher a level in the church's structure than the ordinary. Thus, a question of the remarriage of a divorced person is, according to Canon I.19.3 (2006), decided by the bishop of the diocese in which the individual lives.

Still, the individual layperson does have elements of membership in a general church. For example, since 1835, "all persons who are members of

---

88. Canon 16, Section 1 (1958).
89. *Journal of the General Convention* (1952), 162–64. For an illuminating account of another attempt to define membership made in the 1955 Convention, see "Membership Definition Studied," *Living Church* 131 (September 25, 1955): 9.
90. See White and Dykman (1981), 390–91, and White and Dykman (1991 Supplement), 32–37, and *Constitution and Canons* (2006).

this Church" have been declared by the Constitution of the Foreign and Domestic Missionary Society to be members of the Society.[91] Even more interestingly, regarding the transfer of a person from one parish to another, Canon 16, while not only assuring that the General Convention can make obligatory regulations on so localized a question as the transfer of an individual layman from one parish to another, consistently spoke of "a communicant or baptized member in the parish" rather than "of the parish." Yet, when speaking of a person's relationship to the general church, it uses the phrase, "of the Church." Consequently, the assumption may be fairly drawn that, as far as lay membership is concerned, a person is a member of the church; that is a member of the Protestant Episcopal Church in the United States of America, in a diocese, and in a parish. The canons no longer refer to "a communicant or baptized member in the parish" but to "members of this Church."[92]

Finally, while there is not a great deal of specifically canonical support for this conclusion, the canons of the church and the rites of Baptism and Confirmation contained in the *Book of Common Prayer* of the Episcopal Church seem to infer that a person does not have dual or triple membership in two or three separate jurisdictions, but rather one membership in what is considered to be the church of Christ as organized as the Protestant Episcopal Church in the United States of America. This membership is evidenced by "registration," "enrollment," and "certification," or what is popularly called "membership" in a particular parish, which is canonically governed both by the diocese in which it is situated and by General Convention.

The method of admitting new dioceses into the church, and the governmental responsibility of missionary districts, does not speak unambiguously to the question of the church's constitutional structure. To some extent, the process of admitting new dioceses is similar to that of a federation or confederation. In the early part of the church's history, General Convention was reluctant to act on its own accord in spreading the growth of the church into new territories, and General Convention simply waited for the church in these areas to grow to sufficient strength to ask for admittance into the Protestant Episcopal Church. This exhibits federal or confederal tendencies. General Convention eventually did act, however, in its election of missionary bishops and other activities over missionary districts, in the creation of future dioceses. Though it has been argued that General Convention could not correctly prevent any true diocese from coming into the Protestant Episcopal Church,[93] General Convention, on

---

91. Perry, *Journals*, 2:692.
92. See Canon I.17 (2006).
93. See John H. Hopkins, "Is Dakota a Diocese?" *Church Review* 34 (1881): 135–54.

its own accord, has seldom hesitated from setting any standards for admission that it wishes, including the way in which dioceses may be divided to form two or more dioceses and the manner in which missionary districts may develop into complete diocesan states.

Finally, insofar as General Convention may legally legislate on the admission and definition of dioceses and the status of missionary districts, although the method of diocesan admission may seem to be federal or confederal, the base upon which the method rests is unitary. The absence of dual membership between the general church and the dioceses, or the fact that the individual is member of the Protestant Episcopal Church in the United States alone, strengthens this conclusion.

CHAPTER SIX

SUMMARY *and* CONCLUSIONS

Having in the previous chapters examined in some detail the structure of the American Episcopal Church in relation to the question of the nature of its Constitution, it is now possible to examine that structure in terms of the criteria developed in chapter 1. The examination will be made under five headings: The Written Constitution, General Convention, Executive and Judiciary, Membership, and Locus of Sovereignty. The structural characteristics of the church under each of these five categories will thus be tested for their federal, confederal, or unitary tendencies. At the conclusion, a brief comment will be made on the behavioral actualities within the church's structure.

The Written Constitution

A written constitution is essential for both a federal and a confederal government. It is relatively nonessential, although by no means unique, for a unitary government. The Episcopal Church has a written constitution. Therefore it is necessary to examine it at several points before its implications become clear. How was enacted? What is its nature? How may it be amended? Does it allow nullification and secession, or are the central government's powers supreme over the associated governments'?

The activities leading up to the enactment of a constitution for a federal or confederal government must be carried out by persons who are delegates of the established governments of the units wishing to form the federation or confederation. It is important that they be delegates of the governments and not merely representatives of groups from certain geographic areas. If the persons are not delegates or representatives of governments, the resulting constitution is almost certainly unitary.

Do the circumstances surrounding the enactment of the church's Constitution in 1789 manifest a confederal, federal, or unitary government? There is not sufficient evidence to support a federal or confederal hypothesis. While the approval of conventions of Episcopal clergy and laity in the original states of the United States was sought in framing the Constitution of the church, the evidence does not show that this procedure was grounded on a federal or confederal base.

The church in the states had little or no organized independent existence before the first General Conventions called for conventions in the states to help draw up a constitution for the church in the United States. The state conventions were largely created at General Convention's behest, and were used by the General Convention to ascertain the mind of members of the American Church as a whole in determining the constitutional structure of the church. The church's Constitution, then, reunited the American portion of what had been a single church into an independent branch of the same church in a new nation. It did not federate or confederate previously existing "sovereign" churches into a new body. The only instance of federal-like action during this period was when Bishop Seabury and the New England clergy accepted the Constitution in October 1789; but insofar as the Constitution they accepted had no division or powers or protection of diocesan rights, this single instance cannot be interpreted as evidence of a federal or confederal constitution.

The Constitution of the Episcopal Church does not have the supremacy and rigidity required for a federal government. The Constitution of the church is the written framework of a unitary government, designed to help clarify the structure of that government and to aid it in its self-limitation. There is no pretense that it is exhaustive in its definition. No requirement can be made that General Convention is restricted in its actions to powers either specifically or implicitly delegated to it by the Constitution.

The Constitution did not create the Episcopal Church. The Episcopal Church, in a representative General Convention, created, and subsequently modified, the Constitution for its own more stable governance. Within the Constitution itself there is not a hint of an essential division of powers between the General Convention and some other independent and coordinate exerciser of governmental power. The study of the church's early constitutional history is that the church did *not* follow the obvious models of the Articles of Confederation or the United States Constitution in setting up a confederal or federal government. Indeed, given the primitive state of governmental development of the dioceses at the time, and the constitutional history of the church in England, it is difficult to envision the circumstances under which a federal or confederal government could have been formed.

Aside from a constitutional division of powers, which is the hallmark of both federal and confederal government, the way in which change is allowed in the constitution is the most significant aspect of these governments. That is, the process of amendment is the most crucial institutional feature in the constitution of a federation or confederation. In a federation, constitutional amendment requires the joint participation of the central and associated governments. If the constitution may be amended by the central government alone, even if the process is more difficult than ordinary legislation, the government is probably unitary. If the associated governments, together or singly, are able to amend the constitution, the government is probably confederal.

What, then, is the information of the amending process of the church's Constitution for the question of the church's structure? Nowhere is a unitary structure for the church's government more strongly suggested than in the method of constitutional amendment. No formal participation by the dioceses (or other governmental units) in the amending process is required. General Convention is competent to amend the Constitution itself, although it does take the acceptance of two consecutive Conventions.[1]

Closely connected to the method of amendment is the question of nullification and secession. If an associated government may nullify an act following from the legal powers of the central government that is intended to have effect within or upon the associated government, then the structure of the union is probably confederal. If, on the other hand, the central government legally may modify or eradicate the structure or power of an associated government, then the association is unitary. In a federal government, under the division of powers, the constituent governments must obey decisions of the central government made in accordance with its constitutional powers. There is, however, a deposit of power and an es-

---

1. Because of Edwin White's extensive grounding in John Locke's political theory, it is likely that Locke's theories of representative democracy and limited, constitutional government provided much of the theoretical justification for the church's Constitution. On the other hand, the church's Constitution is very similar to the "weak-mayor" and "weak-governor" American city and state governments being developed at the same time. It has little structural similarity to the Constitution of the United States, however.

sential governmental structure belonging to each associated government, which the central government may not obliterate.

Do the dioceses in the American Episcopal Church possess the power of nullification and secession, or may General Convention legally modify the essential governmental powers of the dioceses, or is the problem handled in accordance with the federal principle? Neither nullification nor secession is specifically allowed or reasonably implied in the Constitution of the Episcopal Church. As noted earlier in chapter 5, until recently, no diocese has specifically attempted to nullify any act of General Convention.[2] The only attempted example of secession occurred during the Civil War and was the result of civil action within the United States. It did not occur because of a desire on the part of the Southern dioceses to leave the American Episcopal Church. Moreover, the church in the United States refused officially to recognize the Confederate Episcopal Church, considering the church in the South as remaining in the American Episcopal Church. Therefore, the confederate principle of secession has neither been vindicated in practice nor allowed in theory as far as the American Episcopal Church is concerned, although various Episcopalians have asserted it on occasion.

On the other hand, the essentially unrestricted power of General Convention over the diocesan governments has been frequently shown. By virtue of the unitary method of constitutional amendment and because General Convention is in no way limited in the exercise or definition of its powers to the Constitution, the governmental structure and powers of the dioceses are possessed by the dioceses according to the actual or tacit decision of General Convention.

In conclusion, then, the nature and provisions of the Constitution, its method of enactment and amendment, and the mutual relationship of governing powers between the dioceses and General Convention are all definitely on the side of a unitary government.

General Convention

The General Convention, in a situation without a separation of powers, is the supreme governing body for the church. It is a primarily representative body of bishops, priests, and laity of the Episcopal Church, combining within it ultimately all legislative, executive, and judicial powers for the church in the United States and its non-domestic dioceses.

---

2. See note 31 in chapter 5 for the attempts by the dioceses of San Joaquin, Pittsburgh, and Fort Worth to remove accession clauses from their diocesan constitutions.

There are, however, three questions about the characteristics of General Convention that must be answered in terms of the problem of the church's constitutional structure. What is the basis of apportionment? To whom do the Convention deputies owe responsibility or accountability? What is the voting procedure in General Convention?

The method of apportionment of the central legislature has significance for the question of federalism because in the central legislature, the federation of the member governments into a common government and the resulting division of power among the governing bodies should be displayed by a bicameral central legislature so that the member governments are represented as such in a part of the central legislature. In a confederate government, the associated states are represented as such in the central legislature, which may or may not be bicameral.

General Convention is superficially bicameral. There is a House of Bishops and a House of Deputies. But it is the Lower House (Deputies) rather than the Upper that seems to exhibit a federal or confederal organization. Moreover, the vote by orders in this House tends more toward producing a tri-cameral than a bicameral legislature. However, the federal or confederal presumption is by no means negated by these peculiarities alone. It is in the method of apportionment in the House of Deputies that a federal or confederal structure for the church seems to be disclosed. Clerical and lay deputies to the General Convention are chosen by diocesan conventions, and in General Convention, during a vote by orders, the votes of the members of both orders in each diocese are counted together. Consequently, in a vote by orders, it is the decision of the orders in the dioceses that is presented in the vote, not merely the sum of a majority of individual wills.

General Convention may seem so far to evince federal characteristics. Indeed, in the fact that each diocese, regardless of size, is entitled to the same number of deputies as every other diocese, a strong confederal presumption is suggested. Coupled with the vote by orders provision, the suggestion may seem overwhelming.

In a confederal government, all of the deputies to the central government are ultimately responsible to the associated governments rather than simply to the "people" of a geographic area. They are *chosen by the member governments* and are expected to attempt to carry out their electors' commands in order that the division of powers and the associated governments' rights may be secured. In a federal government there probably is a similar responsibility on the part of a portion of the central legislature's members. In a unitary government, there definitely is not.

Members of the House of Bishops of the General Convention hold their membership simply by virtue of being bishops. They represent no one and have no legal or formal responsibility to their dioceses. It should be remembered also that bishops have executive, legislative, and judicial governing powers and responsibilities, both in regard to their dioceses and the general church. Their initial election, moreover, is by the diocese over which they are to exercise jurisdiction until the age of retirement, seventy-two. But a majority of all bishops, and a majority of representatives of the whole clergy and laity of the church, either evidenced by Standing Committees or by the House of Deputies of the General Convention, must confirm them in their election.

The election of a bishop is *not* approved by the diocesan conventions, which would be the federal or confederal method. Instead, it is approved by Standing Committees, whose basis and continuance is even more directly dependent upon the canonical legislation of General Convention than is that of the diocesan convention. Indeed, this entire arrangement is subject to the pleasure of General Convention, and may be altered by General Convention, either by constitutional amendment or canonical legislation.

Clerical and lay deputies, however, are chosen by the diocesan conventions, and are responsible to their conventions for reelection. This may seem to be a confederal feature. Notwithstanding this, it appears that the deputies are delegates of their orders in the church in the dioceses, rather than representatives of the diocesan governments themselves.

The voting procedure in General Convention also has interesting ramifications. If voting in the central legislature is tallied in part or entirely on the basis of member state units rather than of individuals voting, a federal or confederal structure, respectively, is suggested. In the House of Bishops there is no formal requirement that dioceses count the vote. Even when one diocese has several bishops in the House, the vote of each bishop counts separately, without regard to diocesan affiliation.

The normal voting procedure in the House of Deputies is the same as in the House of Bishops. However, the vote by orders requirement on some measures, and possibility on all, suggests, it may seem at first, a federal or confederal method. The voting, though, is actually taken of the *orders* in the dioceses rather than simply of the dioceses themselves. This tends to cast the federal or confederal presumption in a different light and suggests that the method may not be essentially connected with the question of federalism or confederalism at all. The vote by orders, instead, is a convenient way to secure the approval of representatives of the church's three orders. This voting method is designed to protect the "veto" rights of each of the orders, rather than that of the diocesan governments. Indeed, the Constitution calls the procedure a "vote by Orders," not a "vote of dioceses."

Considering the structure of General Convention, then, without reference to the question of whether or not the general church's government has a constitutional division of powers between the General Convention and the diocesan conventions, it may appear that some of General Convention's arrangements indicate that the church's government is federal or perhaps even confederal. Yet, these features do not force the conclusion that the church's government is federal, especially in the absence of a constitutionally guaranteed division of power. This division does not exist in the government of the Episcopal Church, and the basis or apportionment and voting procedure in General Convention, when considered both by themselves and in the fact of this absence, does not suggest a federal or confederal structure.

Executive and Judiciary

Some persons feel that the tripartite separation of governing powers into executive, legislative, and judicial branches is essential for the federal government. There is no theoretical reason why this should be so, however. The federal, and confederal, principles should extend into the national executive and judiciary, of course, of a federal or confederal union, as well as into the central legislature; but this is not to argue for a tripartite separation or powers. There is no essential characteristic of the executive in a unitary government.

The chief executive of the Episcopal Church is the Presiding Bishop. This officer, only lately incorporated into the written Constitution of the church, began as no more than the bishop who, according to the seniority, presided over the House of Bishops. Now elective, by the House of Bishops with the approval of the House of Deputies, the Presiding Bishop not only presides over the bishops, but also in his or her presidency over the Executive Council, is the most important executive and administrative officer of the church.

As far as the question of the church's constitutional structure is concerned, it is important to state that the diocesan governments have no control over the election of the Presiding Bishop. He or she is chosen by General Convention and is dependent solely upon the General Convention for the statement of his or powers and responsibilities. The office is like that of a "weak-mayor" or a "weak-governor" in the American system of government. It has no federal or confederal characteristics at all.

In a federal or confederal government, it is necessary to have some instrumentalities by which the law of the member governments and of the central government may be adjudicated in their respective spheres. Both the central and component governments need their own system of courts to decide cases according to their assigned jurisdictions in the division of powers. It is also possible that in a confederation, the central government may be forced to rely upon the courts of the associated governments in the execution of all or part of its adjudication. At the same time, it may be difficult to distinguish between a confederal and a unitary judiciary without considering whether or not there is a constitutional division of powers between associated and central governments. A unitary government may utilize the courts of governmental bodies inferior to it in the same way that the central government of a confederation may be required to use the courts of the associated governments. The question of whether the government of the union is finally confederal or unitary in this instance may be answered by determining whether or not the central government may legally alter this arrangement on its own volition, irrespective of the wishes of the other governing bodies. If it may, the government is unitary. If not, it may be federal or confederal.

According to the Constitution of the church, the diocesan courts handle all cases involving the lower clergy and the national canons, from which there is an appeal no higher than the courts of the provinces. Courts for all cases involving bishops are provided for by procedures established by General Convention, however. Inasmuch as the utilization of diocesan courts is required by the Constitution, it might appear that the church's structure is confederal, were it not that bishops are tried only by methods specifically determined by General Convention, and the Constitution both provides for no division of power and may be amended by General Convention alone. Consequently, the arrangement seems to be that of a unitary government utilizing the judicial systems of inferior bodies over which it enjoys ultimate control.

One of the problems most crucial to the question concerning the church's Constitution is how disputes over the meaning of the Constitution are resolved. In a confederation, constitutional interpretation is, finally, up to each associated government individually. In a unitary government, the central government possesses final interpretative authority. In a federation, there may be either a body independent of both governments so empowered, or the courts of the national government may assume the function.

The Constitution of the Episcopal Church makes no specific provision for a mode of constitutional interpretation. The courts of the church do not perform this function, and the dioceses are not permitted the power. Accordingly, the Constitution is what the General Convention says it is. There is no body in the church that can determine authoritatively whether General Convention has acted constitutionally or not, save General Convention itself. In the American system of church-state relations, moreover, the civil courts in the United States will hear cases of intrachurch disputes where civil or property rights are involved. Consequently, the civil courts may sometimes serve, as it were, as the "supreme court" of the church on all but purely doctrinal matters. The basis upon which the civil courts may be expected to adjudicate is their understanding of the meaning of the church's Constitution and Canons. In a dispute between a diocesan convention and General Convention, then, if the civil courts can be persuaded to take jurisdiction, the conflict will be decided with reference to the Constitution and Canons and the decisions of General Convention itself as "the highest church judicatory" to the dispute.[3] In cases of dispute, consequently, General Convention will probably win the decision, unless the diocese can show specific constitutional support for its position. The diocese cannot rely upon its "sovereign independence" under a supposed federal or confederal division of powers. All governing powers reside in General Convention, although the Convention may delegate its authority, through the Constitution and Canons, to other governing bodies.

Membership

The question of membership is significant for the constitutional problem. In a federation, there is dual membership or citizenship. The individual is citizen both of the central and associated governments. In a confederation, the individual ordinarily is not fully a citizen of the central government, but only of the associated government in which he lives. Under a unitary system, citizenship is determined finally by the central government, although the individual may have special affiliation, ultimately according to national laws, with certain inferior governing bodies.

The exact definition of membership in the Episcopal Church was somewhat unclear until 1961, but one matter is certain. General Convention may authoritatively determine membership.[4] There is no dual citizenship or membership as such, but only membership in the church (meaning that

---

3. The phrase is from *Watson vs. Jones.*
4. See White and Dykman (1981), 390–91, and White and Dykman (1991 Supplement), 32–37. See also note 89 in chapter 5. The canons no longer refer to "a communicant or baptized member in the parish" but to "members of this Church" (see Canon I.17 [2006]).

portion of Christ's church organized as the Protestant Episcopal Church in the United States of America), ordinarily expressed by affiliation with a parish in a diocese.

Both the central and associated governments in a federation should possess constitutionally a complete set of governmental institutions relative to the powers assigned to them by the division of powers. They also should possess sufficient manpower and monetary resources to exercise their powers independently. In a confederation, it often is constitutionally necessary for the central government to rely upon the institutions and resources of the associated governments in carrying out many of its governing powers. Under a unitary system, the central government may utilize the arms and members of inferior governing bodies, but this is not a fundamentally constitutional limitation.

It may appear superficially that the general church is reliant upon the dioceses in several areas for governmental institutions, manpower, and money in carrying out its program. The general church is reliant upon the diocesan courts for the trial of the lower clergy, and upon the provinces for its courts of appeal. The Presiding Bishop, until recently, was simply the oldest diocesan bishop called upon to serve as the general church's executive and administrative head, and there was no full-time, coordinated general-level administration until well into the twentieth century. Finally, the general church appears wholly reliant upon the dioceses and parishes financially. Do these things indicate a confederation?

They do not, because these arrangements, while highly decentralizing and confederal-like, may be altered at any time by General Convention whether by constitutional amendment or simple canonical enactment. The system is not essential. It is dependent upon the pleasure of General Convention, and not upon a constitutional arrangement over which the General Convention has no ultimate control, as would be the case in a federation or confederation.

Locus of Sovereignty

In a confederation, sovereignty, or ultimate legal supremacy, is possessed by each of the affiliated governments to the union. The central government is given permission only to exercise certain sovereign powers for and at the pleasure of the associated governments. On the other hand, in a unitary government sovereignty lies in the central governing body, all other exercisers of governmental powers being inferior and subservient to the central government. The intention of a federation is to divide sovereignty between the central and associated governments. Each is sovereign relative to the powers assigned to it. Consequently, sovereignty resides ultimately in the federation as a whole, though it reveals itself concretely according to the division of powers and finally in the amending process.

Sovereignty in the Episcopal Church lies in the General Convention. General Convention possesses legal supremacy over all other governing bodies in the Episcopal Church. The dioceses and parishes, and the provinces, may enjoy a certain independence guaranteed by the Constitution, but the General Convention alone alters the Constitution.

The basis, or locus, of governing authority in the Episcopal Church is one of the most vexing problems in connection with its polity. While it is admitted by all that the ultimate sources are Christ and the Scriptures, is it believed that these find temporal manifestation in the bishops themselves, in the diocese with its bishop, clergy, and laity, or in the congregation of the faithful as a whole?

That is, as one alternative, is it believed that governing authority flows from Christ, through the apostles, to their successors, the bishops, and thence to the lower clergy and laity? Are bishops held to be the real and correct "government" of the church, and have they simply allowed the clergy and laity to assume certain of the bishops' prerogatives at the bishops' pleasure? Is the College, or House, of Bishops considered to be the real source of government in the American Episcopal Church, and do the House of Deputies and provincial and diocesan conventions but reflect and subsequently participate in this source?

As a second alternative, is it believed that the diocese, with (or even without) its bishop(s), and with its clergy and laity, is the basis of government? Is it plainly evident that each diocese is potentially independent, self-sufficient, and complete? Is the American Church thus a federation (or, more accurately, a confederation) of perfect diocesan churches that have delegated to a central convention power to legislate for certain common matters, but over whose actions each diocese must separately retain final approval?

Finally, does it seem that the laity, clergy, and bishops together are the base? Is all government basically self-government, and are the diocesan, provincial, and General Conventions composed simply of persons representing the clergy or laity, with bishops (and clergy in diocesan conventions) being privileged actually to participate in governmental decisions themselves rather than through representatives?

These seem to be the three possible interpretation of the locus of authority in the Episcopal Church. The church has not made an official and final decision concerning the question of the source of governing authority. All three of these positions may be found passionately argued in the literature of the church.[5]

The evidence from the American Episcopal Church's structural history and development, however, leads to the conclusion that the source of authority is, at least implicitly, assumed to be as described in the third alternative above. The church's own structure seems to presuppose the basis of government in the church to be the self-and/or representative government of the bishops, clergy, and laity of the Protestant Episcopal Church in the United States of America acting, ultimately in General Convention, upon their joint understanding of the catholic faith.

Final Conclusion

The final conclusion, then, about the structure of the church's government is that the government of the Protestant Episcopal Church in the United States of America is unitary. As such, however, it is hugely decentralized. In this decentralization, it takes on confederal, more nearly than even federal, characteristics. This, however, does not make the church structurally confederal. There is no essential division of power between the General Convention and the dioceses. In fact, there is no limit at all upon the Convention's governing powers, unless it is the ancient canons and the necessity for conformity with the catholic faith; but General Convention alone interprets these finally. Thus, the government is unitary.

Concluding Note on Behavior and Attitude within the Church's Governmental Structure
This book has been concerned entirely with the formal, constitutional structure of the Episcopal Church. No attempt has been made to develop in a systematic way the legislative, administrative, and judicial behavior within that framework. This focus may have given an air of unreality to the discussion, because, although General Convention is legally sovereign, it is hardly a governmental behemoth. The Episcopal Church is unitary in structure, but it is highly decentralized, both the dioceses and the parishes participating fully and extensively in the confederal-like decentralization. These confederal features—equal representation according to dioceses and

---

5. The first and second views are chiefly asserted. For examples, see the position of Bishop Samuel Seabury and the statement of Hill Burgwin. This is essentially a "High Church" view. The second view has been argued by many "Low Church" persons, and especially in the literature by Perry, Hawks, Andrews, and Brydon, frequently cited in this work. Bishop William White's position and the structure of the church itself seem to substantiate the third view, however. See also the statement by Loveland.

the vote by orders in the House of Deputies of the General Convention, the method of financing, the court system, and the weak central executive—are probably partly due to the legacy of the spirit of the times when the first Constitutions were being formulated, to the "Founding Fathers'" fear of any government at all, and to the political conservatism of members of General Convention who reflect and intensify the controversies over federalism in the history of the United States and tacitly transfer the controversies to the government of the church. Indeed, the reason for the church's decentralized structure is worthy of careful study.

BIBLIOGRAPHY

A. Confederalism, Federalism, Unitarism

Adams, George B. *Federal Government: Its Function and Method.* New York: Knickerbocker Press, 1919.

Anderson, William. *Federalism and Intergovernmental Relations.* Chicago: Public Administration Service, 1946.

Aron, Raymond. "A Suggested Scheme for a Study of Federalism." *International Social Science Bulletin* 4 (1952): 45–70.

Boehm, Max H. "Federalism." In *Encyclopedia of the Social Sciences,* ed. Edwin R. A. Seligman. Vol. 6, 169–72. New York: Macmillan, 1931.

Bowie, Robert R., and Carl J. Friedrich, eds. *Studies in Federalism.* Boston: Little, Brown, 1954.

Dicey, Albert V. *Introduction to the Study of the Law of the Constitution.* Eighth edition. London: Macmillan, 1924.

Finer, Herman. *Theory and Practice of Modern Government.* Revised edition. New York: Henry Holt, 1949.

Freeman, Edward A. *A History of Federal Government in Greece and Italy.* Second edition. New York: Macmillan, 1893.

Friedrich, Carl J. *Constitutional Government and Democracy.* Revised edition. New York: Ginn, 1950.

Goodnow, Frank J. *Principles of Constitutional Government.* New York: Harper, 1916.

Hamilton, Alexander, James Madison, and John Jay. *The Federalist Papers.* Modern Library edition. New York: Random House, n.d.

Hart, Albert B. *Introduction to the Study of Federal Government.* Boston: Ginn, 1891.

Karve, Dattatraya G. *Federations: A Study in Comparative Politics.* London: Oxford University, 1933.
Keith, Arthur B. *Federation: Its Nature and Conditions.* London: Historical Association, 1942.
Livingston, William S. *Federalism and Constitutional Change.* Oxford: Clarendon, 1956.
MacIver, Robert M. *The Modern State.* London: Oxford University, 1926.
———. *The Web of Government.* New York: Macmillan, 1947.
Macmahon, Arthur W., ed. *Federalism: Mature and Emergent.* Garden City, N.Y.: Doubleday, 1955.
———. "Federation." In *Encyclopedia of the Social Sciences,* ed. Edwin R.A. Seligman. Vol. 6, 172–77. New York: Macmillan, 1931.
Marriott, John A. R. *Federalism and the Problem of the Small State.* London: George Allen and Unwin, 1943.
———. *Second Chambers.* Oxford: Clarendon, 1910.
Mogi, Sobei. *The Problem of Federalism.* 2 vols. London: George Allen and Unwin, 1931.
Newton, Arthur P. *Federal and Unified Constitutions.* London: Longmans, Green, 1923.
Rivero, J. "Introduction to a Study of the Development of Federal Societies." *International Social Science Bulletin* 4 (1952): 5–42.
Sawer, Geoffrey, ed. *Federalism: An Australian Study.* Melbourne: F. W. Cheshire, 1952.
Schaffter, Dorothy. *The Bicameral System in Practice.* Iowa City: State Historical Society of Iowa, 1929.
Sidgwick, Henry. *The Elements of Politics.* Second edition. London: Macmillan, 1897.
Wheare, Kenneth C. *Federal Government.* London: Oxford, 1947.
Willoughby, Westel W. *The Fundamental Concepts of Public Law.* New York: Macmillan, 1924.

B. Histories and Studies of the Episcopal Church

Addison, James Thayer. *The Episcopal Church in the United States, 1789–1931.* New York: Charles Scribner's Sons, 1951.
Benton, Angelo Ames. *The Church Cyclopaedia: A Dictionary of Church Doctrine, History, Organization and Ritual . . . for the Laity of the Protestant Episcopal Church in the United States of America.* Philadelphia: L. R. Hamersly, 1884.
Bolles, James A. *The American Church Catholic.* Boston: E. P. Dutton, 1867.

Boyden, P. M. "The Two Theories of the Church and Inferences Therefrom." *Protestant Episcopal Review* 11 (February–March 1898): 262–69.

Brown, William M. *The Church for Americans*. Fourth edition. New York: T. Whittaker, 1896.

Caswall, Henry. *The American Church and the American Union*. London: Saunders, Otley, 1861.

Chorley, Edward Clowes. *Men and Movements in the American Episcopal Church*. New York: C. Scribner's Sons, 1946.

Coleman, Leighton. *The Church in America*. New York: James Pott, 1895.

Colton, Calvin. *The Genius and Mission of the Protestant Episcopal Church in the United States*. New York: Stanford and Swords, 1853.

Crum, Rolfe P. *A Dictionary of the Episcopal Church*. Eleventh edition. Baltimore: Trefoil, 1954.

Dawley, Powel Mills. *Chapters in Church History*. New York: The National Council, Protestant Episcopal Church, 1950.

———. *The Episcopal Church and its Work*. Greenwich, Conn.: Seabury, 1955.

DeMille, George E. *The Catholic Movement in the American Episcopal Church*. Philadelphia: Church Historical Society, 1941.

———. *The Episcopal Church Since 1900*. New York: Morehouse-Gorham, 1955.

Dilliston, F. W., et al. "The American Church." *Churchman* 62, no. 4 (1948).

Gifford, Frank D. "The Influence of the Clergy on American Politics, 1763–1776." *Historical Magazine of the Protestant Episcopal Church* 10 (1941): 104.

Hawks, Francis L. *Contributions to the Ecclesiastical History of the United States*. 2 vols. New York: Harper and Brothers, 1836.

Hodges, George. *The Episcopal Church*. New York: T. Whittaker, 1892.

———. *Three Hundred Years of the Episcopal Church in America*. Philadelphia: G. W. Jacobs, 1906.

Langdon, William C. "Church Practice and Church Principles." *Church Eclectic* 8 (1880): 504–10.

———. "The Study of Ecclesiastical Philosophy." *Church Eclectic* 8 (1880): 607–11.

Loveland, Clara O. *The Critical Years: The Reconstitution of the Anglican Church in the United States of America: 1780–1789*. Greenwich, Conn: Seabury, 1956.

Manross, William W. *The Episcopal Church in the United States, 1800–1840*. New York: Columbia University, 1938.

———. *A History of the American Episcopal Church*. Second edition. New York: Morehouse-Gorham, 1950.

McConnell, Samuel D. *History of the American Episcopal Church*. Tenth edition. Milwaukee: Young Churchman, 1916.

Murphy, DuBose. "From 'Churches' to 'Church.'" *Historical Magazine of the Protestant Episcopal Church* 25 (1956): 193–200.

Perry, William S. *A Handbook of the General Convention of the Protestant Episcopal Church, Giving Its History and Constitution, 1785–1880.* New York: T. Whittaker, 1881.

———. *The History of the American Episcopal Church, 1587–1883.* 2 vols. Boston: J. R. Osgood, 1885.

Salomon, Richard G. "Mother Church—Daughter Church—Sister Church: The Relations of the Protestant Episcopal Church and the Church of England in the 19th Century." *Historical Magazine of the Protestant Episcopal Church* 21 (1952): 417–46.

Seabury, William J. *Memoir of Bishop Seabury.* New York: E. S. Gorham, 1908.

Stowe, Walter H. "The Scottish Episcopal Succession and the Validity of Bishop Seabury's Orders." *Historical Magazine of the Protestant Episcopal Church* 9 (1940): 322–48.

———. "William White: Ecclesiastical Statesman." *Historical Magazine of the Protestant Episcopal Church* 22 (1953): 372–79.

Temple, Sydney A., Jr. *The Common Sense Theology of Bishop White.* Morningside Heights, N.Y.: King's Crown, 1956.

Tiffany, Charles C. *A History of the Protestant Episcopal Church in the United States of America.* New York: Christian Literature, 1895.

Vail, Thomas H. *The Comprehensive Church.* Hartford, Conn.: H. Huntington, 1841.

White, Edwin G. *Interrelation of Personality and Institution as Exemplified in the Membership of the Protestant Episcopal Church.* East Lansing, Mich.: Michigan State College of Agriculture and Applied Science, 1934.

White, William. *The Case of the Episcopal Churches in the United States Considered.* Annotated edition by Richard G. Salomon. Philadelphia: Church Historical Society, 1954.

———. *Memoirs of the Protestant Episcopal Church in the United States of America.* DeCosta edition. New York: E. P. Dutton, 1880.

Wilberforce, Samuel. *A History of the Protestant Episcopal Church in America.* New York: Stanford and Swords, 1849.

Wilmer, William H. *The Episcopal Manual.* Philadelphia: R. S. H. George, 1841.

Wilson, Frank E., and Edward Hardy. *An Outline of the Episcopal Church.* New York: Morehouse-Gorham, 1949.

Young, John. "The Episcopal Church." *Gospel Messenger* 19 (1842): 39–47, 73–80.

Zabriskie, Alexander C., ed. *Anglican Evangelicalism.* Philadelphia: Church Historical Society, 1943.

C. The Name of the Church

Cavanagh, William H. *The Word "Protestant" in Literature, History and Legislation, and Its Introduction into the American Church.* Philadelphia: G. W. Jacobs, 1899.

McCrady, Edward. *Where the Protestant Episcopal Church Stands.* New York: E. P. Dutton, 1916.

McKim, Randolph H. *Catholic Principles and the Change of Name: The Proposal to Change the Name of the Protestant Episcopal Church Considered in the Light of True Catholic Principles.* New York: E. P. Dutton, 1913.

Nash, Henry S. *"Protestant Episcopal": A Plea for the Constitutional Study of the Church's Name.* Philadelphia: Protestant Episcopal Society for the Promotion of Evangelical Knowledge, 1915.

Randolph, A. M. "Is the Episcopal Church in America a Protestant Church?" *Virginia Seminary Magazine* 2 (1889): 305–29.

Westcott, Frank M. *Catholic Principles as Illustrated in the Doctrine, History, and Organization of the American Catholic Church in the United States, Commonly Called the Protestant Episcopal Church.* Revised edition. Milwaukee: Young Churchman, 1916.

D. Anglican Canon Law: General

Box, Hubert S. *The Principles of Canon Law.* London: Oxford University, 1949.

Church of England, Canon Law Commission. *The Canon Law of the Church of England, Being the Report of the Archbishops' Commission on Canon Law, Together with Proposals for a Revised Body of Canons.* London: SPCK, 1947.

―――. *The Revised Canons of the Church of England Further Considered.* London: SPCK, 1954.

Kemp, Eric W. *An Introduction to Canon Law in the Church of England.* London: Hodder and Stoughton, 1950.

Mortimer, Robert C. *Western Canon Law.* Berkeley and Los Angeles: University of California, 1953.

Winckworth, Peter. *A Simple Approach to the Canon Law.* London: SPCK, 1951.

E. Constitution and Canons of the Episcopal Church

Andrews, John W. *Church Law: Suggestions on the Law of the Protestant Episcopal Church in the United States of America, Its Sources and Scope.* New York: T. Whittaker, 1883.

Barton, William S. "The Constitutionality of the Nineteenth Canon." *Virginia Seminary Magazine* 5 (1892): 343–47.
———. "Virginia's XIXth Canon." *Protestant Episcopal Review* 6 (1893): 487–98.
Baum, Henry Mason. "The Law of the Church in the United States." *Church Review* 49 (1887): 442–49, 552–55, 682–87; vol. 50: 77–89, 230–43, 360–73, 480–502, 610–25, 767–68.
Brydon, G. MacLaren. *Shall We Accept the Ancient Canons as Canon Law?* Richmond, Va.: Virginia Diocesan Library, 1955.
Burgwin, Hill. "By What Laws the American Church Is Governed and Herein Chiefly, How Far, If at All, English Ecclesiastical Law Is of Force as Such, in This Church." *Church Review* 35 (1881): 111–34.
———. "The National Church and the Diocese." *Church Review* 45 (1885): 423–55.
———. "Sources and Sanctions of American Church Law: Reply to Mr. Judd." *Church Review* 40 (1882): 85–107.
C—n, A. "How Far Expediency Is Decisive of the True Polity of the Church." *Episcopal Register* 2 (1827): 81–83, 99–101.
———. "Polity of the Protestant Episcopal Church Perfectly Congenial with the Free Institutions of America." *Episcopal Register* 1 (1826): 175–77, 191–93.
Coke, A. Cleveland. "A Constitutional Congress." *Churchman* 7 (1873): 40.
Coonrad, Ralph E. *The Ancient Canons.* Riverside, N.J.: Burlington Press, 1952.
"The Divine Rule of the Church's Legislation." *Church Review* 4 (1851): 399–414.
"Episcopacy and Republicanism." *Southern Churchman* 3 (1837): 33–34.
Fulton, John. *Index Canonum.* Third edition. New York: T. Whittaker, 1892.
Good, Paul F. "Where Do Church Laws Come From?" *Living Church* 128 (February 7, 1954): 12–13.
Grammer, Carl E. "The Godly Discipline of the Laity." *Virginia Seminary Magazine* 5 (1892): 294–308.
Hanckel, J. S. "Report on Diocesan Autonomy and Federal Relations." In *Journal of the 83rd Annual Council of the Protestant Episcopal Church in Virginia,* 64–72. Richmond, Va.: Clemmitt and Jones, 1878.
Hawks, Francis L. *The Constitution and Canons of the Protestant Episcopal Church in the United States, Annotated.* New York: Stanford and Swords, 1841.
———. "The General Ecclesiastical Constitution of the American Church: Its History and Rationale." In William S. Perry, *The History of the American Episcopal Church,* vol. 2, 383–89. Boston: J. R. Osgood, 1885.

Higgins, H. Ralph. "Is the Church a Democracy?" *Protestant Episcopal Standard* 6 (1958): 7.

Hoffman, Murray. *The Ritual Law of the Church*. New York: Pott, Young, 1872.

———. *A Treatise on the Law of the Protestant Episcopal Church in the United States*. New York: Stanford and Swords, 1850.

Hudson. "Government of the American Episcopal Church." *Protestant Episcopalian* 5 (1834): 48–49.

Inlow, E. Burke. "Studies in Canon Law." *Holy Cross Magazine* 68 (August 1957–March 1958).

Judd, S. Corning. "By What Laws the American Church Is Governed and Herein Chiefly, How Far, If at All, English Ecclesiastical Law Is of Force as Such, in This Church [Reply to Mr. Burgwin]." *Church Review* 37 (1882): 173–216.

———. "Notes on Dr. Hawks's Comments on the Constitution." In William S. Perry, *The History of the American Episcopal Church*, vol. 2, 403–6. Boston: J. R. Osgood, 1885.

Kevin, Robert O. *Sovereign Independence of the Canon Law of the Protestant Episcopal Church in the United States of America—A Rebuttal*. Philadelphia: Episcopal Evangelical Fellowship, 1952.

Meade, William C. *Ecclesiastical Law and Discipline*. Richmond, Va.: H. K. Ellyson, 1850.

———. "Report of the Committee on Canons: On the Boundary Lines of Dioceses." *Journal of the General Convention of the Protestant Episcopal Church in the United States of America* (1862): 253–55.

Muller, James A. *The Government of the Episcopal Church*. Cambridge, Mass.: Episcopal Theological School, 1929.

Norwood, Percy V. "Constitutional Developments Since 1789." *Historical Magazine of the Protestant Episcopal Church* 8 (1939): 282–303.

Observer. "On Church Government." *Gospel Messenger* 12 (1835): 24–27, 53–55, 86–88.

Parker, James. "The National Church and the Dioceses: A Rejoinder." *Church Review* 46 (1885): 35–42.

Patterson, Christopher Stuart. "The Sources and Scope of the Law of the Church." *Church Review* 43 (1884): 119–31.

Percival, Henry R. "Canon Law." *Church Review* 39 (1882): 127–44.

Perkins, Edward N. *Refutation of Dr. Kevin's Rebuttal of "The Ancient Canons."* New York: American Church Union, 1954.

Perry, William S. *History of the Constitution of the American Church*. New York: T. Whittaker, 1891.

Richardson, A. S. "Can the General Convention Prescribe the Qualifications of Members of Diocesan Conventions?" *Church Review* 48 (1886): 131–42.

Seabury, William J. *An Introduction to the Study of Ecclesiastical Polity.* New York: Crothers and Korth, 1894.

———. *Notes on the Constitution of 1901.* New York: T. Whittaker, 1902.

Vaughan, Forrest E. "How Obedient Are the Clergy?" *Living Church* 128 (May 9, 1954): 12–13, 18–20.

Vinton, Francis. *A Manual Commentary on the General Canon Law and the Constitution of the Protestant Episcopal Church in the United States.* New York: E. P. Dutton, 1870.

Wallis, Samuel A. "Some Questions of Canonical Obedience." *Virginia Seminary Magazine* 5 (1892): 447–55.

———. *Synopsis of Lectures on Church Polity in the Theological Seminary of Virginia.* Alexandria, Va.: R. Bell's Sons, 1904.

Wharton, Francis. "How Far Are We Bound by English Canons?" In William S. Perry, *The History of the American Episcopal Church,* vol. 2, 390–403. Boston: J. R. Osgood, 1885.

White, Edwin A. *American Church Law.* New York: James Pott, 1898.

White, Edwin A., and Jackson A. Dykman. *Annotated Constitution and Canons for the Government of the Protestant Episcopal Church.* 2 vols. Greenwich, Conn: Seabury, 1954.

———. *Annotated Constitution and Canons for the Government of the Protestant Episcopal Church.* 2 vols. New York: Church Hymnal Corporation, 1981.

———. *Annotated Constitution and Canons for the Government of the Protestant Episcopal Church,* 1991 Supplement. New York: Church Hymnal Corporation: 1991.

Wilson, W. D. "The Relation of English to American Church Law." *Church Review* 45 (1885): 78–96.

F. General Convention

Addison, James T. "The General Convention of 1880." *Historical Magazine of the Protestant Episcopal Church* 21 (1952): 217–23.

Barnes, C. Rankin. *The General Convention: Offices and Officers 1785–1950.* Philadelphia: Church Historical Society, 1951.

———. "The General Convention of 1919." *Historical Magazine of the Protestant Episcopal Church* 21 (1952): 224–50.

Buozanoski, Michael. "Impressions of a Freshman Deputy." *Living Church* 131 (October 9, 1955): 17–18.

Chorley, E. Clowes. "The Cincinnati General Conventions of 1850 and 1910." *Historical Magazine of the Protestant Episcopal Church* 6 (1937): 337–47.

———. "Dr. Theodore Edson's Journal of the General Conventions of 1838 and 1844." *Historical Magazine of the Protestant Episcopal Church* 15 (1946): 117–32.

———. "The General Conventions of 1785, 1786, 1789." *Historical Magazine of the Protestant Episcopal Church* 4 (1935): 246–66.

A Churchman. "The Special Canon of 1832." *Southern Churchman* 1 (1835): 66.

Cole, Thomas L. "Three Questions and Their Relation." *Virginia Seminary Magazine* 2 (1889): 380–87.

"The Divine Rule of the Church's Legislation." *Church Review* 4 (1851): 404.

"1832 Convention." *Protestant Episcopalian* 3 (1832): 436–41.

Elliott, John H. "Proportionate Representation," *Virginia Seminary Magazine* 3 (1889): 29–35.

G. "Church Liturgy and Government." *Southern Churchman* 1 (1835): 2.

"The General Convention of the Protestant Episcopal Church." *Christian Journal* 1 (1817): 175–76.

Gibson, W. T. "Proportionate Representation." *Church Eclectic* 17 (1889): 523–27.

Grammer, Carl E. "Thoughts on the General Convention: The Representative Element." *Protestant Episcopal Review* 9 (1895): 97–102.

Hopkins, John H. "The General Convention." *Church Eclectic* 5 (1877): 477–90.

———. "The General Convention of 1880." *Church Review* 33 (1881): 77–109.

———. "The General Convention of 1889." *Church Eclectic* 17 (1889): 733–65.

Ingle, Edward. "Conventions of the 18th Century." *Virginia Seminary Magazine* 1 (1888): 303–10.

"Is General Convention Obsolete?" *Living Church* 131 (October 2, 1955): 23–25.

Journals of the General Convention of the Protestant Episcopal Church in the United States, 1785–1958.

Kershaw, John. "The Late Convention in South Carolina." *Church Review* 26 (1885): 466–83.

Kinsolving, Arthur B. "Reminiscences of General Conventions." *Historical Magazine of the Protestant Episcopal Church* 15 (1946): 110–16.

Manross, William W. "General Conventions That Met in Boston, 1877 and 1904." *Historical Magazine of the Protestant Episcopal Church* 21 (1952): 119–216.

———. "The Interstate Meetings and General Conventions of 1784, 1785, 1786, and 1789." *Historical Magazine of the Protestant Episcopal Church* 8 (1939): 257–80.
McKim, Randolph H. "The Democratization of the Church." *Chronicle* 20 (1919): 29–33.
Metcalf, George R. "American Religious Philosophy and the Pastoral Letters of the House of Bishops." *Historical Magazine of the Protestant Episcopal Church* 27 (March 1958).
Parker, E. J. "Some Impressions of the General Convention." *Church Eclectic* 8 (1880): 841–46.
Perry, William Stevens, ed. *Journals of General Conventions of the Protestant Episcopal Church in the United States, 1785–1835*. 3 vols. Claremont, N.H.: Claremont Manufacturing Company, 1874.
Sanford, Louis C. "The General Convention of 1901." *Historical Magazine of the Protestant Episcopal Church* 15 (1946): 90–109.
Seabury, William J. "The System of Representation in the General Convention." *Church Eclectic* 17 (1889): 579–92.
Smith, John Cotton. "The General Convention of the 1880 and the Organization of the Church." *Church Review* 33 (1881): 65–75.
Stotsenburg, John H. "The Governing Power of the Church," *Virginia Seminary Magazine* 4 (1891): 319–30.
Stowe, Walter H. "The General Convention of 1814." *Historical Magazine of the Protestant Episcopal Church* 15 (1946): 132–64.
———. "A Turning Point: The General Convention of 1835." *Historical Magazine of the Protestant Episcopal Church* 4 (1935): 152–79.
"The Value of the Vote by Orders." *Virginia Seminary Magazine* 3 (1889): 91–94.

G. Bishops, Standing Committees, Presiding Bishop, National Council, etc.

Adams, William. "The Cathedral." *Churchman* 33 (1876): 488, 516.
Alpha Centauri. "Quis Custodiet Custodes?" *Chronicle* 18 (1918): 295–96.
Ayrault, Walter. "Proper Place of Episcopacy in the Church." *Church Eclectic* 10 (1883): 961–68.
Barnes, C. Rankin. "The General Convention and the National Council." *Pan Anglican* 8 (1957): 25–29.
———. "The Office of Presiding Bishop: An Evolution." *Pan Anglican* 8 (1957): 21–24.
Batterson, Herman G. *A Sketch-Book of the American Episcopate*. Philadelphia: Lippincott, 1878.

Brydon, G. MacLaren. "New Light on the Origins of the Method of Electing Bishops Adopted by the American Episcopal Church." *Historical Magazine of the Protestant Episcopal Church* 19 (1950): 202–13.

Caesariensis. "On Episcopal Jurisdiction." *Protestant Episcopalian* 3 (1832): 230–35.

———. "The Episcopal Veto." *Protestant Episcopalian* 8 (1837): 206–18.

Carey, Kenneth M., ed. *The Historic Episcopate*. London: Dacre Press, 1954.

Clarkson, Robert H. "The Canon of the Missionary Episcopate—What Changes Desirable." *Church Review* 41 (1883): 401–07.

Corbyn, William B. "A Few Words About Standing Committees." *Church Journal* 1 (1878): 39.

Cross, Arthur Lyon. *The Anglican Episcopate and the American Colonies*. New York: Longmans, Green, 1902.

Delta. "Episcopacy." *Southern Churchman* 1 (1835): 130, 134, 138.

Duncan, Thomas. "Cathedrals and the Cathedral System in the Light of Church History." *Protestant Episcopal Review* 10 (1897): 568–87.

———. "The Historic Episcopate in its Relation to Church Unity." *Protestant Episcopal Review* 10 (1897): 201–17.

Egar, John E. "Cathedrals and Parishes." *Church Review* 29 (1877): 16–42.

Elliott, John E. *The Powers and Responsibilities of Standing Committees*. Baltimore: W. K. Boyle, 1882.

Evans, Hugh D. *An Essay on the Episcopate of the Protestant Episcopal Church in the United States of America*. New Haven, Conn.: S. Babcock, 1855.

Fairweather, Eugene R. *Episcopacy Re-Asserted: A Rejoinder to "The Historic Episcopate."* London: Mowbray, 1955.

Gardner, Wallace John. *What Are Bishops For?* West Park, N.Y.: Holy Cross Press, 1954.

Grammer, Carl E. "Cathedrals and Representative Government." *Southern Churchman* 85 (February 14, 1920): 4–5.

Granger, Francis. "Primitive Cathedrals: Reasons and Hints for Adopting Them." *Church Review* 29 (1877): 283–301.

Hobart, John H. *An Apology for Apostolic Order and Its Advocates*. New York: Stanford and Swords, 1844.

———. *A Collection of the Essays on the Subject of Episcopacy*. New York: T. and J. Swords, 1806.

Hoffman, Murray. "Bishops Elect: The Office of the House of Deputies, and Standing Committees in the Election of a Bishop." *Church Review* 28 (1876): 235–51.

Hopkins, John H. "Assistant Bishops." *Church Review* 42 (1883): 226–50.

"In Defense of Episcopacy." *Chronicle* 47 (1947): 82–83.

Kirk, Kenneth E., ed. *The Apostolic Ministry.* London: Hodder and Stoughton, 1946.
A Layman. "Duties of Standing Committees in the Case of a Bishop Elect." *Protestant Episcopalian* 2 (1831): 384–93.
Littlejohn. "The Parochial Relations and the Episcopate." *Church Eclectic* 8 (1880): 374–77.
Mackenzie, Kenneth D. *The Case for Episcopacy.* London: SPCK, 1949.
Manning, William T. "Episcopal Retirement." *Chronicle* 44 (1944): 183.
Neill, Stephen. *The Ministry of the Church: A Review... of... "The Apostolic Ministry."* London: Canterbury Press, 1947.
O. "Philosophical View of Episcopacy." *Protestant Episcopalian* 8 (1836): 101–4.
Onderdonk, Henry U. *Episcopacy Tested by Scripture.* New York: Protestant Episcopal Tract Society, 1844.
———. "The Presiding Bishop." *Protestant Episcopalian* 7 (1836): 395–96.
———. "The Term, 'Presiding Bishop'." *Southern Churchman* 2 (1836): 154.
Order. "Primary Election of Bishops." *Protestant Episcopalian* 6 (1832): 343–51.
Orrick, William P. "Assistant Bishops: A Rejoinder." *Church Review* 43 (1883): 376–90.
Peck, Arthur Leslie. *This Church of Christ: An Examination of Certain Presuppositions in "The Historic Episcopate."* London: Mowbray, 1955.
Perry, William S. *Bishops of the American Church, Past and Present.* New York: Christian Literature, 1897.
Prichard, Harold A., ed. *The Hartford Papers.* Spencer, Mass.: Heffernan Press, 1932.
Protestant Episcopal Church Congress. *The Church and Its American Opportunity.* New York: Macmillan, 1919.
Richey. "Suffragan Bishops." *Church Eclectic* 5 (1877): 395–97.
Ross, Kenneth N. *The Necessity of Episcopacy: "The Historic Episcopate" Considered.* 1955.
Stowe, William H. "The Cathedral in America." *Historical Magazine of the Protestant Episcopal Church* 19 (1950): 324–39.
Thompson, Robert E. *The Historic Episcopate.* Philadelphia: Westminster, 1910.
Turner, Henry E. W. *Why Bishops? Their Origin, Function, and Traditions.* London: Church Information Board, 1955.
Vail, Thomas H. "Our American Episcopate: Comments on Title I, Canon 15 of Digest." *Church Review* 41 (1883): 301–30.
W. W. "A Defence of the Measure of the House of Bishops." *Protestant Episcopalian* 3 (1832): 68–77.
———. "Evil Consequences of the Admission of Episcopal Resignations." *Protestant Episcopalian* 3 (1832): 33–34.
Warren. "Episcopal Powers." *Episcopal Observer* 1 (1845): 195–201.

Whittemore, Lewis Bliss. *The Care of All the Churches: The Background, Work, and Opportunity of the American Episcopate.* Greenwich, Conn.: Seabury, 1955.

H. Finances

Bonnell, Charles R. "A Positive View of Church Finance." *Church Review* 41 (1883): 573–80.

Brown. "The Church's Financial System." *Church Eclectic* 5 (1877): 357–62.

Craik, James. "The Financial Question in the Church." *Church Review* 38 (1882): 57–66.

Huntingdon, F. D., *et al.* "Symposium on Church Finance." *Church Review* 56 (1890): 11–30.

Langdon, William C. "Reform in Church Finance." *Church Review* 42 (1883): 364–75.

"Quota Apportionment Method Successful." *Living Church* 135 (July 14, 1957): 5.

Wagner, Samuel. "Another Aspect of the Financial Question in the Church." *Church Review* 39 (1882): 19–32.

Winslow, W. C. "Some Financial Considerations." *Church Eclectic* 10 (1883): 1132–37.

I. Courts

Bates, George H. "Courts of Appeal and the General Convention." *Church Review* 48 (1886): 113–30.

Hopkins, John H. "The Illinois Court of Appeal." *Church Eclectic* 8 (1831): 1140–43.

———. "Illinois and the Appellate Court." *Church Eclectic* 9 (1881): 546–53.

———. "The Province." *Church Eclectic* 9 (1881): 160–62.

"Is the Bishop Above the Law?" *Episcopal Churchnews* 121 (June 24, 1956): 20–21.

McLaren, William E. "An Appellate Court." *Church Eclectic* 10 (1882): 142–45.

Nash, Stephen. "The Constitution of Ecclesiastical Courts." *Church Review* 48 (1886): 284–92.

Packard, Joseph, Jr. "Ecclesiastical Courts of Appeal." *Virginia Seminary Magazine* 2 (1888): 8–16.

Patterson, Christopher. "The Legal Enforcement of Conformity to Doctrine and Ritual." *Church Review* 42 (1883): 206–25.

"The Penal Law of the Church." *Church Review* 7 (1855): 530–36.

Perkins, C. "The Judicial System of the Church." *Church Eclectic* 17 (1889): 814–17.
Thall, S. C. "The Province." *Church Eclectic* 9 (1881): 69–70.
Vaughan, Forrest E. "How Obedient Are the Clergy?" *Living Church* 128 (May 9, 1954): 12–13, 18–19.

J. CIVIL COURTS AND CHURCH COURTS

Bayles, George James. *Civil Church Law Cases to Illustrate the Civil Status of American Churches.* New York: Civil Church Press, 1900.
Howe, Mark DeWolfe, ed. *Cases on Church and State in the United States.* Cambridge, Mass.: Harvard University, 1952.
Lincoln, Charles Z. *Civil Law and the Church.* New York: Abingdon, 1916.
Stokes, Anson Phelps. *Church and State in the United States.* 3 vols. New York: Harper and Brothers, 1950.
Torpey, William G. *Judicial Doctrines of Religious Rights in America.* Chapel Hill, N.C.: University of North Carolina, 1948.
Tyler, R. H. *American Ecclesiastical Law.* Albany, N.Y.: W. Gould, 1866.
Zollman, Carl. *American Church Law.* St. Paul, Minn.: West Publishing Company, 1933.

K. PROVINCES

Bristol, L.H., Jr. "Those Provinces." *Living Church* 135 (August 11, 1957): 17.
———. "Those Provinces Again." *Living Church* 135 (November 10, 1957): 20.
DuBois, Albert J. "The Provinces: Groupings of Weakness Under a Canon of Straw." *Living Church* 136 (June 15, 1958): 14–17.
Gibson, W. T., et al. "Report on Federate Councils and the Provincial System." *Church Eclectic* 17 (1889): 422–32.
Hopkins, John H. "Federate Council of the Province of Illinois, Established A.D. 1880." *Church Review* 39 (1882): 167–87.
———. "General Convention and the Provincial System." *Church Eclectic* 8 (1880): 554–58.
McLaren, William E. "The Diocese and the Province." *Church Eclectic* 5 (1877): 384–87.
———. "On the Provincial System." *Church Eclectic* 9 (1881): 693–97.
Nelson, Kinloch. "Diocesan Growth and Diocesan Division." *Virginia Seminary Magazine* 5 (1892): 266–76.
"Provinces and Cathedrals." *Church Journal* 1 (1879): 772–73.
"The Provincial System." *Church Review* 15 (1863): 193–218.

"Review." *Protestant Episcopalian* 6 (1835): 281–95.

Sanford, Louis C. *The Province of the Pacific.* Philadelphia: Church Historical Society, 1949.

Seymour, G.F. "The Provincial System." *Church Eclectic* 8 (1880): 351–52.

Snively, Thaddeus A. "The Need of the Provincial System." *Church Eclectic* 17 (1890): 978–84.

Sontag, Frederick. "Commission Urges Expansion of System of Provinces." *Witness* 45 (February 20, 1958): 4–5.

———. "Many Suggestions on Provinces." *Witness* 44 (November 14, 1957): 3–4.

W. W. "Division of Dioceses." *Protestant Episcopalian* 6 (1835): 328.

Wilson, W. D. *Papal Supremacy and the Provincial System.* New York: James Pott, 1889.

Withers, R. E. "Diocesan Division." *Virginia Seminary Magazine* 5 (1892): 276–82.

L. Dioceses and Missionary Districts

Chorley, E. Clowes. "Minutes of Conventions of the Clergy of Connecticut for the Years 1766, 1784, and 1785." *Historical Magazine of the Protestant Episcopal Church* 3 (1934): 56.

Dalcho, Frederick. *An Historical Account of the Protestant Episcopal Church in South Carolina.* Charleston: E. Thayer, 1820.

Hall, Charles H. "Mexico and Haiti and the Constitution." *Church Review* 49 (1887): 29–31, 150–54, 235–38, 337–40.

Hawks, Francis L. *Contributions to the Ecclesiastical History of the United States of America: A Narrative of Events Connected with the Rise and Progress of the Protestant Episcopal Church in Virginia.* New York: Harper, 1836.

Hopkins, John H. "Is Dakota a Diocese?" *Church Review* 34 (1881): 135–54.

Maryland, Protestant Episcopal Church in. *Journal of the 72nd Annual Convention of the Protestant Episcopal Church in Maryland.* Baltimore: Joseph Robinson, 1855. Journals of the Maryland conventions from 1783 through 1788 were bound separately after the index of the 1855 convention.

Massachusetts, Journals of the Diocese of, 1784–1790. *Historical Magazine of the Protestant Episcopal Church* 9 (1940): 54–55.

New Jersey, Protestant Episcopal Church in. *Journals of the Conventions of the Protestant Episcopal Church in the State of New Jersey, 1785–1816.* New York: John Polhemus, 1890.

New York, Protestant Episcopal Church in. *Journals of the Conventions of the Protestant Episcopal Church in the Diocese of New York, 1785–1819.* New York: Henry M. Onderdonk, 1844.

Pennington, Edgar L. "Colonial Clergy Conventions." *Historical Magazine of the Protestant Episcopal Church* 8 (1939): 178–218.
Stowe, Walter H. "State or Diocesan Conventions of the War and Post War Period." *Historical Magazine of the Protestant Episcopal Church* 8 (1939): 220–50.
Ward, Edward Henry. "The Government of Missionary Jurisdictions." *Church Journal* 1 (1878): 308–9.

M. Episcopal Church in the Confederate States of America

Brydon, G. MacLaren. "The Diocese of Virginia and the Southern Confederacy." *Historical Magazine of the Protestant Episcopal Church* 17 (1948): 386–410.
Burgher, Nash K. "Diocese of Mississippi and the Confederacy." *Historical Magazine of the Protestant Episcopal Church* 9 (1920): 52–77.
Cheshire, Joseph B. *The Church in the Confederate States.* New York: Longmans, Green, 1912.
Constitution of the Protestant Episcopal Church in the Confederate States of America and Digest of the Canons Adopted in General Council in Augusta, Georgia, November 1862. Augusta, Ga.: Steam Power Press Chronicle and Sentinel, 1863.
Fulton, John. "The Church in the Confederate States." In William S. Perry, *The History of the American Episcopal Church*, vol. 2, 561–92. Boston: J. R. Osgood, 1885.
"The General Convention of 1862." *Church Review* 15 (1863): 104–26.
Hoffman, Murray. *What Is Schism? According to the Law of the Protestant Episcopal Church in the United States of America.* New York: E. Jones, 1863.
Journal of the Proceedings of an Adjourned Convention of Bishops, Clergymen, and Laymen of the Protestant Episcopal Church in the Confederate States of America, Held in Christ Church, Columbia, South Carolina, from October 16 to October 24, inclusive, in the Year of Our Lord, 1861. Montgomery, Ala.: Montgomery Advertiser Job Printing Offices, 1861.
Journal of the General Council of the Protestant Episcopal Church in the Confederate States of America, 1862. Augusta, Ga.: Steam Press of Chronicle and Sentinel, 1863.
Lay, Henry C. "The Return of the Southern Bishops to the General Convention of 1865, a Sketch, with Sundry Letters and Documents." *Churchman* 87 (1883): 421–22, 478–79, 534–35, 591–92, 646–47.
Mohler, Mark. "The Episcopal Church and National Reconstruction." *Political Science Quarterly* 41 (1927): 567–95.

Murphy, DuBose. "The Protestant Episcopal Church in Texas During the Civil War." *Historical Magazine of the Protestant Episcopal Church* 1 (1932): 90–101.

———. "The Spirit of a Primitive Fellowship: The Reunion of the Church." *Historical Magazine of the Protestant Episcopal Church* 17 (1948): 435–48.

Pennington, E. L., ed. "Essays on the Church in the Confederacy." *Historical Magazine of the Protestant Episcopal Church* 17, no. 4 (1948).

———. "The Organization of the Protestant Episcopal Church in the Confederate States of America." *Historical Magazine of the Protestant Episcopal Church* 17 (1948): 308–38.

Polk, William M. *Leonidas Polk: Bishop and General.* 2 vols. Second edition. New York: Longmans, Green, 1915.

Shanks, Henry T. "The Reunion of the Episcopal Church, 1865." *Church History* 9 (1940): 120–40.

N. Reformed Episcopal Church

Aycrigg, Benjamin. *Memoirs of the Reformed Episcopal Church.* Third edition. New York: E. O. Jenkins, 1877.

Boggs, Edward B. "The Schism of 1873." *Church Review* 27 (1875): 255–78.

Cummins, Alexandrine M. *Memoir of George David Cummins, D.D.: First Bishop of the Reformed Episcopal Church.* New York: Dodd, Mead, 1879.

Journals of the General Council of the Reformed Episcopal Church. Philadelphia: James Moore, 1874.

"The Late Bishop Cummins." *Church Eclectic* 7 (1879): 282–84.

"The Reason for Starting a New Sect." *Churchman* 43 (1873): 395.

O. Parish, Vestry, Laity, Membership

Anderson, Charles P. *Letters to Laymen.* Milwaukee: Young Churchman, 1913.

Attwood, Albert W. "Church Wardens." *Living Church* 135 (December 1, 1957): 22.

"Bishops and Vestries." *Living Church* 132 (June 10, 1956): 6.

Brydon, G. MacLaren. "The Origin of the Rights of the Laity in the American Episcopal Church." *Historical Magazine of the Protestant Episcopal Church* 12 (1943): 313–38.

Chapin, D. D. "Some Conditions of Permanency in the Pastoral Relation." *Church Eclectic* 11 (1884): 945–48, 1041–45.

Chamberlayne, C. G. "Vestry or Congregation." *Southern Churchman* 85 (January 3, 1920): 5.

"Choosing a Rector." *Living Church* 130 (February 6, 1955): 10–11.

Clericus. "Parochial Elections." *Church Eclectic* 8 (1880): 176–77.
Coddington, Herbert G. *The Rector and His Vestry.* Syracuse, N.Y.: Cornell Printing Company, 1926.
Dix, Morgan. "The Functions of Rectors, and Wardens, and Vestrymen." *Church Eclectic* 8 (1881): 1096–1102.
Edmunds, C. C., Jr. "The Revival of Minor Orders—The True Method of Enlisting Lay Help." *Church Eclectic* 17 (1889): 219–26.
Gibbs, George. "Spiritualities and Temporalities." *Living Church* 136 (June 8, 1958): 11–13.
Hodges, George, and John Reichert. *The Administration of an Institutional Church: A Detailed Account of the Operation of St. George's Parish in the City of New York.* New York: Harper, 1906.
Humphrey, George H. *Law of the Protestant Episcopal Church.* Second edition. New York: James Pott, 1882.
Investigator. "Permanent Deacons as Assistants in Large Parishes." *Protestant Episcopalian* 7 (1836): 383–86.
"The Laity in the Church: Has the Experiment of the American Church Succeeded?" *Church Eclectic* 7 (1879): 374–80.
Larson, Lowell E. "Church Accounting." *Living Church* 136 (January 12, 1958): 20–24.
"Law Representation of the Church." *Southern Churchman* 2 (1836): 113.
Ludlow, Theodore R. *I Am a Vestryman.* Revised edition. New York: Morehouse-Gorham, 1945.
"Membership Definition Studied." *Living Church* 131 (September 25, 1955): 9.
Norman, R. W. "Women's Work in the Church." *Church Review* 36 (1881): 213–40.
The Parish or Vestry System of the Protestant Episcopal Church in the United States of America: The Evils It Involves, and What Will Remedy Them. Buffalo, N.Y.: Barber, Jones, 1896.
Parker, James. "On Rectors, Wardens, and Vestrymen." *Church Eclectic* 9 (1881): 77–81.
Parris, Albion K. "The Place of the Laity in the Church." *Protestant Episcopal Review* 13 (1900): 301–11.
Peoples, Joseph W., Jr. "The Church Office: Management Methods in a Middle-Sized Parish." *Living Church* 136 (January 12, 1958): 16–17.
Ravenscroft. "The Government of the Church Popular." *Southern Churchman* 2 (1836): 61.
"Report of a Meeting of the Standing Committee of the Diocese of M———." *Church Eclectic* 9 (1881): 842–45.
Spalding, John F. "Congregationalism in the Church." *Church Review* 28 (1876): 261–72.

Stowe, Walter H. *More Lay Readers than Clergy: A Study of the Office of Lay Reader in the History of the Church*. Philadelphia: Church Historical Society, 1956.

"Wardens and Vestrymen." *Protestant Episcopalian* 5 (1834): 296–312.

"Why the Vestry." *Living Church* 132 (February 12, 1956): 10–11.

P. Magazines of the Episcopal Church

Bosher, Robert S. "The Episcopal Church and American Christianity: A Bibliography." *Historical Magazine of the Protestant Episcopal Church* 19 (1950): 369–84.

Chorley, E. Clowes. "Archives of General Convention." *Historical Magazine of the Protestant Episcopal Church* 2 (1933): 55.

Mampateng, Charles. "The Library and American Church History." *Historical Magazine of the Protestant Episcopal Church* 5 (1936): 225–37.

Morehouse, Clifford P. "Origins of the Episcopal Church Press: Colonial Days to 1840." *Historical Magazine of the Protestant Episcopal Church* 11, no. 3 (1942).

Pennington, Edgar L. "The General Convention and the Preservation of the Church's Historical Material." *Historical Magazine of the Protestant Episcopal Church* 9 (1940): 171.

Rede, Wyllys. "The Maryland Diocesan Library—A Mine of Historical Material." *Historical Magazine of the Protestant Episcopal Church* 1 (1932): 102.

Rice, Edwin B. "Catalogue of the Archives of General Convention." *Historical Magazine of the Protestant Episcopal Church* 2 (1933): 3, 45.

Sonne, Niels H. "Bibliographical Materials on the Episcopal Church." *Historical Magazine of the Protestant Episcopal Church* 26 (1957): 173–82.

Ward, Julius H. "Church Literature Since the Revolution." In William S. Perry, *The History of the American Episcopal Church*, vol. 2, 611–30. Boston: J. R. Osgood, 1885.

APPENDIX

I. Controversy Concerning the Source of Canon Law
   The Ancient Canons Do Apply to the Episcopal Church
      Hoffman's View
      "The Ancient Canons"
      Analogy to Common Law
      Summary of Hoffman's Position
   The Ancient Canons Do Not Apply to the Episcopal Church
      Andrews's View
      Opinion of Kevin and Brydon
   The Importance of This Controversy

II. The Constitution of the Confederate Episcopal Church
   The Official Draft of October 1861
   The Accepted Constitution

III. The Reformed Episcopal Church
   The Constitution of the Reformed Episcopal Church

IV. Notes and Comments on the Church's Government
   On the Name of the Church
   On Church Parties
   On Parish Government
   On "Divided Votes" in the House of Deputies
   On the Use of the Word "Mission"
   Quotations Showing Conflicting Opinions Regarding the Meaning of the Constitution Enacted in 1789
   Quotations Showing Conflicting Opinions Regarding the Extent of General Convention's Power
   Official Church Acts Showing the Relationship of the Episcopal Church to the Church of England
   Civil Court Cases Involving the Episcopal Church
   On "Sovereignty"

I. Controversy Concerning the Source of Canon Law

There are two opposing views extant with the Episcopal Church regarding the source of canon law in force within the Episcopal Church in the United States. The controversy has existed from an early time in the American Church's history.

There is a body of opinion represented, for example, by Murray Hoffman, Henry R. Percival, S. Corning Judd, Christopher S. Patterson, Edwin A. White, Paul F. Good, Ralph E. Coonrad, Edward Perkins, the American Church Union, and the Clerical Union. Opposed to this is the thought of John W. Andrews, Hill Burgwin, Francis Wharton, Robert O. Kevin, G. MacLaren Brydon, and the Episcopal Evangelical Fellowship.[1]

These two schools of thought will be titled by the name of their earliest major exponents—Hoffman and Andrews—although there is not uniform agreement on all points among adherents of either of the two views.

The controversy revolves around the question to what extent the legislative power of the Episcopal Church in the United States is restricted by the "ancient canons." These canons have been defined as being

> The Canons of the first four General Councils..., plus that body of Western Canon and General Law which was received and promulgated in England, and is now effective through Act 25 Henry VIII, c. 99. In addition there is that body of English ecclesiastical law which has not been outmoded, amended, or superseded, and which has not fallen completely into desuetude.[2]

The Ancient Canons Do Apply to the Episcopal Church

Hoffman's View

Hoffman's argument is that inasmuch as the canon law of the Church of England was in force within the Church of England in the North American colonies before the Revolution, subsequent action by the "daughter church" after the Revolution shows that the ancient canons and the canon

---

1. See the Bibliography for work by these persons on this subject.
2. Ralph E. Coonrad, *The Ancient Canons* (Riverside, N.J.: Burlington Press, 1952), 13 (footnote 35). Also see the Bibliography for other works on the Anglican use and interpretation of canon law.

law of the Church of England were specifically made applicable to the American Church:

> When, then, we find our Church declaring, in one of its most solemn acts, that all which is not of doctrine is of discipline; that she meant not to depart from the Church of England, further than local circumstances required; when we find that the body of English ecclesiastical law was an undoubted part of discipline in that church and in the colonial church; when we find no discrimination made between what of discipline is binding and what is annulled, the conclusion seems irresistible, that this law, with necessary modifications, retained the same authority after the revolution which it possessed before.[3]

In a frequently quoted passage, Hoffman summarizes his opinion thus:

> I may state the result in these propositions:
> 1. The English canon law governs, unless it is inconsistent with, or superseded by a positive institution of our own.
> 2. Unless it is at variance with any civil law or doctrine of the State, either recognized by the Church, or not opposed to her principles.
> 3. Unless it is inconsistent with, or inapplicable to that position in which the Church in these States is placed.
>
> And let it not be thought, that in this loyalty to the English law, we abjure the liberty of a National Church, or admit a subserviency to a foreign authority....
>
> In submitting to the guidance of English authority, we render no other allegiance than every honest judge in the land renders to the decisions of Westminster Hall in civil matters.[4]

"The Ancient Canons"
This position is strongly supported in a pamphlet entitled *The Ancient Canons* by a Joint Committee on Discipline of the American Church Union and the Clerical Union, chaired by Ralph E. Coonrad. *The Ancient Canons* presents the argument as follows at length.

> The Episcopal Church is but one national or regional Church; i.e., a particular church, autocephalous in character, in that stream of catholic Chris-

---

3. Murray Hoffman, *A Treatise on the Law of the Protestant Episcopal Church in the United States* (New York: Stanford and Swords, 1850), 49.
4. *Ibid.*, 64–65. See also Murray Hoffman, *The Ritual Law of the Church* (New York: Pott, Young, 1872), 4; and Edwin A. White, *American Church Law* (New York: James Pott, 1898), Part I.

tendom in which doctrine and law flow to the Apostles and to Christ Himself.[5]

In matters which affect the doctrine and discipline of the catholic Church of Christ, the Episcopal Church is morally as well as canonically bound not to act by or for herself alone, but in harmonious agreement with that heritage through which it retains continuity with the past. The Episcopal Church, its General Convention, its respective diocesan conventions, are not, by virtue of Episcopal orders and the legislative power which accepted them for this church, separate entities in the stream of spiritual, doctrinal, and canonical catholic order and discipline. The ethos and composition of these conventions, however constitutional and democratic in character are homogeneous with the heritage and organic structure of catholic Christendom.[6]

Legislative action which removes souls from the organic and spiritual stream of catholic Christendom must be considered as exceeding the powers of a regional council of the catholic Church. Such legislative action, should it ever occur, must be considered *ultra vires*; it could hardly be imposed without dire results upon the consciences of Episcopal churchmen. Morally, therefore, as well as canonically the sovereignty of a regional church like the Episcopal Church is limited in that it cannot without committing sin separate souls under its care from catholic order and life.[7]

It is desirable to state some facts often overlooked: (1) That the Episcopal Church is a province of the Anglican Communion; (2) that the provinces of this communion share a written and customary canon law (discipline) to which the canons of our General Convention are merely a provincial supplement; (3) that legislation of General Convention which contravenes essential principles of this general law is simply invalid. There is a definite, if not a clearly defined, limit beyond which the enactments ordering the government of a province may not go.[8]

Analogy to Common Law

Considerable emphasis is laid upon an analogy between the use of English common law and canon law in the United States. For example, in *Refutation of Dr. Kevin's Rebuttal of "The Ancient Canons,"* Edward Perkins says:

---

5. Coonrad, *The Ancient Canons*, 1.
6. *Ibid.*, 2.
7. *Ibid.*, 3.
8. *Ibid.*

The "sovereign independence" of the Episcopal Church is not more impaired by having taken over the canon law of the mother church, than the sovereign independence of the states of the United States is impaired by having taken over the common law of the mother country. The common law of England was taken over intact by every one of the thirteen colonies, including Acts of Parliament of general application in force at the time of separation from the mother country, and is basically the law of almost every one of our states today. The proposition that on separating from the mother church the Episcopal Church retained the canon law, which was its law while in the Church of England, is strictly analogous to the proposition that on separating from the mother country the thirteen colonies retained the civil and criminal law which was their law while under British rule.[9]

Moreover, decisions by the United States civil courts are frequently cited to support Hoffman's views.[10]

Summary of Hoffman's Position

Thus the opinion of many within the Episcopal Church is that the church in the United States, while completely free and independent in its "lawmaking and law-enforcing authority,"[11] is morally bound by the ancient canons in the same way the United States or English governments are bound by common law as the highest expression of human wisdom and justice; by "natural law" as the overarching, unwritten, or only partly written law of mankind; or by international law "as a member of the family of nations... without derogation from its sovereign independence."[12]

It is admitted that

> of course no one can physically prevent General Convention from adopting whatever legislation it may wish, whether it be good or bad, sound or unsound. But such departures carry their own penalty. They make us, *pro tanto,* heretics or schismatics, or both, and guilty of another rent in the seamless robe of Christ.[13]

---

9. Edward N. Perkins, *Refutation of Dr. Kevin's Rebuttal of "The Ancient Canons"* (New York: American Church Union, 1954), 3.
10. Coonrad, *The Ancient Canons,* 31–34.
11. Perkins, *Refutation,* 5.
12. *Ibid.,* 4.
13. Coonrad, *The Ancient Canons,* 19. Most of the specific arguments in *The Ancient Canons* were earlier suggested in S. Corning Judd, "By What Laws the American Church Is Governed and Herein Chiefly, How Far, If at All, English Ecclesiastical Law Is of Force, as Such, in This Church [Reply to Mr. Burgwin]," *Church Review* 37 (1882): 172–216.

The Ancient Canons Do Not Apply to the Episcopal Church

Andrews's View

The opinions of John Andrews contradict those of Hoffman. Andrews denies that the canon law of the Church of England has any force within the American Episcopal Church except as specifically incorporated by the church into its Constitution and Canons. He specifically refutes Hoffman's opinion, asserting that the express assent of the church is essential before any law is binding on the church.[14]

As for Hoffman, so with Andrews the analogy between English common law and English canon law is made regarding the applicability of each with the United States. However, Andrews comes to an exactly opposite conclusion in both instances. Andrews shows, with lengthy citations and arguments, that neither English common nor canon law has force within the states or dioceses respectively in the United States except as specifically and expressly adopted by them.[15]

Thus Andrews concludes:

> We have then as laws and regulations for the government of the Protestant Episcopal Church in the United States, as follows:
> 1. The Constitution of the Church, and the canons of the General Convention thereby authorized.
> 2. The constitutions and canons of the several dioceses, of force only in such dioceses, respectively; and subject to the lawful authority of the General Convention.
> 3. The rubrics of the Church, and in some particulars, the articles.
> 4. The civil laws of the states affecting the churches, and their members, in regard to corporate or personal rights, civil privileges, and the acquisition and preservation of property.
> 5. Such forms and usages and laws of the Church of England as have been adopted by this Church, in her constitution and canons.[16]

Opinion of Kevin and Brydon

This view is concurred in by Robert O. Kevin and G. MacLaren Brydon, both writing specifically to refute the writers of *The Ancient Canons*.[17] However, Brydon observes:

---

14. John W. Andrews, *Church Law* (New York: T. Whittaker, 1883), 46–48.
15. *Ibid.*, 8–20.
16. *Ibid.*, 48.
17. Robert O. Kevin, *Sovereign Independence of the Canon Law of the Protestant Episcopal Church in the United States of America—A Rebuttal* (Philadelphia: Episcopal Evangelical Fellowship, 1952), 15. G. MacLaren Brydon, *Shall We Accept the Ancient Canons as Canon Law?* (Richmond, Va.: Virginia Diocesan Library, 1955).

While the American Episcopal Church has frankly declined to give the status of statute law to enactments and customs of past ages, it has very definitely recognized the fact of a mass of custom and tradition as being in its essential parts something very real and vital in the life of the catholic Church.... We do not call it law; because there are things of greater power in life than legal enactments.[18]

On the other hand, "there are many other ancient canons for which we must feel a deep sense of shame and sorrow, as for instance the 'catholic' custom of burning heretics at the stake."[19]

Brydon follows Andrews also in his rejection of Hoffman's interpretation of the common law analogy. He says that the notion that the American colonies "took over" the common law of England at the time of the Revolution or after "must be categorically declared to be untrue to the facts."[20]

Brydon also adds another argument. "Because the government of the Episcopal Church is that of a federated union of dioceses, the analogy of the federal government of the United States in this respect is very striking."[21] He cites Brandeis's dictum in the Erie Railroad case that "there is no federal general common law." Thus there can be none for the Episcopal Church in the United States. He further quotes Brandeis: "The common law so far as enforced in a state, whether called common law or not, is not the common law generally, but the law of that state existing by the authority of that state without regard to what it may have been in England or anywhere else."[22] Thus there can be none for the dioceses.[23]

The Importance of This Controversy

What is the importance of this controversy for this work? This controversy has several ramifications for the federal question to the extent that one view is correct and the other incorrect.

1. If the Episcopal Church in the United States is but "a province of the Anglican Communion" as *The Ancient Canons* states, or "a province in

---

18. Brydon, *Shall We Accept the Ancient Canons*, 24.
19. *Ibid.*, 23.
20. *Ibid.*, 38.
21. *Ibid.*, 36.
22. *Ibid.*
23. W. D. Wilson, "The Relation of English to American Church Law," *Church Review* 45 (1885): 78–96, attempts to show that English canons do apply by the analogy to common law, even though there is no federal common law.

communion with the See of Canterbury" as the same source affirms elsewhere,[24] and if, as a province, the American Church is significantly restricted in its legislative powers by the ancient canons, then the problem of the federal structure of the church in the United States is significantly altered by the questions of:

    a) the exact limits to the legislative power of the American Church;
    b) the extent to which the Constitution and Canons of the church are now "uncanonical" in reference to the ancient canons;
    c) the locus of authority for deciding what exactly is the corpus of ancient canons; and
    d) the precise nature of the structural and constitutional relationship of the American Church to the Anglican Communion (and the catholic faith as a whole) regarding the distribution of governing powers within the Communion.

In short, the question to be considered first might very well first be the nature of the constitutional structure of the Anglican Communion before any decision can be reached concerning the constitutional structure of the Episcopal Church in the United States.

2. If the American Church has complete "sovereign independence" from all other churches in regard to the exercise of its governmental powers, then, of course, the governmental structure of the church in the United States can be studied without essential reference to any other ecclesiastical body or ecclesiastical law.

3. In relation to the problem of General Convention versus diocesan supremacy, it would be informative to see if there is any identity between persons maintaining either that the General Convention of the dioceses are supreme and those holding either that the ancient canons are or are not binding.

    There appears to be no uniformity of opinions, however. Andrews and Brydon, both opposing *The Ancient Canons*' position, also strongly support "diocesan rights."[25] On the other hand, Francis Wharton, rigidly opposed

---

24. Coonrad, *The Ancient Canons*, 3 and 18. Brydon, *Shall We Accept the Ancient Canons*, chap. 6, pp. 26–33, specifically denies these assertions.
25. See Andrews, *Church Law*, chap. 2. Brydon, *Shall We Accept the Ancient Canons*, 32, states: "As all trained churchmen know, the Episcopal Church in the United States came into being and still exists as a federated union of dioceses, in which each diocese is a 'sovereign diocese,' with the right and the power to enact canon laws for its own government; and in which the several dioceses have established a central or federal government having only such powers as have been delegated to it by the dioceses."

to Hoffman's view on the English canons, nonetheless is most emphatic in asserting the complete supremacy of the General Convention:

> I must say that after a careful and anxious scrutiny of the constitution of our general Church, the power of the General Convention seems to me unlimited, while that of the diocesan conventions is only that which the General Convention is pleased to concede.[26]

Hoffman himself is among the first to state that the powers of General Convention are virtually unlimited, and then only self-limited.[27]

Hill Burgwin, "By What Laws the American Church Is Governed and Herein Chiefly, How Far, If at All, English Ecclesiastical Law Is of Force as Such, in this Church,"[28] and his "Sources and Sanctions of American Church Law: Reply to Mr. Judd,"[29] can almost be taken as the models for Brydon's arguments and analysis regarding the English canons. These articles and Brydon's pamphlet are closely parallel. But Burgwin was as ardent a supporter of National Church supremacy over the dioceses as Brydon is a champion of "diocesan sovereignty."[30] For example, Burgwin says that "our dioceses are the creatures of the national church, and have no absolute, reserved, or organic rights, nor any of which they may not be deprived in due legal course of legislation, by the national church."[31]

S. Corning Judd, in an article written in express contradiction of Burgwin's views on the English canons, also stressed national church supremacy over the dioceses. "The national church receives none of its laws or powers from the supposed independent state churches or dioceses."[32]

> The fact is well known to all that, nevertheless, the General Convention legislates in ecclesiastical matters without reserve or hindrance, except so far as restricted by the *limitations* of the Constitution, and in subordination to divine and catholic law.[33]

---

26. Francis Wharton, "How Far Are We Bound by English Canons?" in William S. Perry, *The History of the American Episcopal Church,* vol. 2 (Boston: J. R. Osgood, 1885), 400. Regarding the English canons, see pp. 390–97.
27. Hoffman, *A Treatise on the Law,* 116–17.
28. Hill Burgwin, "By What Laws the American Church Is Governed and Herein Chiefly, How Far, If at All, English Ecclesiastical Law Is of Force as Such, in this Church," *Church Review* 35 (1881): 111–34.
29. Hill Burgwin, "Sources and Sanctions of American Church Law: Reply to Mr. Judd," *Church Review* 40 (1882): 85–107.
30. Hill Burgwin, "The National Church and the Diocese," *Church Review* 45 (1885): 423–55.
31. *Ibid.,* 424.
32. Judd, "By What Laws the American Church Is Governed [Reply to Mr. Burgwin]," 194.
33. *Ibid.,* 197.

While *The Ancient Canons* is not specifically concerned with the problem of national or diocesan supremacy, it is possible to infer a case for national supremacy: "Of course no one can physically prevent General Convention from adopting whatever legislation it may wish, whether it be good or bad, sound or unsound."[34] This seems to say that the church is now so constituted that General Convention is unlimited in its powers.

4. If the ancient canons are binding on the American Church, the Constitution and Canons of the church must be viewed as being incomplete and not full descriptive of the "constitution" of the church. Thus, for a complete analysis of the constitutional structure of the church, the ancient canons might also be examined and evaluated.

The controversy concerning the source of the canon law of the Episcopal Church in the United States has not been solved in this work. However, that there is a marked difference of opinion serves as a caveat to the author. And the warning should extend over all his research and conclusions. This work is concerned only with examining the written Constitution and Canons of the American Episcopal Church in order to determine whether or not the church's government is federal, confederal, or unitary. No other purpose is sought, and any conclusions reached other than those directly bearing on this purpose must be reached only in light of the warning highlighted by the ancient canons controversy.

II. The Constitution of the Confederate Episcopal Church

While the constitution of the Southern church does not have a direct bearing upon the problem of federalism in the American Episcopal Church, there does seem sufficient value in a brief description of it to merit its elaboration for comparative purposes.

The process by which the constitution of the Southern church was finally decided upon is somewhat complicated. Most historians of the church in the Confederate States have not dealt extensively with the constitutional development of the church. Insofar as constitutional features have been their concern at all, their attention has primarily been directed toward:

---

34. Coonrad, *The Ancient Canons*, 19.

1. the attempt to name the Southern church "The Reformed Catholic Church";
2. the inclusion of permission for provinces in the church;
3. the change in the method of constitutional amendment; and
4. the remarkable overall similarity between the final constitution of the Southern church and the one of the Episcopal Church in the United States.

However, this focus tends to overlook certain features in the process of establishing the constitution of the Confederate church that would appear to be highly significant.

The Official Draft of October 1861

The convention of the Episcopal Church in the Confederate States which met in Columbia, South Carolina, from October 16–October 24, 1861, was concerned almost entirely with adopting a constitution for the church.[35]

Among the first matter of business was the constitutional draft presented by a committee on constitution and canons, which had been appointed at the earlier meeting of the convention, for the purpose of drawing up a constitution for the church in the South. This draft, though not accepted, is extremely interesting in the light it throws on possibilities of church polity in the Episcopal Church through the profound structural changes it suggested.

This draft would have done away entirely with the diocese as a basis of apportionment to General Convention, replacing them with a provincial system instead. The General Convention, renamed, very significantly, the "Confederate Council"—the church itself being called "this Confederation" (Article III)—bicameral in form, was to be composed of representatives of the provinces, not dioceses.

Each state in the Confederacy was to be designated a province (Article III). Within each state there would be as many dioceses as practically needed, but new dioceses could be formed within the province only with the permission of the provincial council (Article VII). A bishop was still to be chosen by the dioceses over which he was to have jurisdiction.

---

35. The following, unless otherwise noted, is from *Journal of the Proceedings of an Adjourned Convention of Bishops, Clergymen, and Laymen of the Protestant Episcopal Church in the Confederate States of America, Held in Christ Church, Columbia, South Carolina, from October 16 to October 24, Inclusive, in the Year of Our Lord, 1861* (Montgomery, Ala.: Montgomery Advertiser Job Printing Offices, 1861).

Each diocesan bishop was to be given a seat and a voice in the House of Bishops of the Confederate Council, but all the bishops within a province had only one vote together, and that single vote was to be cast by the senior bishop of the province (Article IV). Each province also was to be allowed to elect up to five lay and clerical deputies to the Confederate Council. The voting procedure was the same was that of the church in the United States except that provinces were substituted for dioceses.

The provincial councils were to be composed of all bishops within the province and clerical and lay deputies from the dioceses as determined by the province. The council of such provinces was to legislate for all dioceses within the province, and its rules were to be of force within all the dioceses embraced within the province. It was also to elect the deputies of the province to the Confederate Council (Article V). Trials of clergy, except bishops, were to be held in the dioceses of the accused clergy, but on the basis of provincial legislation.

The section concerned with constitutional amendment would have required the adoption of a proposed amendment by a majority of both houses in a vote by orders and provinces, the subsequent specific approval of two-thirds of all provincial councils, and the final ratification by the next Confederate Council (Article XII).

This constitutional draft was not accepted by the Confederate church. Immediately after its presentation, three new members were added to the committee on constitution and canons, and the Council adjourned for the day.[36] The proposed constitution was considered the next day by the Council and was subjected to detailed amendment and discussion from the floor for a week.[37]

The Accepted Constitution

The process of metamorphosis from the constitution originally proposed on October 17, 1861, to that adopted on October 24, 1861, is a task meriting the most careful study, which, unfortunately, cannot be here given. Nonetheless, it can be observed that the change was considerable and significantly in the direction of keeping the constitution of the church in the Confederacy similar to that of the American Episcopal Church.

Article I of the constitution took direct notice of the effort that had been made to change the name of the church to "Reformed Catholic"[38] or

---

36. *Ibid.*, 15.
37. *Ibid.*, 16–34.
38. *Ibid.*, 16–17.

to strike the word "Protestant"[39] by stating "this Church, retaining the name 'Protestant Episcopal,' shall be known as the Protestant Episcopal Church in the Confederate States of America."

The name of the central legislative assembly was changed to "General Council." The Council retained its bicameral form, and was almost identical in composition and procedure with the General Convention of the church in the United States. Most interestingly, the basis of provincial rather than diocesan apportionment to the Council was rejected in favor of the older method, although the Confederate church did retain the idea of provinces in altered form (Articles II and III).[40]

Provincial governments could be established within any single state in the Confederacy having more than one diocese, if the dioceses so desired. The Provincial Council could legislate for all dioceses within the province, but it had no representation as such in General Council (Article IV). Provinces were no longer given jurisdiction over the trial of clergy. The General Council legislated for the trial of bishops and the dioceses for their own lesser clergy (Article VIII).

One significant alteration in the Confederate church's constitution of the Constitution of the Episcopal Church in the United States was the process of amendment. The article on constitutional amendment originally suggested by the first Confederate committee on constitution and canons was incorporated entirely into the final draft, with changes only in terminology relating to the "Confederate Council" and "Provinces" (Article XIII).

Thus, the constitution, as suggested in October 24, 1861, and as finally adopted in Augusta, Georgia, in November 1862,[41] was similar in most respects to that of the church in the United States. It would take a careful analysis of that constitution to determine whether or not alterations affected the problem of federalism, although the method of amendment adopted for the Confederate church's constitution was decidedly on the side of a federal government. The changes suggested on October 16, 1861, were far more revolutionary that those of October 24, 1861.

---

39. *Ibid.,* 18.
40. It should be remembered that the American Episcopal Church did not at this time have a provincial system, though it had been the subject of Convention debate for some time. The experience in the Confederate church no doubt served as a precedent for the American Church.
41. See *Journal of the General Council of the Protestant Episcopal Church in the Confederate States of America, 1862* (Augusta, Ga: Steam Press of Chronicle and Sentinel, 1863), appendix containing constitution and canons adopted during the Council's meeting.

III. The Reformed Episcopal Church

It was not necessary to detail the causes for the development of the Reformed Episcopal Church because it was not formed upon the basis of a diocesan protest. That is, the Reformed Episcopal Church was created by a number of discontented "Low Church" members of the Protestant Episcopal Church in 1873 and not by discontented dioceses.[42] While there was some thought at the time that perhaps a few dioceses might attempt to remove themselves and join with the Reformed Episcopal Church—Virginia and Ohio were especially mentioned[43]—no formal action toward this end by any diocese appears to have been consummated.

The Reformed Episcopal Church was organized on December 2, 1873, by one bishop and seven other clergymen[44] and seventeen laymen who felt that the Protestant Episcopal Church was helplessly in the control of those who wished to adopt and perpetuate "Romish" errors that all Protestants, they felt, must abhor.

The movement to form a new and "pure" church by the evacuation of Low Churchmen from the Protestant Episcopal Church did not attract as many followers as the founders of the Reformed Episcopal Church had anticipated. Most Low Churchmen in the Protestant Episcopal Church rejected the notion, preferring to remain in the older body.[45]

The Constitution of the Reformed Episcopal Church

Even though the founding of the Reformed Episcopal Church does not have a direct bearing on the problem of federalism in the Protestant Episcopal Church, it does appear valuable to note a few of the characteristics

---

42. The Reformed Episcopal Church should not be confused with the Evangelical Episcopal Church formed in 1815–1816 by the Rev. George Dashiell of Maryland and seven or eight other clergy. This movement ended in 1826.
43. See Benjamin Aycrigg, *Memoirs of the Reformed Episcopal Church*, third edition (New York: E. O. Jenkins, 1877), 62 (line 14), 63 (line 23), and 76 (lines 4, 5).
44. All deposed clergy of the Protestant Episcopal Church. See Edward Clowes Chorley, *Men and Movements in the American Episcopal Church* (New York: C. Scribner's Sons, 1946), 417–18.
45. See Aycrigg, *Memoirs*, and Alexandrine M. Cummins, *Memoir of George David Cummins, D.D., First Bishop of the Reformed Episcopal Church* (New York: Dodd, Mead, 1879). These are the major original sources on the founding of the Reformed Episcopal Church. See also Chorley, *Men and Movements*, 393–424; and Edward B. Boggs, "The Schism of 1873," *Church Review* 27 (1875): 255–78. This is a review article of Cummins's letter of resignation, his edition of the "Proposed Book of 1785," and the "Union Prayer Book" of 1872.

of the constitution adopted by the Reformed Episcopal Church in 1873–1874.[46] An attempt may have been made by the Reformed Episcopalians to remove particular dissatisfactions felt by some Protestant Episcopalians in their polity.

One of the most significant differences in the constitutions of the two churches, as far as the federal question is concerned, is that of the basis of apportionment for the unicameral General Council, so called, of the Reformed Episcopal Church. Article II of the constitution of the Reformed Episcopal Church declared that all bishops and all priests of the church were to be admitted to the Council, and one layman was to be admitted for each fifty communicants. Voting was normally decided by a majority of all members voting regardless of orders, but when required by any five persons, it could be taken by orders, the concurrence of "both orders" (*i.e.,* clergy and laity) being necessary for a measure to pass. There was no requirement for diocesan or congregational agreement in this vote by orders, however.

Bishops, according to Article III, were not to form a separate House, nor to exercise any veto power over the acts of the laity and other clergy in Council. Rather, each bishop was to have no more power than any other clergyman, except that a "Presiding Bishop of this Church" was to be chosen by ballot of Council, to serve for one year with right of succession.

Another significant departure from the polity of the Protestant Episcopal Church was that bishops were to be chosen by the General Council, which Council also had exclusive rights to determine the jurisdiction of each bishop (Article IV). No mention was made of a diocesan substructure. Rather, six or more adjoining congregations were permitted in Article V to form a synod under a bishop with its own constitution and canons.

All ecclesiastical trials were to be provided for by the General Council (Article VI). And in order to amend the constitution it was necessary to have either the simple consent of two General Councils or the unanimous consent of only one.

Thus the structure of the government of the Reformed Episcopal Church, as outlined in its first constitution, was strikingly different from that of the Protestant Episcopal Church. There was no question of a federal form. The General Council was supreme, synods (rather than dioceses) being permitted by the Council under certain circumstances. The basis of the Council's apportionment was congregational, not diocesan or provincial. Bishops had few special governing prerogatives different from other ministers. The amending process was decided by that of a unitary constitutional government.

---

46. The following is from the *Journals of the General Council of the Reformed Episcopal Church* (Philadelphia: James Moore, 1874).

IV. Notes and Comments on the Church's Government

On the Name of the Church

Through this work, the church whose government is the subject of analysis is called promiscuously "the Protestant Episcopal Church in the United States of America," "the Episcopal Church," "the American Episcopal Church," etc. In distinguishing between the government of the church as expressed in the General Convention, Presiding Bishop, National [Executive] Council, etc., and the government of the church in the various dioceses, the author uses the term "national [or "general"] church" to designate the former and "diocesan church" to mean the latter. The author hopes, in this way, to use terminology that will not presuppose an answer to the problem of this work.

More especially, by not using the full, legal title of the church in every instance, the author does not necessarily mean thereby to be expressing a theological predisposition, but rather he is only using an abbreviated title for the sake of convenience and variety.

The name of the church is, and has been, the subject of dispute for some time. Apparently the name "Protestant Episcopal Church" was first used officially to designate the successor of the Church of England in the state of Maryland after the American Revolution. In any event, as far as church titles are concerned, it came into use in a time when the word "catholic" meant "Roman Catholic" and the word "Protestant" meant, at least, "not Roman Catholic."

Since the development of a reemphasis upon the catholic—but non-Roman Catholic—aspect of the church's faith and practice, beginning probably with the Oxford Movement of the 1830s, in many General Conventions of the Episcopal Church there have been suggestions made either to drop the word "Protestant" from the church's title and/or to add the word "Catholic" at some point, possibly with some modifying word. In 1862, the Episcopal Church in the Confederacy considered seriously adopting the name "The Reformed Catholic Church in the Confederate States of America."

On the other side, many persons in the church have insisted that that full title of the church should always be used to emphasize the church's Protestant faith, and that to drop the "Protestant" in speaking about the church is to show a disposition to minimize the church's Protestant heritage.

This author does not intend to be entering this debate by using shorter names for the church, on occasion. His only interest here in using popularly accepted short-hand terms is to conserve space and appropriate the merits of variegated language.[47]

On Church Parties

While it is difficult and dangerous to generalize about this matter, it should be understood that there are within the American Episcopal Church, broadly speaking, two or three distinct "parties." That is, there are two or three groups that stress different aspects of the church's faith and doctrine. Generally these are distinguished as "High Church" (or "catholic" or "Anglo-catholic"), "Low Church" ("Protestant" or "Evangelical"), and "Broad Church" ("Liberal").

These parties tend to express different and often mutually exclusive opinions about the church's discipline, worship, doctrine, and faith. Thus it is generally impossible to determine an "official" church view on any particular point, or to describe the church's faith, worship, doctrine, and discipline without offending one party's views by not expressing the point in exactly the party's terms.[48]

The author has sincerely attempted to present the polity of the church fairly without consciously adopting one of these groups' viewpoints, nor, on the other hand, expressly rejecting any of them. And he has tried to describe fairly differing views where necessary.

On Parish Government

In the interest of a more nearly complete analysis of the government of the Episcopal Church, it seems desirable to include this note on the place of the parish in the church's government. In describing parish government, it is necessary first to summarize briefly the structure of General Convention and the dioceses to show their interrelation with the parishes.

This work has shown that the government of the Episcopal Church, rather than being a federation or confederation of dioceses with a com-

---

47. For a list of works discussing the implications of the church's name, see the Bibliography.
48. For the most thorough analyses of the church's parties, see Chorley, *Men and Movements*; George E. DeMille, *The Catholic Movement in the American Episcopal Church* (Philadelphia: Church Historical Society, 1941); Alexander C. Zabriskie, ed., *Anglican Evangelicalism* (Philadelphia: Church Historical Society, 1943); and P. M. Boyden, "The Two Theories of the Church and Inferences Therefrom," *Protestant Episcopal Review* 11 (February–March 1898): 262–69.

mon central governing body empowered to deal only with matters of common concern to the members of the association as defined in a written Constitution, is in fact an ecclesiastical organization in which all matters of faith and discipline are finally referable to a single, sovereign, and only self-limited representative assembly.

The government of the church is now, indeed, quite similar in structure to the essence of the framework that Bishop William White outlined in his *Case of the Episcopal Churches in the United States Considered* of 1782. In its totality the government of the church is composed of a series of four interrelated representative bodies from the parish vestry, through the diocesan conventions, and the provincial synods, to the General Convention.

The provincial synod is the newest and most incomplete of the four, being a late creature of General Convention whose life is dependent upon the mutual support of the General Convention and the diocesan conventions. The other three groupings are more intimately interconnected historically, however. The General Convention, at the peak of the governmental structure, is composed of all bishops of the church and representatives of the clergy and laity chosen by the diocesan conventions. The governing power of the General Convention extends to all areas of church life: national, diocesan, and parochial. The diocesan conventions are primarily concerned with ecclesiastical affairs within the limits of their respective geographic territories. However, on the one hand, in their participation in the provinces, and in their function as electors of the representatives to the synods and to General Convention, they also have responsibility that extends out beyond their boundaries. On the one hand, the dioceses have extensive discretionary powers over the parishes and missions within their jurisdictions, and, under the restrictions set by General Convention, may legislate for them. However, the diocesan convention itself is composed of the diocese's bishop(s), all clergy of the diocese, and lay representatives from the parish churches. The basis of lay apportionment in diocesan conventions may be that of equal representation for each parish regardless of size, or proportionate representation according to church membership, finances, or some other measure. Thus there is about as much reason to call the dioceses themselves federations of parishes as it is to call the national church a federation of dioceses.[49]

The parish church is also representatively governed in accordance with diocesan and national canons. The parish wardens and vestry are chosen

---

49. See George H. Humphrey, *Law of the Protestant Episcopal Church,* second edition (New York: James Pott, 1882); and White, *American Church Law.* Both of these deal with parish law. See also Charles P. Anderson, *Letters to Laymen* (Milwaukee: Young Churchman, 1913).

generally by the whole adult membership of the parish. The parish's rector, however, is member and chair *ex officio* of the vestry, and while major governmental decisions are made for the parish by the vestry, the rector is given, by the national canons, considerable power over the use of church property.[50]

Still, the vestry's role is very significant. In the absence of a rector, the vestry controls the parish and is alone responsible for the calling of a new rector. The diocese's bishop (according to the canons) only offers "advice" in this procedure. Of course, the extent to which that advice is compelling varies considerably from diocese to diocese and bishop to bishop.[51]

For financial and legal reasons, most states of the United States allow churches to form corporations under state law. While some states forbid incorporation of religious bodies, most states require or permit it. In the Protestant Episcopal Church, it is the vestry which is incorporated, forming a trustee corporation of clergy and laity.[52]

The government of the United States does not incorporate religious associations except in the District of Columbia and its other exclusive jurisdictions. And, interestingly, state laws apparently do not include the diocesan bishop, Standing Committee, or other representative of the diocese in a parish's incorporation. Thus, Episcopal parishes are incorporated by most states on the parish level through the vestry—elected representatives of the parish. Episcopal churches do not form corporations out of the total membership of the parish.

But the important feature of parish government is that it is representatively democratic and not directly democratic. That is, the vestry makes the

---

50. See Herbert G. Coddington, *The Rector and His Vestry* (Syracuse, N.Y.: Cornell Printing Company, 1926); Morgan Dix, "The Functions of Rectors, and Wardens, and Vestrymen," *Church Eclectic* 8 (1881): 1096–1102; George Gibbs, "Spiritualities and Temporalities," *Living Church* 136 (June 8, 1958): 11–123; *The Parish or Vestry System of the Protestant Episcopal Church in the United States of America: The Evils It Involves, and What Will Remedy Them* (Buffalo, N.Y.: Barber, Jones, 1896); James Parker, "On Rectors, Wardens, and Vestrymen," *Church Eclectic* 9 (1881): 77–81; "Wardens and Vestrymen," *Protestant Episcopalian* 5 (1834): 296–97; "Why the Vestry," *Living Church* 132 (February 12, 1956): 10–11; and Theodore R. Ludlow, *I Am a Vestryman*, revised edition (New York: Morehouse-Gorham, 1945).
51. See D. D. Chapin, "Some Conditions of Permanency in the Pastoral Relation," *Church Eclectic* 11 (1884): 945–48 and 1041–45; "Choosing a Rector," *Living Church* 130 (February 6, 1955): 10–11 (see a reply to this article by G. MacLaren Brydon on page 5, March 6, 1955); "Bishops and Vestries," *Living Church* 132 (June 10, 1956): 6; and John F. Spalding, "Congregationalism in the Church," *Church Review* 28 (1876): 261–72.
52. George Hodges and John Reichert, *The Administration of an Institutional Church* (New York: Harper, 1906); Lowell E. Larson, "Church Accounting," *Living Church* 136 (January 12, 1958): 20–24; Joseph W. Peoples, Jr., "The Church Office: Management Methods in a Middle-Sized Parish," *Living Church* 136 (January 12, 1958): 16–17.

policy decisions. The parish as a whole meets governmentally to elect its representatives to the vestry.[53]

Hence, one feature of the total structure of the church's government stands out prominently. That feature is its representative nature. The purpose of the three governmental bodies below the General Convention is to govern, to a considerable extent on their own initiative, but, otherwise, through the commands of General Convention, the area over which they have jurisdiction. But each of them is composed of members chosen from the area which they govern, having responsibility both downward to their electors and upward to General Convention.

On "Divided Votes" in the House of Deputies

The interpretation that divided votes should count in the negative, mentioned earlier in this book, has been attacked by some and the object of attempted constitutional revision by others.

Vinton, in his *Manual Commentary*, devotes several pages attempting to show, by civil and ecclesiastical precedent, that a divided vote should count only as a blank vote; that is, as no vote cast. He cites the record of an aye-nay vote in the 1786 Convention:

> New York (Clergy *aye*, Laity *no*), divided; New Jersey, *aye*; Pennsylvania (Clergy *aye*, Laity *no*), divided; Delaware (Clergy *divided*, Laity *divided*), divided; South Carolina, *aye*. And so the words [under consideration] are to be restored [to the creed], there being two ayes and no negative.[54]

Plainly, this is evidence of divided votes being considered blank, or uncast. However, the constitutional requirement for voting in 1786 was different from that in 1789 and later. Constitutionally, votes were not required to be taken by orders, but by dioceses only. Vinton admits to this elsewhere, but still concludes that divided votes should be counted as blank, rather than in the negative.[55]

White and Dykman cite several unsuccessful attempts to change the Constitution to allow divided votes to be counted as one-half for and one-half against. These writers conclude, from a casual examination of some voting instances, that counting divided votes in this manner would probably not affect the outcome of many voting decisions anyway.[56]

---

53. See C. G. Chamberlayne, "Vestry or Congregation," *Southern Churchman* 85 (January 3, 1920): 5.
54. Francis Vinton, *A Manual Commentary on the General Canon Law and the Constitution of the Protestant Episcopal Church in the United States* (New York: E. P. Dutton, 1870), 119.
55. *Ibid.,* 121.
56. White and Dykman (1954), 1:26–30.

On the Use of the Word "Mission"

The use of the word "mission" in the American Episcopal Church may be confusing. The term "mission" has been used before in this book to refer to the power that a bishop receives at consecration. It is also used in certain instances to describe a religious settlement, church, or group of churches overseas, subject to the American Episcopal Church. These foreign missionary districts may either have been specifically set up by the General Convention, or by a diocese, a religious community, a seminary, or by an "independent" group of clergy. Or an existing group of native clergy in a foreign area may have requested to come under the care of the American Church. The degree of actual control that General Convention exercises over these varying types of foreign missions differs considerably.

The aim of most foreign missions is that they may eventually set up ecclesiastical bodies in their own area formally independent of the American Church. This has been done in the case of both the Japanese and Mexican churches, for example.

There are also domestic missionary districts. Again, these may have had the varying origins as above or have been given to the General Convention by a diocese unable to provide for the area. The aim of these districts is to become self-supporting dioceses in the American Episcopal Church.

Both foreign and domestic missionary districts are under the control of General Convention and largely supported finally by the church through the General Convention and the Executive Council. Within each diocese, however, there are also mission churches. These missions are generally small, non-self-supporting churches for which the diocese is primarily responsible governmentally and financially.

For example, whereas a parish may "call" its own rector, the diocesan bishop may assign a vicar to a mission. Whereas a parish is largely financially self-supporting, the diocese aids in the support of a mission. Finally, whereas each parish is entitled to full representation at the diocesan convention, a mission may be permitted only a smaller representation, if any at all.

Unlike the case of foreign and domestic missionary districts, the General Convention has no more especial power or responsibility over a diocese's missions than it does over the ordinary parish. That, of course, does not mean that General Convention is thereby restricted from legislating for the diocesan missions.

Quotations Showing Conflicting Opinions Regarding the Meaning of the Constitution Enacted in 1789

The following quotations show that various students of the church's government have had widely varying opinions regarding the meaning of the Constitution of 1789, and whether or not it set up a federal or confederal government:

> They were then the representatives of the Churches in the respective states assembled in state or diocesan conventions and the Constitution they enacted was adopted in their representative capacity as representing the said state or diocesan churches in convention assembled.
> (William S. Perry, *History of the Constitution of the American Church* [New York: T. Whittaker, 1891], 285.)

> [The General Convention of 1789] was composed of deputies, professing to represent ten state churches—not dioceses. Of these only five had any form of organization, and even that wholly voluntary, without law or precedent to authorize it. Of the other five not one of them had even a formal organization; their so-called deputies were appointed by a few of the clergy and laity, or of the clergy alone, who found it convenient to meet for the purpose at the call of some leading zealous clergymen.
> (Hill Burgwin, "The National Church and the Diocese," *Church Review* 45 [1885]: 433.)

> The union of the Church in this country was not a federal league of independent and separately existent colonial churches, but it was in fact a union of individual congregations in one Church, which for convenience of administration is divided into dioceses, but in whose governing body there is vested, but not by delegation, a general power of legislation, subject to certain organic restrictions.
> (Christopher S. Patterson, "The Sources and Scope of the Law of the Church," *Church Review* 43 [1884]: 124.)

> It was a confederation of ecclesiastical jurisdictions, whose metes and bounds conformed to the lines of the states, under the government of the college of bishops, presided over by one of their number, *primus inter pares*, viz.: the senior member; and to this was added a house of clerical and lay deputies representing each diocese and endowed with certain powers of concurrent action.
> (William E. McLaren, "The Diocese and the Province," *Church Eclectic* 5 [1877]: 384.)

The Convention of 1789 convened through the several states with full powers, according to the understanding of churchmen, for establishing a central government in accordance with the fundamental principles that had been discussed, and to perpetuate a body with power to legislate on all matters pertaining to the church.

In theory the powers of the General Convention extend to any legislation not in conflict with the Divine Constitution of the Church and the Canons of the ecumenical councils, but in fact, such powers, owing to the broken unity of the church, are unlimited.

Fifty years ago it might have been necessary to have stopped here to discuss what was called the doctrine of "state rights." But this theory, which many tried to apply to the dioceses in their relation to the General Convention, happily has become a matter of the past, by reason of its disappearance in national politics."
(Henry Mason Baum, "The Law of the Church in the United States," *Church Review* 50 [1887]: 768.)

Quotations Showing Conflicting Opinion Regarding the Extent of General Convention's Power

Earlier in this work, the author concluded that the governmental powers of General Convention are and always have been virtually unlimited, as far as the formal, constitutional structure of the church is concerned. Below are some conflicting opinions by other students of the church's government regarding the extent of General Convention's powers:

> Our national church, within the proper scope of ecclesiastical legislation, and subject to the Divine law and that of the One Catholic Church, is under no restrictions or limitations whatsoever, as to its power of legislation. Our dioceses are the creatures of the national church, and have no absolute, reserved, or organic rights, nor any of which they may not be deprived in due legal course of legislation, by the national church.
> (Hill Burgwin, "The National Church and the Dioceses," *Church Review* 45 [1885]: 424.)

The national church is a church of delegated powers, and its authority rests upon the consent of what the Constitution of the General Convention styles, "the Church in each diocese."

The national church is the creature of the diocesan, or (as they were then called) the state conventions, which latter were, in turn, the creations of the clergy and congregations within that state; and that all powers not then and since delegated to the General Convention remain with the state or diocesan conventions.

(James Parker, "The National Church and the Dioceses:
A Rejoinder," *Church Review* 46 [1886]: 35.)

The rights and powers derived from the dioceses: The rights and powers of the diocesan conventions are not derived from the Constitution or from the General Convention, but are original and inherent.

(Carl E. Grammer, "The Godly Discipline of the Laity,"
Virginia Seminary Magazine 5 [1892]: 284.)

[The General Convention of 1789,] under the powers given to its delegates, was constituted and appointed as a body of nearly supreme absolute powers to establish an ecclesiastical government for the whole church of the United States.

(William S. Barton, "Virginia's XIXth Canon,"
Protestant Episcopal Review 6 [1893]: 496.)

Official Church Acts Showing the Relationship of the Episcopal Church to the Church of England

The Protestant Episcopal Church was reconstituted as the direct successor to the Church of England in the American colonies. This has been generally recognized by the civil courts in the United States and has been officially so stated by the American Episcopal Church itself. The following are two of the most important statements of the relationship of the Protestant Episcopal Church to the Church of England.

The quotation below was originally written to enable the Diocese of Vermont to receive land that had belonged to the English Society for the Propagation of the Gospel in Foreign Parts (SPG) in Vermont before the Revolution, but had since fallen into other hands.[57] Subsequently, it has been cited frequently to show that General Convention has stated officially the continuity of the Protestant Episcopal Church with the Church of England, yet its independence therefrom:

The following declaration was proposed and agreed to:

It having been credibly stated to the House of Bishops, that on questions, in reference to property devised before the Revolution to congregations

---

57. According to Walter H. Stowe, "The General Convention of 1814," *Historical Magazine of the Protestant Episcopal Church* 15 (1946): 155–56.

belonging to "the Church of England," and to uses connected with that name, some doubts have been entertained in regard to the identity of the body to which the two names have been applied, the House think it expedient to make the declaration, and to request the concurrence of the House of Clerical and Lay Deputies therein—that "The Protestant Episcopal Church in the United States of America" is the same body heretofore known in these states, by the name of "The Church of England"; the change of name, although not of religious principle in doctrine, or in worship, or in discipline, being induced by a characteristic of the Church of England, supposing the independence of the Christian churches, under the different sovereignties, to which, respectively, their allegiance in civil concerns belongs. But that when the severance alluded to took place, and ever since, this church conceives of herself as professing and acting on the principles of the Church of England, is evident from the organization of our conventions, and from their subsequent proceedings, as recorded on the journals; to which, accordingly, this Convention refer for satisfaction in the premises. But it would be contrary to fact, were any one to infer, that the discipline exercised in the church, or that any proceedings therein, are at all dependent on the will of the civil or of the ecclesiastical authority of any foreign country.

The above declaration having been communicated to the House of Clerical and Lay Deputies, they returned for answer that they concurred therein.[58]

The Preface of the *Book of Common Prayer* of the Protestant Episcopal Church in the United States, as written in October 1789, and still prefixed to all American Prayer Books, is concerned with justifying the alteration of the English liturgy for use by the American Episcopal Church:

> But when, in the course of Divine Providence, these American states became independent with respect to civil government, their ecclesiastical independence was necessarily included; and the different religious denominations of Christians in these states were left at full and equal liberty to model and organize their respective Churches, and forms of worship, and discipline, in such manner as they might judge most convenient for their future prosperity; consistently with the constitution and laws of their country....
>
> In which it will also appear that this Church is far from intending to depart from the Church of England in any essential point of doctrine, discipline, or worship; or further than local circumstances require.

---

58. *Journal of the 1814 General Convention*, in Perry, *Journals*, 1:431–32.

Civil Court Cases Involving the Episcopal Church

The following is a list of some of the cases involving the Protestant Episcopal Church that have been adjudicated by the civil courts of the United States. It is not a complete listing by any means [and reflects only cases up to and until the original writing of this work in the late 1950s], but is only illustrative of the extent to which the civil courts in the United States serve as an authoritative arbitrator of some of the Episcopal Church's internal disputes. Future research should be done to describe in more detail the extent and manner of the civil judiciary's role in the totality of ecclesiastical government.

Bartlett vs. Hipkins
  Maryland 76 (1892): 5–40.
Batterson vs. Thompson
  Philadelphia Reporter 25.
Bird vs. St. Mark's Church of Waterloo
  Iowa Reports 62 (1883): 567–75.
Brown vs. Protestant Episcopal Church
  Federal (2nd) 8 (1925): 149–151.
Carter vs. Papineau
  Massachusetts 222 (1916): 464–69.
Fiske vs. Beatty
  (New York) *Appellate Division* 206 (1923): 349–61.
Jennings vs. Scarborough
  New Jersey Law Reports 56 (1894): 401–11.
Lynd vs. Menzies
  New Jersey Law Reports 33 (1868): 162–69.
Rector, etc. of Church of the Holy Trinity vs. Melish (New York)
  Miscellaneous 194 (1949): 1006–18; *Miscellaneous* 195 (1949): 377–79; *Appellate Division* 276 (1950): 1088–89; *Appellate Division* 277 (1950): 783; *Miscellaneous* (2nd) 1 (1956): 933–37; *Appellate Division* (2nd) 1 (1956): 978 and (1957): 256–57; *New York* (2nd) 3 (1958): 476–85; *Miscellaneous* (2nd) 12 (1958): 321–25.
Rector, etc. of the Church of the Nativity vs. Fleming
  (New York) *Miscellaneous* 174 (1940): 473–75; *Appellate Division* 260 (1940): 930; *New York* 285 (1941): 706.
Rector, et al of St. James' Church, etc. vs. Huntington
  (New York) *Hun* 82 (1894): 125–28.
Terret vs. Taylor
  United States 13 (1815): 43–55.
Young vs. Ransom
  (New York) *Bars* 31 (1876): 49.

www.ingramcontent.com/pod-product-compliance
Ingram Content Group UK Ltd.
Pitfield, Milton Keynes, MK11 3LW, UK
UKHW041919140426
5217IPUK00013B/222